Pynchon Character Names:
A Dictionary

Pynchon Character Names: A Dictionary

PATRICK J. HURLEY

McFarland & Company, Inc., Publishers
Jefferson, North Carolina, and London

LIBRARY OF CONGRESS CATALOGUING-IN-PUBLICATION DATA

Hurley, Patrick J., 1969–
    Pynchon character names : a dictionary / Patrick J. Hurley.
       p.   cm.
    Includes bibliographical references.

    ISBN 978-0-7864-3458-9
    softcover : 50# alkaline paper ∞

    1. Pynchon, Thomas — Characters — Dictionaries.
    2. Characters and characteristics in literature — Dictionaries.
    3. Names, Personal, in literature — Dictionaries. I. Title.
    PS3566.Y55Z665   2008
    813'.54 — dc22   2007051517

British Library cataloguing data are available

©2008 Patrick J. Hurley. All rights reserved

No part of this book may be reproduced or transmitted in any form or by any means, electronic or mechanical, including photocopying or recording, or by any information storage and retrieval system, without permission in writing from the publisher.

Cover design by Mark Durr

Manufactured in the United States of America

McFarland & Company, Inc., Publishers
  Box 611, Jefferson, North Carolina 28640
    www.mcfarlandpub.com

To Teresa

Acknowledgments

I would like to thank all those involved in Pynchon scholarship and apologize to any who offered something I missed on a name. The fine companions written by Steven Weisenburger and J. Kerry Grant have been invaluable, as my many references to them indicate. Thanks also to Ray Benoit who directed the dissertation that was the basis of this dictionary. Special thanks to my parents for all the support they have given me over the years. And most of all, I thank my wife Teresa for the typing, organizing, programming, and help with proofing, as well as for her loving support. Without her, nothing would be possible for me, least of all this book, and so, I dedicate it to her.

Table of Contents

Acknowledgments vii

A Note on Citation x

Abbreviations xi

Preface 1

Introduction 3

The Dictionary 13

Bibliography 183

A Note on Citation

With the exception of one reference to a short article by Weisenburger, which is clearly identified, all citations of Weisenburger referring to *Gravity's Rainbow* reference his Gravity's Rainbow *Companion*. Citations of Grant referring to *V.* and *The Crying of Lot 49* refer, respectively, to his *A Companion to* V. and his *A Companion to* The Crying of Lot 49.

I have not included citations for given names that I deem common. Common given names include Andy, Maria, Charles and Sylvia, as well as the common German name Lotte and the common French name Ghislaine. I have also not noted many common ethnic surnames, such as Rodriguez (Hispanic), MacGregor (Scottish), Pizzini (Italian), and Feldman (Jewish). Many of these "common names" are used throughout Pynchon's fiction.

When a word or term is not used functionally but is used as the word or term itself, it is italicized and definitions and translations are in quotation marks. There are, therefore, many short bits of quoted matter not followed by citations because they are not direct quotations from particular sources, but commonly held definitions.

Abbreviations

Works by Pynchon

- E: "Entropy"
- GR: *Gravity's Rainbow*
- Lot 49: *The Crying of Lot 49*
- LL: "Low-lands"
- M&D: *Mason & Dixon*
- MMV: "Mortality and Mercy in Vienna"
- SI: "The Secret Integration"
- SL: *Slow Learner*
- SR: "The Small Rain"
- UR: "Under the Rose"
- V: *V.*
- Vine: *Vineland*

Reference Works

- AH4: *The American Heritage Dictionary of the English Language* 4th edition
- CID: *The Cambridge Italian Dictionary*
- DNB: *The Oxford Dictionary of National Biography* (online)
- EB: *Encyclopaedia Britannica* (online)
- ODEE: *The Oxford Dictionary of English Etymology*
- OED: *The Oxford English Dictionary* (online)
- W3: *Webster's Third New International Dictionary*

Preface

When I first read Thomas Pynchon in the late 1980s, I was struck especially by the bizarre character names — Tyrone Slothrop, Pig Bodine, Oedipa Maas, Benny Profane — and the great number of them. Most existing Pynchon criticism pays some attention to names, but no one had yet settled on Pynchon's character names as his or her sole subject. Kelsey Harder and Terry Caesar had written short essays focused on the names, and Steven Weisenburger and J. Kerry Grant eventually produced readers' guides to *Gravity's Rainbow*, *V.*, and *The Crying of Lot 49* that offer glosses on some of the names. But clearly what was needed was a single, exhaustive guide to every one of Pynchon's named characters — over 2,000 in all.

From 2001 to 2004 I attempted to create such a guide. It was my Ph.D. dissertation. When *Against the Day* came out in 2006, I took the opportunity to add the character names from that novel as well as those from Pynchon's published short fiction. At every stage, my goal has been to provide the widest range of possible readings for each name, without privileging a particular reading. This has been the fault of the attention paid to the names in the existing criticism: the brief explanations of names were always subservient to a larger critical agenda, so potentially rich names were given narrow, apparently definitive descriptions. This dictionary differs, then, by being an objective reference book on character names in Pynchon, rather than a set of critical readings, where names are merely tools used as part of some definable project and the entries are all visions refracted through a set, limited range of lenses. I have tried to cull as many plausible readings of names from existing criticism, often offering additional possible interpretations.

As I assembled names and glosses, I began to think about how Pynchon created and used these names, considering the possibility of embedding my dictionary within a larger poetics of naming, but I ultimately decided against this. Offering a clear description of naming in Pynchon necessitates fitting all of the names into this strategy, rather than letting the names speak for themselves. My compromise is the discussion of naming found in the introduction and the set of categories that seem to account for most of the names.

Over the past few years, the dictionary has grown and developed. In addition to scouring Pynchon criticism, I checked likely background source material. Many of Pynchon's sources have been identified, but *Mason & Dixon* and *Against the Day* presented the pleasant challenge of tracking down sources on my own. I have made great use of numerous dictionaries both English and foreign, as well as encyclopedias. General dictionaries of names have also proven quite helpful. Finally, the Internet has been a valuable tool, useful for finding how common names are and in what countries certain names are commonly used.

So this final dictionary is a marked improvement over its early predecessor. Time, research, and sometimes merely mulling over a name and its sound have strengthened many of the character name glosses found here. Quite late I often found "the best reading" that had eluded me before, saving me from the humiliation of skipping over what eventually seemed so obvious. There are undoubtedly cases where "the best reading" is still elusive. I count on those readers who use this dictionary to fill in the gaps. Such a dictionary would have been a great boon to me when I first encountered Pynchon almost 20 years ago. I hope that it helps readers new to Pynchon, but that old hands, too, may find it a useful companion.

Introduction

Thomas Pynchon is considered by many to be one of the most important post-war American novelists. His first three novels have already spawned thorough reader's guides, and numerous books and articles augment these with additional annotations and explanations. While these studies pay at least passing attention to the naming of at least some of Pynchon's characters, there is no exhaustive guide to them. Any attempt to understand naming in Pynchon involves two components: the possible readings of individual names and the broader concerns of Pynchon's naming strategies. While these two components are clearly connected, there are sound reasons to offer an exhaustive guide to the names themselves without embedding it within a theoretical poetics of naming in Pynchon. In order to argue any fixed strategy of naming on Pynchon's part, one must necessarily favor particular readings of individual names where multiple readings (which are sometimes contradictory) are possible. What follows is an attempt to provide an exhaustive dictionary of the names of Pynchon's characters, offering as many readings as possible, yet to look toward an understanding of the practice of naming in Pynchon as a coherent strategy.

Before turning to specific names, we should do four things. First, we should consider the philosophy of naming in general. Second, we should look briefly at the history of literary naming in order to see how Pynchon fits into this tradition. Third, we should attempt to set out, however rudimentarily, some logical scheme describing the main ways in which the characters' names function. And finally, we must be aware of the problems and inherent limitations of such a study.

The philosophical study of naming seeks to identify a logic connecting the vocal utterance or written representation (the word) to the thing or concept described by the word. Alfred Korzybski was fond of beginning his lectures on general semantics by gesturing toward a chair and saying, "Whatever this is, it is not a chair." To what does this word refer? Is a chair a pair of perpendicular pieces of some material elevated from the ground by four legs? Eero Saarinen's famous tulip chair consists of a piece of molded plastic, curving from seat to backrest, elevated by a single pillar connected to a platform. So perhaps the word chair should describe function rather than form: a chair is something on which one sits. Yet if I sit on a case of wine, as I am doing as I write this, it is not a chair in part because when I finish this sentence I will stand up, open the case of wine, remove a bottle, uncork it, and begin drinking (a trick regrettably impossible with more traditional chairs). The study of naming involves similar problems. Even proper names reveal problems of definition and classification. For a compact introduction to some of the major approaches to names (particularly by Wittgenstein, Kripke, and Searle), see Boersema. The fundamental question is whether names have meanings, and specifically, whether a name be a definite description or combine a number of descriptions. Various examples complicate a clear answer to the question. Literary naming, however, demands a modified approach. The characters an author creates are all named by the author, presumably for specific reasons. We will see a strand of Pynchon's naming that reflects the view of name as description (see below on charactonymic/descriptive names). But this is a single strand. And in Pynchon's case, we face a specific problem: with over two thousand names in six novels and six short stories, some characters exist as little more than names. In such cases, it is impossible to determine whether a name is descriptive. Consequently, we will have to consider such names from alternative perspectives. But Pynchon should be considered within the broader tradition of literary naming, which, as we will see, has as one of its central trends names as descriptions.

The history of literary naming is a long one (a full description of which is far beyond the scope of this introduction) and has involved the use of motivated character names from early on. Passage offers some background on the Greek and Roman roots of literary naming (11), while Malone, focusing on English works, cites Old English literature as the genesis of meaningful names along with an assertion that "[f]ictitious characters with characterizing names are to be found in all literatures known to me" (53). In addition to names meant to describe a quality of a character, Malone cites personified abstractions (such as those found in *Piers Plowman*) and occupational, social class, or character type names as other early examples of meaningful character names (54–5). Pynchon employs these early types of names but often in a different manner than in older texts. One aspect of Pynchon's method concerns comic names. Both Malone (55, 60) and Passage (11) maintain that comic names were typically reserved for lower-class characters. Pynchon uses comic names throughout his fiction, but they apply to all social classes. Interestingly, his use of derisive comic names for lower-class characters can actually be read as a radical gesture against class. It is a critical commonplace to read Pynchon through his ubiquitous theme of the conflict between the elect (those who are saved according to the Puritan worldview) and the preterite (those passed over or denied salvation). Where Pynchon uses a comic-derisive name for a lower-class character, and if no qualities of the character bear this description out, the name may be read as how he or she is viewed by the elect. There is a similarity in this respect to Rabelais, if we follow Bakhtin's reading of *Gargantua and Pantagruel*. Comic-derisive names associated with the lower bodily stratum in Rabelais do not mock individual minor characters as much as they are part of a larger project of overturning social hierarchy. Indeed, Pynchon's naming is often closer to that of the sixteenth century Rabelais than of the twentieth century Céline, some of whose derisive names from *Journey to the End of the Night* translate roughly to words such as "fool," "half-witted," "whore," "coward," and many others, all of which seem to stem from misanthropy. Pynchon will use names in this way, too, but their use is part of a larger satirical structure.

Pynchon clearly borrows from the broad history of fictional name giving, but his approach is not so narrow as that of many writers. While Pynchon takes from the naming tradition, he also distorts it:

> In Pynchon's texts names do not operate as they do in, for example, Fielding in which Thwackum or Allworthy are — or do — exactly what their names indicate.... We usually expect to find the person in his or her name. In a realist book as in life, the name comes to signify a real character with unique characteristics. This goes along with a very tenuous notion of the unique individual. Pynchon blows all this up. "Character" and identity are not stable in his fiction.... Pynchon indicates that he can see how, in various ways, people are subject to the authority of naming: how a whole society can exercise its power through naming. As an author he also has to confer names on his figures, but he does so in such a way as to sabotage the conventional modes of naming [Tanner 60].

And he does this largely by refusing to use character names in one consistent way. Having said that, there are some basic ways naming tends to be used by Pynchon.

Even as we let the names speak for themselves, we should look for some unifying thread that weaves the individual names into the overall pattern of Pynchon's naming. It is true that naming in individual novels can be viewed from a dominant perspective, but as I have stressed, the perspective from which names from each novel were introduced suggests only one component of naming among many. Without characterizing Pynchon's naming in too narrow a fashion, we may view the pattern of naming in all the novels as one driven largely by a subversive instinct: odd-sounding names in general subvert realism and highlight the fictionality of the text, and each category into which individual names may be placed can be said to have a subversive function.

The persistent use of absurd or wildly comic names must be viewed as an act of subversion regarding general readerly expectations as well as the realist tradition. It is, of course, a postmodern commonplace to discuss how works of fiction (or metafiction) highlight their own fictionality, but the sheer scope and range of Pynchon's character names defy his easy placement in any simple school or trend. As Caesar, Tanner, and others have suggested, Pynchon's wild names amount to an attack on naming itself. In this sense, Pynchon uses names to subvert the inherent power of naming. Thus, even odd-sounding names that do not quite fit into any established category still suggest that naming is being used to some end, and that we cannot quite identify that end may make the tactic even more subversive. Categories and taxonomies are, after all, tools used to tame and control.

But our use of categories to understand naming in Pynchon need not be viewed as an attempt to render these names harmless by confining them to cozy pigeonholes. This is partly because Pynchon does not allow us to do so. If we acknowledge a range of possible readings of any given character name, we are faced with the possibility that it can fit into several different categories. Indeed, the fact that one can read the names in different ways sometimes makes it impossible to determine exactly what the function of the name is. This problem offers an odd defense of a set of loose categories; even if we cannot state with certainty which category explains the function of a name and which categories cannot apply, we can look at the names as a group in order to determine the possible functions of naming in general. So even if a single name cannot be placed in, for example, the category of irony with any degree of certainty, the fact that many names *may* be read ironically suggests that one strand of Pynchon's naming involves irony. More than anything, then, the categories point to general trends in naming, and these trends can all be understood as tactics of subversion.

For Pynchon's names, a rigid set of mutually exclusive categories is a reductive fiction, but we can and must identify some loose categories that point toward the logic of naming in Pynchon. Character names may be charactonymic or descriptive when they describe some qualities associated with the character (function, appearance, personality, ideology). Of these names, some, which I call metonymic, describe not directly, but by association. In some cases two parts of the name will repeat the description — I refer to these by the term doubling. Other names appear paradoxical in that the component parts appear to cancel one another out. This is particularly evident in V where, as Harder points out, some names combine references to animate things with inanimate ones (65). Ironic names are opposed to charactonymic/descriptive ones in that the name does not match the character at all, but refers to qualities seemingly absent from him or her. Many names are comic in nature; some are comic-derisive, some are puns, some jokes. Some names suggest social class in some way and may identify a character as preterite or elect. Names sometimes allude to actual people, things, or phenomena, and some "characters" are actual historical figures (which presents a special problem for M&D). A special category is the occupational/descriptive epithet, in which a character is introduced with a name connected to a title revealing a job or interest. There are, of course, some ordinary names that would not be out of place in any work of realist fiction (common names) and some names that do not seem to fit any of these categories. I have tried to resist the invention of categories based on insufficient examples and the practice of forcing a character name into a particular category.

While charactonyms and descriptive names are quite old, their use can be viewed as subversive in that they represent the resurrection of an ancient literary tradition. It is true that they have been used on and off throughout literary history, but Pynchon does not always use them in traditional ways. In addition to using names that directly reflect some aspect of the characters (the definition of charactonym), Pynchon sometimes employs a name that should be read as charactonymic, but then dismisses the character as a name only, often as a joke, so we have no way of knowing if the name is appropriate. This tactic undercuts our very understanding of how this type of name is supposed to work. At other times, Pynchon uses the tactic indirectly through what I call a metonymic charactonym by indirectly describing the character through a word that is related to something that can be said to characterize, even though the word itself does not. Just as Pynchon can use names to undercut the act of naming, he uses traditional types of character names in ways that bend their accepted definitions.

Another way Pynchon distorts traditional character names is by using them very insistently. He often uses two words that provide the same description in order to intensify or double the effect of the characterization. This doubling creates an onomastic redundancy that produces comedy as well as a heightened sense of the fictionality of the work. If a charactonym is jarring, one that repeats itself is even more so.

On the other side of intensified description is the practice of offering an apparently descriptive name to a character whose qualities are nearly the opposite of what the description implies. Such names are used ironically, partly as a comic effect and partly to further problematize prominent notions of how character names have been used historically. This is one of many strategies that suggests that naming cannot be limited to a small set of straightforward functions.

Not all names, of course, reflect or counter any qualities of the characters to which they refer. We might call these unmotivated references: see, for example, the entries for Webley Silvernail or Ronald Cherrycoke. Sometimes a name will allude to something quite external to the novel. These allusive names can become subversive by allowing the real world to leak into the fictional one and especially by referring to popular culture or brand names. The use of popular culture within literature, while not limited to Pynchon, reflects an attack on the notion that there can be a rigid boundary separating high and low culture; indeed, the practice questions whether such exclusive cultures can even be said to exist. That Pynchon sometimes draws on monster films, comic books, consumer products, and television for character names and references shows a healthy contempt for literary convention.

The greatest contempt for convention of any sort often presents itself in Pynchon through comedy. Comic naming is central to all of Pynchon's novels; many names that can be said to fit into some other category can also be said to be comic. These names take many forms, ranging from puns and simple jokes to obscene references. Perhaps the most fascinating subset of comic names is the comic-derisive category. Pynchon's use of these names makes him a literary descendent of Rabelais. Bakhtin terms this type of name praise-abuse and discusses it in terms of some of the lists of characters in *Gargantua and Pantagruel*:

> Still another part of the list is composed of nicknames of an abusive nature founded on various physical disabilities, monstrosities, or signs of uncleanliness.... The formation of proper names from abusive terms is one of the methods most frequently used by Rabelais as well as by folk humor in general.... All Rabelais' names are in a way understood as nicknames of praise abuse. The only exceptions are the names of historic persons or the author's friends ... or of those who remind us of real people [460–61].

We see, then, a connection between Pynchon and western folk humor in general — a liberating laughter. While these names are used to refer to people of all backgrounds, they are usually meant to debase the upper class, but to liberate the lower class; however, both cases demonstrate the subversive power of humor as that which can overturn.

Similar to the use of comic-derisive names is the use of names that somehow mark the social status of their bearers. These names fit into Pynchon's ubiquitous theme of the conflict between the preterite and the elect. Pynchon is a champion of the downtrodden, dispossessed, and forgotten. He continually attacks the system of values instituted by the elect to keep the preterite in their places. So, in Pynchon's overturned world, popular elect symbolism is reversed and the elect marker or white hat becomes a sign of evil, while the preterite marker or black hat stands for the good. Names that function in this way help situate characters within Pynchon's unique moral framework.

Not all names, however, are unambiguous. Even if a character's moral position is discernable, the meaning of the name itself may not be. In some instances Pynchon combines elements within a name that contradict one another. This tactic is especially prevalent in V, where character names sometimes combine animate and inanimate elements. In cases such as this, Pynchon subverts our understanding of names by making a clear, unidirectional meaning impossible to uphold with certainty.

Another somewhat specialized case occurs in M&D, where names may often be said to be anachronisms. The names of some eighteenth-century characters derive from twentieth-century sources. This makes it impossible to read the work as a straight historical novel. The ultimate effect on the reader is to cause a constant application of the novel's criticisms of the eighteenth century to our own time. And this was clearly Pynchon's intention. Such names, then, raise local and historical questions to universal and timeless status. There is an important subversion of history inherent in this process; the sustainability of finished or stable versions of history is revealed as sham. Of course the division between history and fiction is constantly called into question as well-known figures such as George Washington mingle on the page with a reverend named Cherrycoke.

Certainly M&D relies on a large cast of fictionalized figures from history, but all of the novels include references to real historical figures who can, in some cases, be said loosely to operate as characters (at least as much so as fictional characters who appear for a line and vanish). The presence of real figures in fiction that is not patently historical can have a disconcerting effect on the reader. Certainly Pynchon is not alone in this practice, but he manages to emphasize the problem of categorizing a text as fact or fiction, historical interpretation or authorial fancy. Given the fact that this dictionary's aim is primarily to define the possible meanings of fictional characters whose names Pynchon invented, I offer only very brief entries on real figures from history, identifying only generally who each is. Certainly existing guides to V, Lot 49, and GR offer very good background on such "characters" and background figures.

In the case of ATD, I have stretched what it means to be a "character" beyond commonly accepted notions, at times even including entries on figures who could not be said to function as characters in any meaningful way. I have done this to help the reader of the novel to avoid any possible confusion as there has not yet been time for any body of critical commentary to develop around the novel. While not quite as chock-full of historical figures as M&D, ATD still presents us with a good number of actual figures, some with brief walk-on roles. And like M&D and Pynchon's earlier novels and stories, ATD continues to use characters and names in much the same way as he has in the past, and the categories discussed above still apply here.

Not one of these tactics or categories could be said to be an original contribution to literature by Pynchon, but taken together, they represent a unique approach to naming. Not only can the names in his novels be said to function in a variety of different ways, the sheer volume of named characters (about 500 in GR alone) suggests an approach that beggars the reader's understanding of what a novel is. Kharpertian's reading of the works of Pynchon as contemporary versions of Menippean satire is useful and telling, for satire always attempts to subvert the status quo, but subversion itself, while it may be behind Pynchon's strategies of naming, cannot be thought of as the single, unifying element behind the names. This dictionary aims above all to be a reference on the names themselves. It cannot offer a conclusion to the discussion of naming in Pynchon; it attempts to provide an introduction.

A final note on categorizing names may be in order. Like the entries on the names themselves, the categories, too, represent possibilities, sometimes mutually exclusive or contradictory ones. The categories themselves must be somewhat flexible, but, equally important, the explanation of each name must not preclude other meanings and competing categories. Some names can be said to fall into several different categories depending on which reading of the name we accept. And this confusion is, I think, deliberate on Pynchon's part. As Tanner points out, the overall pattern of Pynchon's naming is "a gesture against the tyranny of naming itself" (60). But we still must confront individual names. Offering an explanation of each name forces one to navigate between the Scylla of reading too much into a name and the Charybdis of reading too little. At times I have probably fallen victim to both of these fates. In defense of stretching the material as far as possible to provide possible meanings, I will quote the character Sir Stephen Dodson-Truck, who speculates why a particular rocket is named Hawaii I: "There's a poetry to it, engineer's poetry ... it suggests *Haverie*— average, you know — certainly you have the two lobes, don't you, symmetrical about the rocket's intended azymuth ... *hauen*, too — smashing someone with a hoe or a club" [ellipses in the original] (GR 207). The author behind this passage would surely recognize whimsical or far-reaching etymologies. Of course, reading too much into a name presents its own dangers as the following anecdote illustrates. At a crossword-fanatic convention, one puzzler told of his rapture over the impending contract between pop singer Britney Spears and the Pepsi-Cola company: "You see, 'Pepsi-Cola' is an anagram of 'Episcopal' and 'Britney Spears' is an anagram of 'Presbyterians'" (Bilger 66). One can imagine the look of deranged triumph on his face as he awaited an appropriate response from his interlocutor. I do not expect the reader to accept all or even most of the glosses I have quoted and provided. I have tried to provide a *range* of possibilities for the meanings of names wherever possible. While I think some readings are more plausible than others, I have tried not to force a single reading or to promote an overriding interpretive scheme for the names. The purpose of this dictionary is to provide possibilities and outline trends and groupings, not to insist on a preferred reading or to clearly define a poetics of naming in Pynchon. It is meant to be a helpful resource. Of course, some names might not *mean* anything at all; if, like the crossword fanatic, we insist on finding meaning everywhere, we will descend into a state of paranoia more profound than that experienced by Oedipa Mass and Tyrone Slothrop.

The Dictionary

187 (Vine)
See Barf, Billy and the Vomitones.

2-A Lagoo (M&D)
While Lagoo is a relatively common surname, the meaning of the prefix 2-A is unclear. We could sound the whole name as "due lagu," approximating Italian/Sicilian for "two lake." The surname may also be a rhyming reference to myopic cartoon character Mr. Magoo. Like other references and jokes, these are unmotivated in that the character is only mentioned, so we have no context for any allusions embedded in the name.

Abdul (M&D)
This common Arabic name is formed on the root *abd*, meaning "servant" (Ahmed 3). This seems appropriate for a character who acts as bartender and is seen only briefly taking orders for drinks and pipes.

Abraham (M&D)
Pynchon provides a name for each Indian escort who accompanies Mason and Dixon to the western terminus of the line. Mason's journal confirms that there were 14 Indians, but he does not name one of them, nor does he mention any women (Pynchon includes two in addition to the 14 chiefs and warriors). Other general accounts of the Mason-Dixon line mention these Indians but do not name them. The names may very well be real, but Pynchon's source is uncertain.

Ace (Vine)
This character is only mentioned as a member of Hub's crew. The name, probably a nickname, seems to have no special meaning for the character.

Ace, Mr. (ATD)
The positive associations of the word do not seem appropriate here. The name he uses to refer to himself may be a shortened form of "Ace of Spades," the playing card widely associated with death. His description supports this: "Glossy black eyes, presented like weapons in a duel. The gently damaged, irrevocably educated eyes we associate with the visiting dead" (415).

Achtfaden, Horst (GR)
As Weisenburger points out, the surname is German for "Eight-thread" (209). But *Faden* can also mean "string," so the surname Achtfaden can be read as "eight-string," a reference to a guitar that features two more strings than the common six. *Horst* is common enough that it need

not refer to anything, although it may recall famous Nazi culture hero and small-time thug, Horst Wessel.

Addle, Ed (ATD)

As an adjective, *addle* may mean "muddled," "unsound," even "crazy" (OED). It is appropriate for a member of a "small Ætherist community" (60) in Cleveland. They are a harmless group of crackpots (one might even say addle-pates, though Pynchon does not intend to denigrate any of them, least of all Merle Rideout). The less common meaning of "crazy" may be especially relevant to this character whom Merle helps to escape from the Newburgh Insane Asylum (61).

Adelina, Aunt (ATD)

She is only mentioned and has a common name.

Adolf (ATD)

Along with Ernst, he is a bartender in Pap Wyman's saloon, which actually existed, as did Wyman (Noel 175). Whether Adolf or Ernst were actual historical figures is uncertain. Neither first name is included in MacKell's thorough study of Colorado brothel culture during the period. But Pynchon's description of Mayva Dash's job at Pap Wyman's saloon as a "saloon girl" (88) and Mayva's characterization of the loneliness of Ernst as opposed to the expectation that bartenders be paid off, coupled with the claim that Ernst (and presumably Adolf) wanted all the girls to be his concubines, suggests that these characters also acted as pimps for some of the girls, a common practice in many Colorado saloons at the time (MacKell 13–14 et al.). Both Adolf and Ernst are common names, but if they were real, the source is uncertain.

Aghtina, Mrs. (V)

The name is Maltese for "give us" (Cassola 330). Significantly, the name is drawn from the Maltese version of the Lord's Prayer, and it puts us in mind of "give us this day our daily bread." Mrs. Aghtina is praised for her generosity and dignity after she provides a hearty porridge for a starving Maijstral after an air raid (332).

Aghtina, Saturno (V)

Aghtina means "give us" in Maltese, alluding to a line from the Lord's Prayer, and *Saturno* is the Italian for Saturn (Cassola 330). *See* Aghtina, Mrs.

Aïeul, P. (V)

Aïeul means "grandparent" in French. There is obvious humor in that this name is attached to a character described as a libertine (63). Since only his first initial is given, we are also invited to read the name as a paronomastic encoding of the expression of olfactory disgust (*peeyew*).

Aksashi, Baron (ATD)

Colonel Motojiro Akashi was a Japanese spy and member of the Black Dragon Society (Richard Spence 46).

Al Mar-Fuad (ATD)

The sound of the name gives us "Elmer Fudd," the cartoon hunter who managed to bag neither Bugs Bunny nor Donald Duck. He shares with his Islamized counterpart both the deerstalker cap and the speech impediment.

Albanian, the (ATD)

See Ramiz.

Alberto (ATD)

This common name is Italian for Albert.

Albrecht (GR)

Common German name.

Alexandrevna, Feodora (GR)

Weisenburger identifies the historical Russian empress (175).

Alexandrine of Rye (Lot 49)

Wife of Count Leonard II von Taxis (*Thurn und Taxis*).

Alexei (Vine)

Common Russian name.

Alexei, Mouse (GR)
Of all the laboratory animals used and named by Pointsman, Alexei is one of the only ones who could be said to be a character. Like most of the others, he has a Russian name chosen to honor Pavlov, the famous Russian behaviorist and Pointsman's hero.

Alfonsito (ATD)
Alfonso is a common name, but the diminutive ending *-ito*, making the name the equivalent of "little Alphonso," gives the name an ironic cast as it is applied to a gunman. It could be meant as a description of his size, which is not described in the text, or a charactonymic reference to his character: this "dutiful" lieutenant comes off as something of a yes-man.

Algernon (M&D)
As this very minor character is one of the many effeminate fops populating the novel, we might read the name as a reference to Wilde's character Algernon Moncrieff from *The Importance of Being Earnest*, more as a reference to the Wilde-type than to this character himself. The name itself, however, is not anachronistic as it developed at the time of William the Conqueror and started to gain popularity in the fifteenth century (Withycombe 14).

Algernon (ATD)
According to Withycombe, the name derives from the French for "with whiskers" or "moustaches" (14) and "has remained a mainly aristocratic name" (15). Pynchon seems to use the name for characters who are really more caricatures of certain aristocratic excesses. This character appears in three scenes: associated with Ruperta's indignation at being exposed to a low, black jazz club (369); portrayed drivelling and giggling in conversation with Hunter Penhallow (729); described as "a flâneur" (an idler, but often associated with foppish dress and manners) (672). The character recalls the minor character Algernon in M&D (22); both are described or portrayed in terms of effeminacy and foppishness.

Algie (ATD)
Described as "a flâneur of Ruperta's acquaintance" (672), this must be the Algernon who appears on 369 and 729. See Algernon.

Alice (V)
Grant mentions that the name "may have been influenced by speculations regarding the creator of *Alice's Adventures in Wonderland* and his relationship with the children to whom he told his stories and whom he photographed" (47). It is certainly a reference to Alice Liddel, the putative child love of Lewis Carroll. Another bit of evidence of this connection may be found in Alice's response to MacBurgess's advances: "a game, she'd *carol*— such fun" [emphasis added] (70).

Alice (GR)
See Girls, Slothrop's.

Allan (GR)
Common name.

Allègre, Armand (M&D)
Allègre is French for "cheerful" or "lighthearted"; the name is rather inappropriate for a character so gloomy as chef Armand. The name Armand is quite common.

Allen, Ethan (M&D)
The DNB identifies this American revolutionary army officer (Bellesîles).

Allison (GR)
See Girls, Slothrop's.

Amber the paralegal (Vine)
According to the Social Security Administration, "Amber" remained among the top 20 female names from 1981 to 1993 ("Popular Baby Names").

Amelia (Amy) (M&D)
Ware demonstrates that the character's name refers to Amy Fisher, the infamous

Long Island Lolita, who was involved with Italian mechanic Joey Buttafuoco and tried to murder his wife; our Amelia runs off to Massapequa with an Italian Waggon-Smith ("*Mason & Dixon*").

Amp, Lucifer (GR)

Larsson mentions *amp* as a measure of current, a kind of match, and a brand name of lightbulbs and cites Lucifer as the first rebellious Angel (V542.40). This last point is especially important as Lucifer Amp defects from the Special Operations Executive and joins the Counterforce (542–3).

André (M&D)

Common French name.

Andreas (V)

It is ironic that this typical German name is applied to a slave, but it does emphasize the force of colonialism in Africa.

Andreas (GR)

Common German name.

Andrée, Salomon (GR)

Weisenburger identifies the historical Arctic explorer (254).

Andy (V)

Common name.

Angelo (V)

Common Italian name.

Angelo (M&D)

Common Italian name.

Angelo, Duke of Squamuglia (Lot 49)

Angelo is Italian for "angel" (*see also* Niccoló for a brief description of reversal in the names of characters in *The Courier's Tragedy*). Squamuglia does not appear to describe any province of Italy and may come from *squaghiàre*, "to melt down, or liquefy" and *mugliàre*, a variant of *mugghiàre*, "to bellow," together, suggesting Angelo's evil reign.

Angevine, Miss (V)

The name simply means "from the region of Anjou, France." The significance seems to be that she and most other named tenants in Profane's parents' apartment building are immigrants, or still have ethnic names.

Annes (GR)

See Girls, Slothrop's.

Annunziata, Sister Maria (V)

The nun's name honors the Annunciation of the Virgin Mary. She is apparently one of Fina Mendoza's teachers, and Profane asks Fina what the good sister would think if she saw Fina offering herself sexually to him (145). The situation is ironic, given the nun's name especially, but the name is not.

Antonia (V)

Common name.

Aquilina (V)

Although *aquilino* is Italian for "aquiline," that gloss does not seem meaningful. Surely it derives from the Latin/Italian words *acqua* meaning "water" and *linea* meaning "line." A water line is a "line on the hull of a ship to which the surface of the water rises" (AH4), a point of critical concern to a shipfitter, this character's trade. Cassola says that Aquilina is also a Maltese surname (331).

Arch (GR)

Arch is probably short for Archibald, an ordinary name. There may be some mild description of this child whose mother "keeps trying to smack him but he's too fast" (171). The adjective *arch* can mean "clever, crafty, roguish" and is often used to describe children and their expressions (OED).

Archer, Mr. (ATD)

Common name.

Arnold (M&D)

Common name.

Arrabal, Jesús (Lot 49)
Hollander glosses the name as "Jesus of the suburbs" ("Pynchon, JFK and the CIA" 95). Grant suggests that "suburbs" is misleading in that in Mexico the word refers to "that part of the city occupied by the latest arrivals from the countryside — the poorest and most neglected inhabitants of the urban sprawl" and that the combined name refers to the redemption of the preterite (103). We might further speculate, given the character's connection to anarcho-syndicalism, a reference to the redemptive potential of anarchism. There may also be an allusion to Fernando Arrabal, the Spanish playwright.

Arriaga, Camilo (ATD)
Liberal Mexican intellectual and friend to Ricardo Flores Magón (Cookcroft 95–97).

Arvin (ATD)
The name comes from the Anglo-Saxon for "man of the people" (Kolatch 22), appropriate for this common miner and minor character.

Asaph (M&D)
This biblical name meaning "to gather" or "assembler" (Hamilton 23) is mildly appropriate for a preacher who looks beyond the days of deism to when Christians will be brought together again.

Asch, Walter (GR)
As Larsson points out, the name derives from the German *Asche*, meaning "ashes or cinders" (V152.16). He has some connection to the I.G. and other power structures that will be behind every aspect of the war, and, as such, represents the forces of death over life.

Ashkil, Danilo (ATD)
Danilo is a common Slavic name. The character descends from Sephardic Jews and ends up in Salonica because it is a haven for "Jews on the run" (827). The surname embodies the fate of European Jews later in the century: "ashes, killed."

Assunta (ATD)
Common Italian name.

Astounding Galvanic Grandpa (ATD)
A charactonymic carnival name capturing the essence of this old performer's act: he sprouts "electric plumes of many colors" with the help of a generator (184). *Galvanic* means "relating to direct-current electricity" (AH4).

Atildado, El (ATD)
Günther von Quassel's nickname is explained in the text: it refers to his "flawless personal toilette" (637). The Spanish verb *atildar* means "to tidy up or adorn." But it also means "to mark with a tilde." His duelling scar is mentioned in this passage, and Kit remarks earlier on the appearance of the scar: "looks like a Mexican tilde" (600). The nickname is pure charactonym: "The one marked with a tilde."

Atman, Weed (Vine)
In addition to mentioning a possible reference to Steven Weed, one-time boyfriend of Patty Hearst who was famously kidnapped by the Symbionese Liberation Army, Diebold and Goodwin gloss *weed* as slang for "marijuana" and *atman* as Hindu for "breath, the principle of life, the World Soul." While the term *atman* itself is rich with meaning, the name can be read as a simple joke in the comic-derisive tradition (in the Bakhtinian sense): "marijuana breath." Other glosses begin with these same definitions, including Rushdie, who defines the name as "marijuana soul" (36), Cowart, who reads the name widely as a depiction of the 1960s Zeitgeist: "The soul of this counterculture — or rather its *atman* (for it favored an Eastern spirituality) — was a substance properly known as 'weed'" ("Continuity" 181), but goes on to offer the possibility

that *atman* should still be read as "supreme spiritual essence," but that *weed* could refer to the Anglo-Saxon word for "garment," together suggesting body and soul, both of which are destroyed by Vond through Frenesi (186), and Tabbi who reads the surname *Atman* as an indication of "the influence of Hindu religion on *Vineland*" (97–8). In an interesting article on the role of Group Theory in Vine, Slade connects the character of Atman to the French mathematician Galois through *weed* meaning "tobacco, cigarettes," a reference to the popular French cigarettes Gauloise ("Communication" 84). As far-fetched as this sounds, he offers strong evidence that the character Weed Atman is at least partially based on Galois.

Aubade (E)

An aubade is a song accompanying daybreak, but also a poem "about lovers separating at dawn" (AH4). She is associated with music; all sensation for her is reduced to sound: "of music which emerged at intervals from a howling darkeness of discordancy" (84). And since the name refers to songs of a new day, there seems to be an element of hope implied in this ambiguous story. But the second meaning of *aubade* is called up by the story's end, when Aubade shatters the glass of their hemetically sealed world, turns to Callisto to "wait with him until the moment of equilibrium was reached ... and resolve into a tonic of darkenss and the final absense of all motion" (98). The separation of the lovers, with dawn fast approaching, seems inevitable and permanent.

Aubergine, Madame (ATD)

A comic name for a dance instructor, *aubergine* is French for "eggplant"— somehow Mrs. Eggplant sounds less refined than Madame Aubergine. There is also a reference to the novel's theme of bilocation by way of another character, Baklashchan, whose foreign name means "eggplant."

Augustine (V)

See also Bartholomew, Ignatius, Paul, Teresa, and Veronica. Augustine is one of Fairing's anthropomorphized rats. The reference is obviously to St. Augustine of Hippo, whose prolific writing addressed, among other things, politics — appropriate for the potential mayor of New York.

Austra (M&D)

Austra ("'tis a common name here for Slaves") (65) means, as Mason points out, "The South." The root forms such words as *austral* and *Australia*. The name points toward the North-South dichotomy in the novel and also suggests the parallel between slavery and all the southern regions visited by Mason and Dixon.

Avalanche, Father (V)

New suggests that this name is no accident:

> for the effect of the priest, the father, the artist, the reader, is always to overwhelm, to bury the future with his own constructs, not through viciousness or even insensitivity, but because it is the act of love by which the past speaks to the future about the elusive present which neither can penetrate nor possess, but where the "something of value, some truth to tell a son," is always located [410].

Harder claims that the name is another scientific allusion, referring to the Townsend avalanche, "a process in which the ions of one generation have collisions that produce a greater number of ions in the succeeding generation" (77).

Avery (ATD)

A relatively common name for a very minor character. Kolatch lists Avery as a variant of Aubrey, from the Anglo-Saxon for "elf-ruler" (24), but this has no obvious application to a mine inspector, unless one reads it as ruler over little people, a reference to the corporate attitude toward workers.

Aychrome, Vance (ATD)

The character is a parody of the overfed policeman stereotype. The name, too, has an element of stereotype and is charactonymic. Vance is "a form of the British name Vans, meaning 'high, high places'" (Kolatch 236), suggesting his role in the police, while the uncommon name Aychrome seems formed around *chrome*, suggesting hardness, although certainly not bodily hardness, given his description.

Azeff, Monsieur Yevno (ATD)

Evno Fishelovich Azef was an infamous Russian police spy (Richard Spence 11).

Aziz, Abdel (ATD)

Porch identifies the historical Sultan but gives the name as Abd el-Aziz (106).

Babington-Smith, Constance (GR)

Weisenburger identifies the historical British surveillance photo analyst (300).

Baby Igor (Lot 49)

Metzger's name from his days as a child movie star is perfect: the combination of the cute and the monstrous aptly describes numerous apple-cheeked young stars who end up involved in drug addiction, prostitution, pornography, alcoholism, or the practice of law.

Bad (Vine)

See Barf, Billy and the Vomitones.

Bad Priest, The (V)

This title refers to an unnamed incarnation of V. The bad or evil modifying her priestly impersonation refers simply to her conception of religion, which is grounded in sterility and abortion, qualities associated with her own descent into the inanimate. There is also a likely literary allusion here: Fr. Rolfe, in his eccentric novel *Hadrian the Seventh*, refers to a minor figure in the past of the main character as "the bad priest" who "ruined himself. He persisted in his career of crime until the bishop found him out.... He's in one of the colonies now" (316). This bad priest is modelled on an actual Jesuit who told an author of a biography of Rolfe, in reference to the preceding quotation, "I was sent to Malta for two years" (Symons 100), the final sight of V's Bad Priest.

Baffy, Ellsworth (SI)

If this "candy magnate" is real, the source is uncertain. He is not listed in the Federal Writers' Project guide to the Berkshires, which is Pynchon's source for so much in this section of the story. Both names are common. Perhaps Baffy was chosen because it rhymes with *taffy*, or it may combine *batty* and *daffy*, suggesting an eccentric. The word *baffy* is a golf term describing "a short wooden club used to hit the ball into the air" (OED) and there seem to be many golf courses named Ellsworth. These associations may rely on the reputation of golf as a form of recreation for the wealthy, characterizing this magnate obliquely.

Baglione, Gino and the Paisans (Vine)

This band alias for Billy Barf and the Vomitones is meant to make them seem Italian as they play at a Mafia wedding. Baglione is a relatively common Italian surname. Gino, of course, is quite common. *Paisan* is actually an American expression used by those of Italian descent and means "fellow-countryman" (OED). It is descriptive, in that the band members are impersonating Italians.

Baker, William (M&D)

Headlee identifies the historical packhorse driver (7).

Baklashchan (ATD)

This Russian agent's alias most likely refers to a Russian word more properly transliterated as *baklazhan*, meaning "eggplant." He asserts that the name is an alias and that "the more threatening ones were all spoken for" (1022). Agent Eggplant does sound laughably non-threatening. It also forms part of the theme of bilocation as there is another character, Madame Aubergine, whose name is a foreign word for "eggplant."

Bakto (ATD)

Bakto does not seem to be a very common name. It appears to derive from the Serbo-Croation verb *bàktati* ("to struggle with"), an apt characterization of him as a member of the "Black Hand" (834).

Banks, Sir Joseph, [Baronet] (M&D)

The DNB identifies this British naturalist (Gascoigne).

Barbie (Vine)

The name refers to the eponymous doll introduced by Mattel in 1959 and presenting the stereotypical image of what a woman should be, although this Barbie is a beleaguered mother, the very fate Frenesi had hoped to avoid.

Barf, Billy and the Vomitones (Vine)

The band is a parody of punk rock bands of the era. The names of the members (with the exception of Lester and the ironically named Isaiah Two Four) are extensions of this parody: Bad, 187 (named, as the narrator explains "after the California Penal Code section for murder" [98]), Meathook (the device from which slaughtered animals are suspended), and the eponymous Billy Barf.

Barfstable, Inigo (Lot 49)

The first name of this seventeenth-century printer recalls the famous British architect (and near contemporary of the character), Inigo Jones. The surname, while likely formed from the name of the Massachusett's town Barnstable, seems to suggest contempt for him or his works by Pynchon, but most likely it is another name functioning purely as a joke.

Barkhausen, H. (V)

Grant identifies the historical physicist (117).

Barkley, [John] (M&D)

Browne identifies the historical witness to the melee described in the text (156).

Barnes, Moses (M&D)

Headlee identifies the historical overseer of the axmen (5).

Barnes, Mr. (M&D)

See Barnes, Moses.

Barnett (M&D)

See Johnson, Barney.

Barrington, Carl (SI)

Both given- and surname are common, suggesting in the context of the story a fundamental humanity that transcends race, and therefore the ridiculousness of racism and segregation. Barrington may also be a play on *barren*— the Barringtons are childless, so the other children invent a child for them, Carl, their imaginary black playmate. Or the whole name may reflect on the values of the town itself— it is a "barren town." The source for the surname, however may come from the actual town of Barrington in the Berkshires, named for Viscount Barrington, "famous apostle of religious tolerance" (Federal Writers' Project of the Works Progress Administration for Massachusetts 152). This same WPA guide to the Berkshires (a source Pynchon acknowledges using [SL 21]) describes Barrington House as the "showplace of the community" (157), thus giving the name of the black family a nobility absent from many of the whites, with their often ridiculous names.

Bartholomew (V)

See also Augustine, Ignatius, Paul, Teresa, and Veronica. Bartholomew is one of Fairing's anthropomorphized rats. Two Saints Bartholomew (of the first and twelfth centuries) inspired cultic followings in England (Farmer 39–40), appropriate for the British Fairing. The first-century Bartholomew is the patron saint of tanners and those who work with skins, because he is said to have been martyred by flaying (Farmer 40). This, too, is appropriate as Fairing skins and eats some of the rats.

Basilisco the cop (V)

In Italian *basilisco* means both "a type of lizard" and the mythical "basilisk," whose breath and glance were said to be fatal. As part of a list of rapidly introduced names, the function is largely comic, although there is undoubtedly an element of derisive typing of the police officer.

Basilisk, Maynard (V)

This alias for the escapee from Devil's Island, who is on his way to Vassar to teach beekeeping, is glossed by Harder as "mighty lizard" (73). Of course, *Basilisk* is just as likely to refer to the mythical creature of fearsome breath and glance, and *Maynard* comes from the Old German, *Magenhard*, combining "strength" and "hardiness" (Withycombe 205). It is an appropriate name for a Devil's Island escapee.

Basnight, Lewis (Lew) (ATD)

The surname and given name are both fairly common. There is a hint that some joke, comic sound, or something similar is intended, though, by the comment that newsboys "pronounc[ed] his name disrespectfully" (37). The only obvious deliberate mispronunciation would yield "Lube Ass Night," and the obvious sexual connotations. Given the prevalence of the practice of sodomy in the novel, this is a reasonable enough reading of the name as a joke.

Basnight, Troth (ATD)

The name of Lew Basnight's wife is both charactonym and an ironic reference to her character. *Troth* means "betrothal" or "pledged fidelity" (AH4); one thinks of the word primarily in the context of the marriage ceremony, "unto thee I pledge my troth." The name defines her as a wife, but the pledge of fidelity is ironic as she leaves Lew (38). Basnight is a common surname. Troth, too, however, was somewhat common as a name from the seventeenth century on (Withycombe 269).

Baxter (SR)

Common as both a given- and a surname. Hollander suggests an allusion to seventeenth-century "nonconformist-English clergyman" Richard Baxter ("Pynchon's Politics" 25) as part of a reading showing the importance of a range of religious rituals in the story. There may also be an allusion to Pynchon's creative writing teacher at Cornell, Baxter Hathaway (SL 17).

Beatrice the barmaid (V)

Although all the barmaids at the Sailor's Grave are called Beatrice — including the owner, Mrs. Buffo — we are first introduced to one as "Beatrice the barmaid" (11). This is the first of many instances where the "full" name of the character links a name with an occupation. Grant cites Madsen in interpreting the use of the name to refer to all barmaids as an indication of "[t]he debased condition of language as a referential medium" (6). The allusion to Dante's Beatrice is clear, although Grant reads this, coupled with the wide use of the name in the bar, as a warning to question "grand ordering structures of all kinds" (7). But Beatrice does act as a guide to the sailors, albeit one whose offer of redemption consists of drunkenness and sexual gratification. The name Beatrice means "bringer of joy" (Withycombe 42), surely an appropriate name for a barmaid.

Beatriz the Bulb (GR)

See Byron the Bulb.

Beaver (GR)

See Jeremy (Beaver).

Beaver, Boyd (Lot 49)

Hollander observes that the character is "reduced to a woman's crotch" ("Pynchon,

JFK and the CIA" 69). Boyd is typically a Scots surname and less common as a given name. Given his use of the celebrated Pynchonian kazoo, the vaginal reference may celebrate transgression (as a vulgar body-part name in the Rabelaisian tradition).

Beck, Professor (GR)
Weisenburger identifies the historical engineering professor (119).

Beck, Rhodie (M&D)
Rhodie is a variant of *rhody*, "rhododendron." It is not an uncommon name and has no clear meaning for this character. Beck is a common name.

Beck, Zepho (M&D)
Although the character, who turns into a beaver during the full moon, is not real, the name may be. *Zepho(n)* is a biblical name meaning "watchtower" (Hamilton 121) and Beck is quite common. There is no clear application to this character.

Becker, Eula (Vine)
Tabbi claims that the character "may have been named after Eula Varner in Faulkner's Snopes novels" (97). We really do not learn enough about Eula Becker to establish this with any certainty. Becker is a common surname.

Becker, Mr. (ATD)
Although a common surname, Becker creates a clear link to the Traverse family genealogy. Vine details the Becker-Traverse family reunion (369–75) and tells how Eula Becker (grandmother of Frenesi Gates) met Jess Traverse (76). While not stated, the pro-worker school teacher Mr. Becker is meant to be a direct ancestor of the whole Becker-Traverse clan, even if not a literal one.

Beláustegui (GR)
Weisenburger states that the origin of the name is unknown (188). It appears to be a fairly common Hispanic surname.

Benito the Bulb (GR)
See Byron the Bulb.

Beppo (ATD)
Dally's male alias in Venice is a fairly common nickname for Giuseppe. It is also an allusion to Lord Byron's poem *Beppo*, which appropriately takes place in Venice.

Bergomask, Oley (V)
Bergomask is an alternative spelling of *bergamask*, which refers to a rustic dance imitating the people of Bergamo, Venice, who were "ridiculed as clownish in their manners and dialect" (OED). While the name Oley has no clear significance (its source may be a place by that name in the Berkshires), it approximates the word *oily*. Taken together, the parts of the name may be read as "oily clown."

Bernie the Bulb (GR)
See Byron the Bulb.

Bert (GR)
Weisenburger identifies this hypothetical name applied to the Lord of the Sea as being from Grimm's *Teutonic Mythology* and referring to Berchtold, a white figure who promotes navigation (50). White also links the figure/name with death as the color does throughout the novel.

Betts, [Joseph] (M&D)
British mathematician elected as Savilian Professor of Geometry at Oxford University in 1765, a position previously held by Nathaniel Bliss and Edmund Halley (*The Honours Register* 89).

Beukes, Tim (V)
Grant identifies the historical Bondel chief (118).

Bevin, Ernest (GR)
Weisenburger identifies the historical labor minister (69).

Bevis, [John] (M&D)
The DNB identifies this physician and astronomer (Clerke).

Bezumyoff (ATD)

This know-it-all of the crew has a name formed on the Russian word for madman (*bezumeshch*) with a common Russian name ending.

Bianca (GR)

The last name is uncertain since her mother's last name is an alias of sorts and her father is unknown. *Bianca* is the Italian version of the name *Blanche*, and ultimately means "white" (Withycombe 48), although there may be a connection to *biancàna*, Italian for "waste land." White is ironic in connection with a young girl with so much sexual experience, but Weisenburger points out repeatedly that the color white is associated with death throughout GR. This connection may prefigure Bianca's fate.

Bibescue, Countess (GR)

The reference to Bucharest makes certain that Pynchon refers here to the Romanian noble family Bibescu. There seems to be no special reason for the allusion (the character is another very minor one), and may just be another bit of arcana.

Biddle, "Gobbler" (GR)

Larsson identifies the Biddle family as "one of the leading families of Philadelphia" (V65.15). Such a family could presumably send a son to Harvard (he is identified as Slothrop's classmate). Another possible reading is paronomasia: a "gobbler" is a turkey and a "biddy" is any fowl, especially a chicken. A typical Harvard nickname?

Big Knife (SI)

A charactonymically appropriate name for one of Carl McAfee's former cellmates.

Bing, Liu (ATD)

Common Chinese name. *Thomas Pynchon Wiki* wishes to hear the name as "lubing" with sexual connotations. Given characters such as Lew B. and Lube Car-

nal and other references to sodomy, this seems plausible.

Birch, Thomas (M&D)

The DNB identifies this Royal Society secretary and "compiler of histories" (Miller).

Bird, John (M&D)

The DNB identifies this "maker of scientific instruments" (McConnell).

Birdbury, Pharmacist (GR)

The surname is not an uncommon one and does not seem to suggest anything about the character. There is a Bradbury Pharmacy chain in the UK, but this reference seems unlikely.

Black, Penelope ("Penny") (ATD)

The common name Penelope Black is transformed by the nickname Penny: in 1840, England issued the first prepaid postage stamps, the penny black and the two penny blue, both with the likeness of Queen Victoria in profile ("philately"). This is an appropriate pun from an author whose interest in philately has persisted from its pervasive role in Lot 49 to the character Ewball Oust, Sr. in ATD, "a stamp collector of average obsessiveness" enraged by his son's devaluing inverted 1901 Pan-American Issue Stamps by using them to mail letters (978). There may, however, be another allusion related to a larger theme in the book rather than this minor character. Joseph Hergesheimer's 1917 novel *The Three Black Pennys* tells "the story of three generations of the wealthy, mine-owning Penny family" ("Hergesheimer, Joseph").

Black-Powder (Blackie) (M&D)

The name of this revolutionary clearly refers to gunpowder, an important tool of his trade. It also refers to his explosive temper: on meeting Mason he says "I'll kill him, if you lot would rather not" (402).

Blackner, Mr. (M&D)

Common name.

Bladdery, St. John (GR)
The OED defines the adjective *bladdery* as "thin and inflated; inflated and hollow." One of the two competitors in the runcible spoon fight, Bladdery realizes how close he and Purfle are to meaningless death, a universal condition, one would think, during a war. The name seems to reflect this precariousness. But the situation is also ridiculous, given that the weapon is a runcible spoon, a sort of fork-spoon-knife combination invented by Edward Lear, British author of nonsense verse (OED).

Blaine, James G. (SI)
Hollander identifies the 1884 presidential candidate ("Pynchon's Politics" 46).

Blamm, Helga (Lot 49)
The surname undoubtedly derives from the German root *blam-*, meaning "shame" or "disgrace" and probably refers either to Hilarius's past as a Nazi, or Helga Blamm's sharing in this secret past through her devotion to him. It may, however, be meant as a comic/onomatopoeic sound, imitating the sound of a gun being fired, although more as it is depicted in comic books than in reality.

Blanca, La (ATD)
La Blanca (Spanish for "the white") is the local nickname for Bob Meldrum's wife. It is explained in the text: "named for a white horse of supernatural demeanor she was always seen to ride" (287). The wife and horse were real: "In the saddle of her beautiful white horse, she made a romantic picture riding the trails, but her withdrawal from all contact with any of us on the hill caused some comment" (Backus 69). The source of the nickname is uncertain; Backus does not even mention a name.

Bland, Buddy (GR)
Buddy seems another ordinary name. Given the similar first name, there may be on echo of Bobby Bland, the famous blues singer. *See* Bland, Lyle for the surname.

Bland, Clara (GR)
Clara is a common name. *See* Bland, Lyle for the surname.

Bland, Lyle (GR)
Given Bland's role in Tyrone Slothrop's being "sold to the I.G." (286), the name seems inappropriate in its association of mildness or insipidity. There may be an allusion to the comic-fictional "Bland Corporation" mentioned in the 1964 film, *Dr. Strangelove*, modeled on the actual Rand Corporation. The name also belies Bland's eventual interest in the occult and astral projection. Bland, however, is a fairly common surname.

Bland, Lyle, Jr. (GR)
See Bland, Lyle.

Bland, Margaret (M&D)
Mentioned in Dixon's will along with her daughters, presumably fathered by Jeremiah Dixon as Pynchon says in the novel (Robinson "Jeremiah Dixon" 274).

Blaskó, Béla (ATD)
This character from Lugos, Hungary who plays a vampire on stage is of course Béla Lugosi, who played the Bram Stoker character Dracula on stage and in film; Béla Lugosi is the stage name used by Blasko Béla Ferenc Dezso ("Lugosi, Béla").

Blaze (ATD)
Blaze is essentially a charactonym, though its descriptive value refers more to the nature of her relationship with Darby: "Blaze and Darby were a furiously passionate 'item' right from the beginning" (1032). The romantic figurative use of the noun *blaze* is well-known: "a sudden kindling up of passion as of a fire" (OED).

Blazzo (GR)
The name of this Italian stuntman derives from a character in a Burnand and Sullivan opera called *The Chieftain*. There

does not seem to be any connection between these two characters, and the name is probably another bit of arcana; perhaps Pynchon liked the sound of it.

Bleagh, Dr. (GR)
The name may be a pun on the word *bleak*. Larsson reads the name as an "expression of disgust" (V91.27). In either case, the name could refer loosely to the character of this doctor who performs lobotomies and pursues his nurse. Most likely, it is a simple joke.

Blicero, Captain (GR)
Weissman chooses the German nickname for death as a code name. Blicero/Weissman is everywhere associated with death. Although his deeply perverse sexuality could be tied to transgression (usually a positive in Pynchon), his desires are too tied to control to be read positively. The perverse sexuality associated with the character should probably be read as a sign of sterility.

Blicero, Dominus (GR)
More a personification of death than a character, the name literally means Lord (from the Latin *Dominus*) Death (from a German nickname for death) (Weisenburger 31).

Blinky (M&D)
The word means "prone to blinking," but this is not relevant to this "Youth of loutish and ungather'd appearance" (35). The name may be meant as comic, although it is not terribly rare. It does look forward to the actual crook Blinky Morgan who appears in ATD.

Bliss, Nathaniel (M&D)
Cope identifies Bliss as Bradley's successor as Astronomer Royal ("Some Contacts" 234).

Bloat, Teddy (GR)
An ugly name for an ugly character. Besides the connotation of intestinal gas, *bloat* is also American slang for a "conceited or contemptible person" (OED).

Blobadjian, Igor (GR)
Winner cites a Kazakh delegate at the VTsK NTA conference who claimed the strength of the Arabist movement against Latin script by the name of Badzhbildin (141). Thomas Moore points out this is the probable source of the name Blobadjian (100). In the context of the novel, however, Blobadjian is not depicted as an Arabist (353-5). Of course, if this is meant to be an ironic allusion to the historical Arabist, it is so obscure as to be missed by everyone.

Blobb, Augustine (Lot 49)
The first name may suggest his vocation as minister by recalling St. Augustine. Although we have no information about the Reverend Blobb's denomination, the combination of the two names could be a derisive reference to the Puritans, who spawned the notions of election and preterition so central to all of Pynchon's work. Hollander wishes to read the name as a reference to a particular way of exegeting *City of God* whereby the fate of contemporary figures could be deduced ("Pynchon, JFK and the CIA" 100), but this only makes sense in the context of his reading of Lot 49 as political allegory.

Blobb, Dr. Diocletian (Lot 49)
"To name a character Diocletian Blobb is to mock the very act of naming" (Caesar 7). *Blobb* is obviously a joke, and possibly charactonymic to some extent: Oedipa describes him as "an insufferable ass" (158). Hollander suggests the name Diocletian refers to the Roman emperor from 284 to 305 C.E., whose government was characterized by dictatorship, massive military, loss of autonomy, weak senate, and a change in government ("Pynchon, JFK and the CIA" 99-100). Presumably these qualities refer both to circumstances around the Thurn and Taxis monopoly and to fears about the

direction of the United States at the time of the novel.

Bloggins (ATD)

Both *Wikipedia* and *Urban Dictionary* define the name as a word for a soldier or a name for a hypothetical Canadian soldier. The reading is tempting and certainly fits the context of the passage and the description of this constable, yet these online sources do not provide solid sources. The term is not listed in several dictionaries of slang, dictionaries of military slang, Canadian English, or Canadianisms. It could merely have been used for its comic Dickensian sound.

Blondelle, Sister (M&D)

An ironic name for a Gypsy, *Blondelle* means "blond woman" (*elle*—"she, her"). A better English approximation might be *Blondie*. Like the other sisters in Las Vinetas de Cristo, she is trained to please men, so the name might hint at a character meant to be an object of desire.

Blope, Dr. Templeton (ATD)

Templeton is fairly common, though more as a surname. Together, the names have a comic Dickensian sound. Blope suggests *bloat* and *blimp*, appropriate to this pedantic windbag. The name also recalls that of Diocletian Blobb in Lot 49.

Bloth, Mindy (GR)

Bloth means "blood" in both Gothic and Old Norse. The Rocket City of the future has disturbing Teutono-Nordic overtones.

Blowitt (GR)

A punning name for a dead airman: he blew it.

Blundell, Miles (ATD)

Both given- and surname are common, but given his description as "suffer[ing] at times from a confusion in his motor processes, often producing lively results, yet as frequently compromising the crew's physical safety" (4), we cannot help but hear in the surname *blunder*.

Boaz (ATD)

Katie's jocular nicknames for the two doormen at the I. J. & K. Smokefoot department store, Jachin and Boaz, are from 1 Kings, as she says: "And he set up the pillars in the porch of the temple: and he set up the right pillar, and called the name thereof Jachin: and he set up the left pillar, and called the name thereof Boaz" (1 Kings 7: 21). Twice in the paragraph describing these doormen, Pynchon uses the word "pillars" (346), deliberately echoing the language of the Bible reference. 1 and 2 Kings are widely held "to explain how Yahweh's people came to be in exile.... [They] were guilty of cultic infidelities so numerous and so terrible that destruction was the only fit punishment" (Brown, Fitzmeyer, and Murphy 161). Solomon's temple is reimagined as a temple of consumerism, for which we may infer the "fit punishment." *Jachin* and *Boaz* mean "solid" and "strength," respectively (Brown, Fitzmeyer, and Murphy 1264), appropriate to pillars or doormen.

Bodine, Fender-Belly, Captain of the Foretop (M&D)

Clearly the character is meant to be Pig Bodine's ancestor (*see* Bodine, Seaman Pig). Fender-Belly is a wonderful Bakhtinian celebration-of-the-lower-bodily-stratum name. A fender is "something that serves to fend or keep off something else" (OED). Thus his massive stomach (earned through the consumption of copious quantities of beer) protects him.

Bodine, O.I.C. (ATD)

Pig Bodine or an ancestor/relative has appeared in Pynchon's short fiction, V, GR, and M&D. We should not be surprised to find him here. The *Thomas Pynchon Wiki* suggests the common naval abbreviation Officer in Charge and very cleverly suggests that if one renders it OinC rather than O.I.C., it reads oink, most appropriate to Pig Bodine. The *Wiki* voices the obvious objection that no

Bodine would ever be an officer. In fact, he is a stoker, and not even the chief stoker at that (517); officers do not shovel coal. The initials sound "Oh, I see," anticipating readers' reactions "upon encountering this old favorite: 'Oh, I see Bodine!'" (*Thomas Pynchon Wiki*). Indeed the character bears the standard Bodine features, from drinking liquor of dubious quality to preparing to sleep during his watch (517). *See* Bodine, Seaman Pig.

Bodine, Seaman Pig (LL, V, GR)

The character first appeared in Pynchon's 1960 story, "Low-lands," reappeared in V, and shows up both as a kind of ancestor as Foretopman Bodine in M&D and O.I.C. Bodine in ATD. Many critics have commented on this name. Harder's emphasis on the character's obscene and swinish qualities (71) is typical. Others have emphasized positive aspects as well as the necessary ambivalence in reading such a character. In contrast to negative images in GR, "the life force, only surviving in its most earthly, mindless states, is symbolized by the Pig (and pig-figures such as Pig Bodine)" in V (LeVot 115). Pig's atheism, criminality, womanizing, and so on contrast with "conventional" characters, who are often portrayed as evil in the Pynchonian universe. Pig is the supremely transgressive character (*see* White 56–8). The name *Pig* seems obvious enough, but *Bodine* does not necessarily suggest anything. I would like to suggest that the full name *Pig Bodine* (as far-fetched as it may seem) is a simple anagram of *Ping Bodie*, the name of a New York Yankee from 1918 to 1921 (*Baseball Encyclopedia* 587). Bodie is best known as Babe Ruth's spring training roommate (Sobol 17). The Bodine/Bodie anagram alludes to Babe Ruth. A troubled American hero, larger than life, known as much for heavy drinking and womanizing as for hitting homeruns, Ruth captured the nation's imagination during the 1920s. Pig Bodine is meant to mirror the qualities of a popular American hero, one whose popularity is tied to transgression. Clearly the character is meant to be positive, if flawed. All the previously discussed shades of meaning seem relevant, but there is not one overriding interpretation of the name. Like several other major character names in Pynchon, this one is overdetermined.

Bodley, Mr. [Sir Thomas] (M&D)

The DNB identifies this scholar and founder of the Bodleian Library at Oxford (Clennell).

Boeblich (V)

This pseudo-German name may connote *boobish*, but the German does not seem to mean anything.

Boggs, Robert (M&D)

Headlee identifies the historical axman and instrument bearer (5).

Boilster, Chloe (ATD)

Chloe, a common name, derives from the Greek for "a young green shoot" (Withycombe 60). It is an appropriate name for a baby. *See* Boilster, Tace for the surname.

Boilster, Eugene (ATD)

Eugene is a common name. If Boilster is a perversion of *bolster* (to prop up or support), the name is somewhat charactonymic. He is first seen waiting for a deputy to arrive and assist him in his duties as sheriff. That Deuce Kindred, a murderer, is mistaken for this man explains why the name and its meaning are perverted. *See also* Boilster, Tace.

Boilster, Tace (ATD)

Kolatch claims that the name Tace is short for Tacita, deriving from the Latin for "to be silent" (426). The OED gives *tace* as "be quiet" and lists the phrase, "tace is latin for a candle," which means "keep it quiet." It is an ironic description for one as talkative as this character, who, within minutes of meeting Lake Traverse, reveals that her own father "Ha[d] his way" with her (480). Boilster is not a common name, perhaps a perversion of *bolster*, "to support," which she attempts to do for Lake. The name could also be a play on similarly formed occupational names, like *maltster* (one who malts grain for brewing). The name would mean "one who boils," referring perhaps to her temper: when she thinks Deuce Kindred is beating Lake, she appears at their door with a loaded shotgun (487). The name might also be read as a comic combination of *boil* and *blister*.

Bolingbroke (LL)

Hollander relates the probable source for this name: "To Flange the dump is 'a discrete kingdom with Bolingbroke its uncontested ruler' [LL 67]. Pynchon's choice of the name 'Bolingbroke' (the historical Bolingbroke became England's Henry IV) for the night watchman signals some inversion" ("Pynchon's Politics" 32). But there is another "historical Bolingbroke": Henry Saint John, First Viscount Bolingbroke, an exiled Jacobite writer (AH4). Our character Bolingbroke is also a kind of exile, albeit a self-imposed exile, escaping social responsibilities, conventional expectations, and "three or four [wives] scattered around the country and glad to be rid of them all" (64).

Bongo (M&D)

The captain asks him to sniff the wind for evidence of Frenchmen in the area, saying "ancient Beliefs will persist" (37). *Bongo* links the character to ancient beliefs and a form of primitivism (through the simple drum recalled by the name). Perhaps there is an echo of the Bongo-Shaftsburys in V.

Bongo-Shaftsbury, Eric (V)

Owner of a preposterous sounding name, Bongo-Shaftsbury is one of several British characters with odd hyphenated names. Pynchon's mock-British hyphenated names may be modelled in part on those of Evelyn Waugh, such as Mrs. Beste-Chetwynde from *Decline and Fall*, for example. *Shaftsbury* has obvious sexual connotations and *Bongo* adds a disturbing percussive rhythm. Of course *Shaftesbury* (notice the slight spelling variation) is an old British name (Reaney 336), a reality that heightens the derisive humor. There may be an allusion to the seventeenth-century writer, the Third Earl of Shaftesbury.

Bongo-Shaftsbury, Hugh (UR, V)

See Bongo-Shaftsbury, Eric.

Bonk, a Functionary of the V.O.C. (M&D)

This Cape-Dutch police official's name is a Dutch word meaning "lump" or "lumpish fellow." He answers this description very nicely. That he is introduced with the title "Functionary" suggests widening the name's derisive connotations to characterize colonial administration in general.

Bonnifoy, Cleveland ("Blood") (Vine)

Cleveland and Bonnifoy are not terribly uncommon names. *Blood* is slang for "brother," typically referring to a friend. *Compare with* Gomez, Eusebio ("Vato").

Bopp, Karl (Vine)

Both first- and surnames are German, but if this character is real, there is no ready information on this "notorious" ex-Nazi officer. The surname also has an onomatopoeic sound connoting violence, albeit cartoonish-sounding violence.

Borgesius, Katje (GR)

The surname is common in Dutch. It could refer to any number of historical figures, perhaps two brothers and mathematicians of the seventeenth century (Johannes and Joachim). Given Katje's connection to sado-masochistic sex throughout, the name might refer to the character from the Marquis de Sade's *Juliette* named Borghese, the same name as the famous Italian noble family. Although Katje is a common first name, Hohmann suggests that the name and associations with "the wheel" recall St. Catherine (12).

Borowicz, Professor Bogoslaw (ATD)
The name is a comic-derisive one, with the first name built around the sound *bogus* (fake) and the surname built around the sound *bor* (bore), an apt description of his "Floor Shows" (343-4).

Borracho (V)
The name is the Spanish adjective meaning "drunk." This does not have any connection to his description ("aristocratic looking"). The name would be more appropriate for Mantissa's friend Césare who is always drinking, or perhaps the Gaucho, if one reads it as drunk on revolutionary action. It is probably a purely comic name.

Borrasca (ATD)
The name of Frank's colt is the Spanish for "storm." It hints at the theme of bilocation through a meaning that echoes Webb's phrase describing Lake — "child of the storm" — repeated in several places.

Bortz, Charles (Lot 49)
The given name is common. *See* Bortz, Emory for the surname.

Bortz, Emory (Lot 49)
This is another obvious pun: the name is voiced as "emery boards." Is there significance in the fact that this name means "nail files"? Is it a reference to English professors or literary critics in general? Perhaps the professor takes a literary work and files away at it until what is left is smooth, but artificial. More likely the name is a simple joke, one of several in the novel.

Bortz, Grace (Lot 49)
Given the visible stress associated with Grace Bortz's raising of her children (on the phone she jokes to Oedipa about infanticide) the name Grace is highly ironic. Grant focusses on Oedipa's brief appropriation of the name, suggesting she uses it to attempt to find grace in her situation (121). Colvile also looks at Oedipa's appropriation of the name, under which she makes an appointment to see the gynecologist, reading the name as "A Bortz," or *aborts*, suggesting that Oedipa's "gestation" with the Tristero ends in an abortion (28).

Bortz, Maxine (Lot 49)
The given name is common. *See* Bortz, Emory for the surname.

Bosanquet, [Bernard James Tindal] (ATD)
The reference is to a famous cricket player of the era.

Boscovich, [Ruggero Giuseppe] (M&D)
EB identifies the Jesuit astronomer and mathematician ("Boscovich, Ruggero Giuseppe").

Boswell, James (M&D)
The DNB identifies the biographer of Samuel Johnson (Turnbull).

Botha, brothers (M&D)
The name of these gin-swilling hunters may derive from the Dutch *botheid*, "stupidity." There may also be a reference to former South African prime minister/president during the 1980s decade of apartheid, P.W. Botha. Botha also seems to play on *both*: "both brothers," essentially referring to the two of them twice.

Bouguer, [Pierre] (M&D)
EB identifies the French scientist ("Bouguer, Pierre").

Bounce, Hilary (GR)
A vaguely comic name with no clear meaning. Hilary is a common male given name in England.

Bounce, Roswell (ATD)
The name is a comic Dickensian one which echoes Hilary Bounce of GR. Roswell recalls Roswell, New Mexico, thought to be near the site of a UFO crash and subsequent government cover-up, discussed to this day by heated crackpots not unlike Bounce and his fellow aetherists.

Bouquet, General [Henry] (M&D)
Danson identifies the historical officer, but refers to him as a lieutenant-colonel (82).

Braddock (M&D)
Edgar identifies the historical English military commander (passim).

Bradley, James (M&D)
The DNB identifies this astronomer (Williams).

Bradley, Miss (M&D)
Bradley and his wife Susannah Peach had a daughter named Susannah in 1746 (Williams).

Brain, Mr. (M&D)
This surname is quite rare, so it may be intended as comic, but the meaning of the noun *brain* has no clear application to the character, either directly or ironically. On the other hand, he is the innkeeper of the Cudgel and Throck. A cudgel is a short stick used as a weapon and a throck is a large piece of wood used in a plow (OED), but certainly capable of being used as a weapon. If we read the name as the verb *brain*, meaning "to dash someone's brains out" (OED), we can see some relevance.

Brain, Mrs. (M&D)
See Brain, Mr.

Breedlove, "Dope" and his Merry Coons (ATD)
The band name is similar in construction to earlier Pynchon band names such as Eddie Enrico and his Hong Kong Hotshots (Vine 78). Breedlove is a common surname and the name of a guitar company, appropriate for a musician. The surname joins with the nickname to form a comic reference to marijuana as aphrodisiac: "dope breed(s) love." *Coon* is a derisive term for African-Americans and "Merry Coons" suggests the stereotype of the smiling "happy negro."

Brenda (GR)
Common name.

Brenda the Bulb (GR)
See Byron the Bulb.

Brennan, Paul (MMV)
Common name.

Brennan, Peewee (GR)
The names of the four great "thumbs" are all relatively ordinary. Weisenburger reads them as pinball players (251), but the context suggests the game marbles. As Weisenburger points out, Pynchon lived in or near three of the four locations associated with these names, so it is conceivable that the names come from people Pynchon knew, perhaps in his boyhood, given the reference to marbles.

Brice (ATD)
Although a common surname, it may refer to the St. Brice's day massacre: "in 1002 King Ethelred the Unready ordered the Danes in England to be massacred on St. Brice's Day [13 November]" (Farmer 70). The character Brice will presumably take part in the coming massacre at the tent colonies at Ludlow. But Farmer's account of the life of St. Brice may undermine this reading: "Brice became a critic of his master, but eventually his successor," and his apparent expiation for earlier wrongdoing helped him to be made a saint (70). The character Brice lets Jesse go, even though he knows he has been shooting at Brice and his colleagues. There is a moment of bonding between them, but Brice's attitude

is far from certain. So we can read the name as a reference to the saint or the massacre.

Bridget (M&D)
Common name.

Briggs, Estrella (ATD)
Estrella is a common name from the Spanish word for star. Briggs is also a common name, but may allude to English mathematician Henry Briggs, "who devised the decimal-based system of logarithms and invented the modern method of long division" (AH4). The name could also be one of Pynchon's nautical references: a brig is both a ship and a term for naval prison.

Brooks, [Thomas] (M&D)
Browne identifies the historical "security" given to Justice Price by Catherine Wheat to maintain possession of her child (132).

Bruce, who got burned (GR)
Another person betrayed by Pirate in his work, the name Bruce seems chosen solely for its alliteration when joined with "burned."

Brum Kiddy, the (M&D)
Brum is "a slang contraction of brummagem" meaning "counterfeit" (OED). As the character is part of a group of highwaymen sorting the day's spoils, it is an appropriate name, a kind of criminal type name: it could be rendered "The Counterfeit Kid." *Kiddy* could suggest his youth — his interlocutor says "You're too young, yet" (767) but *kiddy* is also thieve's cant for "a professional thief who assumes a 'flashness' of dress and manner" (OED). Thus a doubling of sorts.

Brunhübner (GR)
"Unknown, or fictional," according to Weisenburger (199). If the name is made up, it seems derived from variations on two German words: *braun* ("brown") and *hübern* ("over there, on this side"). Perhaps it is meant to suggest "on the side of the brown shirts" or even "brown nose" as he is characterized as "trying to suck up to Hitler" (415).

Bruno (ATD)
A common name, but as it applies to one of Vibe's bodyguards, it may be meant to connote the Germanic-bruiser type, in part through its sound.

Bryant, Alexander (M&D)
The name of this owner of a house on Mason and Dixon's path to establish the boundary line is mentioned in Mason's journal, but Mason consistently spells it "Bryan" (47).

Buffo, Beatrice (V)
See also Beatrice the barmaid. The Italian *buffo* means a "squall of wind; a low comic opera singer; funny or droll; odd or laughable" (CID). All these meanings are relevant, reflecting her boatswain's pipe playing ability, the seedy nature of the Sailor's Grave, the "suck hour" tradition, and the image of her in a kimono, toppling into an ice tub. Grant cites Hawthorne, who glosses the character as an asexual toad (seeing an etymological connection to *bufo* or "toad," but this reading is not convincing, and Allen, who sees Mrs. Buffo as a "corrupted" but "balancing female character" (6). Given the carnivalesque qualities of the scene where she appears, the name should be regarded positively.

Bummer, Emile ("Säure") (GR)
Another example of a nickname joining a surname to make a joke or pun. Although the narrator explains that the "nickname which means 'acid' in German, developed back in the 1920s, when he was carrying around a little bottle of schnapps which, if he got in a tight spot, he would bluff people into thinking was fuming nitric acid" (365), the joke is still obvious. "Emil is an 'acid bummer,' American 1960s slang for an unpleasant

experience while under the influence of LSD" (Weisenburger 179). He is a "bad trip."

Bung the foreman (V)
Not only is this an occupational epithet, the character always identifies himself as "Bung the foreman." W3 gives the older slang definition of *bung* meaning "anus." His name would carry the same vulgar force as *asshole*. This is an appropriate name for a boss who only gives orders.

Burchell, Mrs. (ATD)
British medium who visualized the assassination of King Alexander Obrenovich of Serbia at a séance held by W.T. Stead (West 563), as depicted by Pynchon (228).

Burgess, Sheriff (ATD)
Common name.

Burgher King, the (ATD)
This character in an operetta of the same name is a king who disguises himself as "a member of the middle class" (914), in other words, the king disguises himself as a burgher, a comfortable member of the mercantile or middle class (AH4). Besides this charactonymic meaning, there is an obvious pun on the Burger King Restaurant chain, supported by the fact that he is referred to as B.K. on 915, an abbreviation used widely by Burger King both in identifying products and as an abbreviated nickname for the restaurant.

Buster (Vine)
Common name.

Bute, Jack [John Stuart, 3rd Earl of] (M&D)
The DNB identifies this prime minister (Schweizer).

Buttercup, little (SR)
This name adopted by Levine's blonde is clearly an allusion, as Levine refers to "Spot this Quote" (43). The reference is to the character Mrs. Cripps in Gilbert and Sullivan's *H.M.S. Pinafore* whose first act aria begins "I'm called Little Buttercup," stated literally by the blonde (42), although Pynchon leaves the *l* in *little* lowercase. Pynchon's little Buttercup carries a basket of sandwiches for the soldiers while Gilbert and Sullivan's Little Buttercup has a basket of varied wares (from "Snuff and tobaccy" to "ribbons and laces") to sell to sailors (Bradley 121).

Byrd, Colonel [William] (M&D)
Clerc identifies the historical farmer and Virginia historian (*Mason* 81).

Byron the Bulb (GR)
Like the other bulbs, Byron has an alliterative name, but his also seems to be a pun: Lord Byron burned brightly, but died young, having achieved his immortality through verse. Byron the Bulb shines brightly and permanently, being literally immortal.

Cabot, the elder [John] (M&D)
The DNB identifies the historical navigator (Quinn).

Caesarini, Cardinal (M&D)
Ware identifies the fifteenth-century cardinal and crusade instigator ("*Mason & Dixon*").

California Peg (ATD)
MacKell's study of Colorado brothels does not mention a California Peg or a Silver Orchid bar, although there was a Silver Bell Saloon near Popcorn Alley in Telluride (106). Assumed names must have been common among both prostitutes and madams, and California Peg sounds as plausible as such real names as "Mexican Jennie" (MacKell 219).

Calkins, Minnie (GR)
The surname may derive from the name of early female psychologist Mary Whiton Calkins. Pynchon may have come across the name in his psychology

readings, but there is no apparent connection between the historical figure and the minor character.

Callisto (E)

Callisto is a figure from Greek mythology, "a nymph in the train of Artemis" (Harvey 88). Artemis was goddess of wildlife and childbirth (Harvey 52). Given the density of flora and fauna in Callisto's enclave, the name is somewhat appropriate. But he and Aubade are childless, negating part of the name's potential meaning. Hollander claims "he has a regal name, similar to that of three popes. Callisto believes he is the sovereign in his hothouse" ("Pynchon's Politics" 37).

Calvert, Cecilius (M&D)

He is said to be "styl'd by some, for his unreflective effusions, 'The Silliest' Calvert" (301). The character was the historical uncle and secretary to Lord Baltimore (Cope "The Jersey Quadrant …" 566). The epithet "The Silliest" is presumably Pynchon's invention and stems, obviously, from the sound of the name *Cecilius*.

Campas, Don Emilio (ATD)

Former Madero supporter who, along with José Inés Salazar, fought to overtake Ciudad Juárez (Gonzales 88).

Candlebrow, Gideon of Grossdale Illinois (ATD)

Gideon means "warrior or destroyer" (Hamilton 48), and there is an Old Testament judge by the name. The inescapable reference is to the Gideons International, who are responsible for those Bibles in every motel nightstand in America. The meaning may involve his great zeal for the dubious synthetic fat from which he made his fortune. The surname is one of those ridiculously Dickensian ones we find more in this novel than in Pynchon's previous ones. *Candle* suggests illumination, while *brow* (in general, any ridge) suggests something that covers or shades. It could be read as "lampshade." *Thomas Pynchon Wiki* suggests a phallic reading, seeing a ridged cylinder. Grossdale may be a derisive parody of some other small Illinois town, Carbondale for example. The town name could also be rendered "Fat Valley."

Cantor, Dr. [Georg] (ATD)

While not strictly a character, he is introduced in a section dealing with the fictional Sfinciuno Itinerary, described as "impl[ying] a degree of the infinite not even Dr. Cantor in our own time is certain of" (250), referring to Cantor's controversial theory of infinite sets (Bell 555).

Cappy, Mrs. (Vine)

Common name.

Capsheaf (ATD)

The word *capsheaf* refers to "the top sheaf of a stack of grain, or the crowning point" (W3). The name may also be a joke referring to a condom by way of *cap* (head covering) and *sheaf* (a quiver for arrows).

Capucci (SR)

Common Italian surname. Hollander suggests that the name recalls the Capuchins, an order of Franciscan monks, as part of an underlying layer of the story invoking Catholic, Protestant, Jewish, and pagan rituals ("Pynchon's Politics" 25).

Carnal, the Reverend Lube of the Second Lutheran (Missouri Synod) Church (ATD)

This reverend in the moral desolation of Jeshimon is appropriately named. *Carnal* refers both to sexual appetites and worldly or earthly things (AH4). The first meaning of the surname joined with the given named Lube, short for *lubricant*, is strongly suggestive of sodomy. The character is portrayed as a hypocrite whose name embodies the opposite of Christian virtue. That he is linked in his introduction to a specific church suggests that Pynchon also wishes to satirize Missouri Synod Lutherans, widely held to be the most conservative group of Lutherans, both theologically and socially. The initials L.C. can also refer to Lutheran Church. Lube Carnal also functions as a simple joke name tied to its association of perversion.

Carolines (GR)
See Girls, Slothrop's.

Carothers, [Wallace Hume] (GR)
Weisenburger identifies the historical chemist (133).

Carpenter, John (M&D)
Headlee identifies the historical packhorse driver (7).

Carruthers-Pillow (V)
On the surface, this is another of many hyphenated British names. Pynchon's mock-British hyphenated names may be modelled in part on those of Evelyn Waugh, such as Mrs. Beste-Chetwynde from *Decline and Fall*, for example. If it is a joke, however, the immediate source is American. In his 1955 novel *The Recognitions*, William Gaddis includes a joke about Carruthers and his horse in numerous conversations. The punchline does not come until the novel is nearly finished (page 941). Steven Moore identifies the joke: "two stuffy British majors are discussing the latest scandal: 'Heard about Carruthers?' 'No, what?' 'Been drummed out of the Army.' 'God, what for?' 'Caught in the act with a horse.' 'Ghastly! Mare or stallion?' 'Mare, of course — nothing queer about Carruthers!'" "Carruthers's Pillow," then, would be the horse's crupper. The name would then mean "horse's ass." The situation is echoed in ATD where Cyprian Latewood's friend Crayke is carrying on a relationship with a Shetland pony (492).

Cassar (V)
Cassola identifies the name as a common Maltese surname (331).

Cassidy, Butch (ATD)
This famous outlaw, whose real name was Robert LeRoy Parker, was active in the Colorado area, among other locales (O'Neal 250).

Catfish (Chief of the Delaware Nation) (M&D)
Actual chief mentioned in Mason's journal (174).

Cavendish, Henry (M&D)
The DNB identifies the natural philosopher (Schaffer).

Cavi (ATD)
The reference is to Pierre Louis Napoleon Cavagnari, who was a British military administer at Kabul who was killed ("Sir Pierre Louis Napoleon Cavagnari"), or "ate the sausage" as Halfcourt says (758).

Cesare (V)
This is a typical Latinate name. The Spanish for *Caesar* is *César*, the Italian *Césare*. There is probably no allusion or special meaning.

Chandrasekhar, O.D. (ATD)
The name is taken from American astrophysicist of Indian descent, Subrahmanyan Chandrasekhar, who developed the Chandrasekhar limit (the maximum mass of a white dwarf star) and for whom was named the Chandrasekhar number (a dimensionless number used to measure magnetic field strength). This last seems the most relevant reference, given the novel's exploration of other dimensions. O.D. is the abbreviation for overdose, perhaps referring to his impenetrable speech on ether and religion (63), or simply one of Pynchon's many drug-related puns.

Chantry, Mr. (M&D)
Although a fairly common surname, *chantry* also means "the daily singing of a mass for specified souls" (OED). This meaning has no apparent reference to this minor character, a lawyer. The name may

be a modified form of "chancery" or court, appropriate for a lawyer.

Chapman, Major Percy (V)
The name is completely ordinary and may refer to an actual person, but the source is not clear. It could refer to the famous cricket player of that name.

Chardin, Teilhard de (GR)
Weisenburger identifies the historical Jesuit philosopher (234).

Charisma (V)
See also Fu and Winsome. Like *winsome*, *charisma* denotes charm at one level. But the word is much stronger, describing pronounced magnetism. This quality seems absent from what little we see of the character (largely silent, wrapped in a blanket), and from the crew itself, and so should be read ironically.

Charles (GR)
Common name.

Charles the homosexual constable (GR)
Common name.

Chase, Ed (ATD)
Chase owned a saloon/gambling hall/house of prostitution called the Navarre, formerly the Hotel Richlieu (MacKell 62). Perhaps "Ed's Arcade" (176) refers to the Navarre.

Chase, John (ATD)
Osur identifies this Colorado National Guard general (21).

Chastain, Darryl Louise (DL) (Vine)
While Chastain is a fairly common surname, Pynchon may be playing with the connotations of two words suggested by the name: *chaste* with *stain*, suggesting a flawed purity. In Pynchon, flawed purity is the only type of purity, and the name seems to place her among the preterite.

Chastain, Moody (Vine)
The name Moody aptly describes this character's disposition. *See* Chastain, Darryl Louise for the surname.

Chastain, Norleen (Vine)
Norleen is a common name. *See* Chastain, Darryl Louise for the surname.

Chauncey (M&D)
Common name.

Ché (Vine)
With another comical name bestowed by children of the 1960s on a child of the 1980s, Ché is of course named for revolutionary hero Ché Guevara.

Cheeseley, Thrapston III (ATD)
The name sounds Dickensian and seems meant to mock the effete aristocrat. It is Reef Traverse's alias when he impersonates an "East Coast nerve case" (367). Thrapston comes from the name of a town in Northamptonshire, England, and Cheeseley is a fairly common surname, although it suggests the derisive adjective *cheesy* by sound association.

Cheezy (ATD)
Comic name formed on the derisive adjective *cheesy*.

Chen, Miss (M&D)
Common name.

Cherrycoke, Reverend Wicks (M&D)
Perhaps the ancestor of the Ronald Cherrycoke who appears in GR, this Cherrycoke's surname anachronistically refers to the popular carbonated beverage. Dewey compares the name *Wicks* to other light-related names in the novel (LeSpark and Tenebrae) and glosses it as "a steady if fragile illumination" (119–20). Ware suggests a connection with wiccans, "practitioners of white magic" ("*Mason & Dixon*"). Certainly the Reverend fills his tale with many supernatural elements. *See also* Cherrycoke, Ronald.

Cherrycoke, Ronald (GR)

The surname is a reference to the carbonated, cherry-flavored cola beverage, but the name, besides sounding somewhat funny, has no specific application to the character. We meet his "ancestor," the Reverend Wicks Cherrycoke, in M&D. We could view the name as an allusion to either popular culture or a brand. While Coca-Cola has been around since the 1890s, Cherry Coke, as a proprietary name, did not exist until the 1980s. The beverage would have been created at a soda fountain before that time. The name may also refer to burning coal, from *coke* (an impure form of charcoal) and *cherry* as both the color red and "to redden" (OED).

Cheryl (Vine)

Common name.

Chesterfield, [Philip Dormer Stanhope, 4th Earl of] (M&D)

The DNB identifies the politician and diplomatist (Cannon).

Chew, Benjamin (M&D)

Mentioned throughout Mason's journal and appearing as a signatory on several letters to Mason and Dixon (first mentioned on page 138), Benjamin Chew was one of the line commissioners.

Chiave Lowenstein, Margravine di (V)

Harder identifies the parts as "wife of a margrave," "key," and "stronghold of lions," respectively, glossing the entire name as "the woman who holds the key to the lion's cage" (78), or perhaps, we might render it as "mistress of the lion's den." There is too little information about the character to determine whether the name is charactonymic, but clearly it is an elect identifier.

Chick (Vine)

Chick is a fairly common form of the name Charles. The name is chosen solely to rhyme with Rick, his twin brother's name. Twins are often given rhyming or alliterative names.

Chickeeta (Vine)

This name is apparently a variant spelling of the popular brand of bananas, Chiquita.

Chiclitz, Clayton "Bloody" (V, Lot 49, GR)

Readers of Pynchon first come across this character in V. But GR takes place at an earlier point in history. Chronologically, Chiclitz still manufactures toys during WWII. He had appeared in V as a former toy-maker turned defense contractor and again in Lot 49 solely as the Yoyodyne chief. The name operates on many levels. Grant identifies the joke combined in nick- and surname: "Do you want a mouthful of bloody Chiclets?" (66). The joke apparently stems from the fact that those flat, vaguely tooth-shaped pieces of gum were originally white, before other colors were marketed. We can also read "Bloody" as an appropriate nickname for a defense contractor. Hollander claims that the name Clayton refers to Henry De Lamar Clayton of the Clayton Anti-Trust Act of 1914 ("Pynchon, JFK and the CIA" 87). Given the nature of the defense industry and the military-industrial complex, this reading of Clayton becomes somewhat ironic.

Chilkes, Maud (GR)

For a character whose only major appearance in the novel is the scene where she fellates Pointsman, we expect a name of comic, obscene, or charactonymic character. Chilkes is not an uncommon surname, and Maud does not appear to have any special significance. Alas.

Chinchito (ATD)

The chinch or chinchbug is a very small insect and the diminutive ending *-ito* exaggerates this description, making the name appropriate for a midget.

Chingiz (ATD)

The name is a variant of Ghengis and common in parts of the former Soviet Union, but Pynchon may also be playing on the sound "chingas" (a conjugation of the Spanish verb *chingar* [to fuck]).

Chiquita (ATD)

Fairly common as both a given- and surname, *chiquita* is Spanish for "little one." There is no way to know if this applies to the fandango girl Frank Traverse meets in Texas. As with the variant spelling Chickeeta, applied to a character in Vine, the name may refer to the popular brand of bananas, a fruit featuring prominently in the opening scenes of GR.

Chirpingdon-Groin, Ruperta (ATD)

Ruperta is the feminine form of Rupert, a variant of Robert. It is common enough, but the second syllable is suggestive. As a verb, *pert* means "to exalt oneself," appropriate to this character and her sense of superiority, and as an adjective, it is often applied to firm, shapely breasts or buttocks (OED), appropriate, too, for this very sexual creature. To chirp is to utter a sharp sound (OED); the *-don* ending is supplied to make the name plausible. As one of Pynchon's mock-British hyphenated names, which may be modelled in part on those of Evelyn Waugh, such as Mrs. Beste-Chetwynde from *Decline and Fall*, for example, the addition of groin makes it sound ridiculous, but also adds to the sexual associations, and since the chirping is connected to the groin, the name suggests cries of sexual pleasure. Altogether the name is fairly charactonymic. That chirping is primarily associated with birds is appropriate as well, since *bird* is British slang for "girl."

Chobb, Nasty (V)

As Harder and others have pointed out, this is a paronomastic encoding of "nasty job" (74). Harder takes it to mean that he does a poor job of baking, citing his use of salt instead of sugar to discourage people from stealing pies (74). But this is deliberate, not an indication of incompetence. The name is probably a simple joke with no charactonymic meaning.

Chong (ATD)

This Chinese-sounding alias of Sidney Reilly is probably chosen to allude to Tommy Chong, co-star of the Cheech and Chong films, beginning in the late seventies with *Up in Smoke*. The films celebrated the Herculean consumption of marijuana by the duo, just the kind of pop culture/drug reference Pynchon seems to enjoy.

Christian (GR)

Seed remarks that some of the Herero names "ironically reflect their colonized states" (*Fictional Labyrinths* 182). This name reflects the general influence of Western Christian ideology over the primitive (and, according to Pynchon, healthier) social structures destroyed by colonialism.

Christian, Abraham (V)

Grant identifies the historical Bondel chief (131).

Christian, Jacobus (V)

Grant identifies the historical Bondel leader (118).

Chuck (ATD)

Common name, typically substituted for the proper name Charles.

Chunko, Sheriff Willis (Vine)

This name of the Vineland County Sheriff sounds like a contrived comic-sounding name, but Chunko is a not-uncommon surname. Contrary to assertions by Leithauser (7), preposterous-sounding names are not always at Pynchon's whim—he seems to have an ear for the interesting within the everyday.

Cinoglossa (V)

Harder translates the name as "Chinese-glossary" (77). It is unclear how this name applies to an epileptic homosexual poet. Perhaps it is a joke.

Claire

Claire (GR)
Common name.

Claire (Vine)
Common name.

Clasper, Harry (M&D)
Dixon places this Tyne rowing champion of the nineteenth century more than one hundred years before his time (Clasper passim).

Claude the assistant chef (GR)
Common name.

Clementia, Sister (ATD)
This nun's name comes from the Latin for gentle or compassionate. It may also be a feminized form of Clement, the name for a few Roman Catholic saints.

Clissan, Vlado (ATD)
Vlado is a common Slavic name from a root, *vlad*, meaning "ruler." As he says, Clissan derives from the town Clissa.

Clive, Lady (M&D)
See Maskelyne, Peggy.

Clive, [Robert] of India (M&D)
The DNB identifies the East India Company officer (Bowen).

Clothilda (ATD)
The name derives from Old German words meaning "loud" and "battle"; its use in England is largely by Roman Catholics and it occurs in France as Clothilde (Withycombe 66), suggesting it would not be out of place in Roman Catholic Italy, although the etymology has no clear application to this character.

Clovis (M&D)
He is not listed in any of the obvious sources, so the name may be contrived. Clovis could refer to a prehistoric North American people circa 12,000 to 9,000 B.C.E. or the fifth to sixth century Frankish king (Clovis I) who unified the Gauls (AH4). Neither reference seems to have any relevance to this minor character.

Withycombe does not mention the name, so it was probably not a common English or American name at the time of the novel.

Cognomon, Artie (SI)
A cognomon can be either a surname (making his own self-reflexive) or a nickname. The sound-alike adjective *arty* can mean "showily or affectedly artistic" (AH4). Thus this clearly contrived character name means "clearly contrived name."

Cohen, Genghis (Lot 49)
When novelist Roman Gary claimed Pynchon had stolen the name "Genghis Cohn" [*sic*] from one of his novels, Pynchon responded that he had never read anything by Mr. Gary:

> I took the name Genghis Cohen from the name of Genghis Khan (1162–1227), the well-known Mongol warrior and statesman. If Mr. Gary really believes himself to be the only writer at present able to arrive at a play on words this trivial, that is another problem entirely, perhaps more psychiatric than literary, and I certainly hope he works it out [Letter 22, 24].

Grant, Caesar and others have pointed to this passage to indicate the playfulness of some of Pynchon's names. We may take it as a warning against reading too much into many of the names.

Colman Smith, Pamela ("Pixie") (ATD)
Pynchon hyphenates Colman-Smith on her first mention (186) but not subsequently. She was the illustrator of the popular Rider-Waite tarot deck, sometimes referred to as the Rider-Waite-Smith tarot deck. The nickname Pixie is not Pynchon's invention; it was apparently meant to capture "the artist's lively spirit and imagination" ("Pamela Colman Smith Collection, 1896–1900").

Colonel, The (ATD)
The use of a title rather than a name by Khäutsch here is perfectly natural, given

his involvement with male prostitutes. *See* Khäutsch, Max.

Colonel, the (ATD)
This nickname for an unscrupulous gambler has no clear application to the character. Such general (anonymous) nicknames were frequently used by gamblers, outlaws, etc., as a glance through O'Neal will attest.

Colonna, Pompeo (V)
The *Catholic Encyclopedia* identifies this historical cardinal (Loughlin).

Conflans, [Hubert de Brienne, Count de] (M&D)
The DNB entry for Edward Hawke identifies this French admiral (Mackay, "Hawke, Edward, first Baron Hawke (1705–1781)").

Considine, Debby (MMV)
Both given- and surname are common, but Considine suggests the Latin *considere* (to sit down, but figuratively, to die out). The name's figurative association applies more to the partygoers in general than this character, and to humanity, by extension. It is linked to the overall sense of doom that hangs over the story.

Consuelo (ATD)
Not a character, but a role Edwarda hopes to play in *Mischief in Mexico*, Consuelo is a "lively *bandida*" (16). Appropriately, Consuelo is a common Latina name.

Contango, Johnny (V)
Harder defines *contango* as "a fee paid by a buyer of securities to the seller for the privilege of deferring his payment" (72). This is strangely appropriate for the officer who rose from the ranks of the enlisted, but acts as a fixer for his friends.

Cookson, Sir Charles (UR)
British consul-general at Alexandria, Egypt during the time period covered in the story (Baedeker 5).

Cookworthy (M&D)
The character is, of course, a ship's cook. His soup is "worthy" of Dixon, but not Mason, on whom its smell acts as an emetic. It is unclear if the name is descriptive or ironic.

Cooper (ATD)
A common name, usually a surname, it may allude to actor Gary Cooper, star of many westerns.

Cope, [Jonathan] (M&D)
Mentioned in Mason's journal (74). Like Pynchon, Mason always speaks of Cope and Darby together except one instance when Cope appears alone (191). Headlee identifies him as a chain/instrument carrier (13).

Counterfly, Chick (ATD)
Counterfly is a mechanical term for "a fast-moving, heavy fly-wheel" (OED). It is appropriate for one described as a "Science Officer" (141). But the name also embodies his initial characterization in that he "flies counter" to the other balloonists. Before becoming the mature scientist, he is depicted as constantly speaking against the good-boy-scout mentality of the Chums of Chance (4–5). Chick is a common familiar name for Charles, and was chosen to rhyme with father "Dick." This is also a clear echo of Rick and Chick, the twins in Vine.

Covess (V)
The name refers to a school chum of Sidney Stencil's. Covess derives from an obsolete term, *covess-dinge*, meaning "prostitute" and functions solely as comedy ("Covess-Dinge"). But the word *cove* refers to "a fellow" or "chap," making the name based on this word appropriate for "a school chum" (189).

Crawfford, Hugh (M&D)
This historical Indian interpreter who accompanied Mason and Dixon and the Indian deputies is mentioned in the

introduction to Mason's *Journals* (19), where the surname is spelled Crawford.

Crayke (ATD)

Crayke is not a common personal name, but the name of a parish in North Yorkshire. The character is said to have "retired up north" (492).

Creepham (GR)

This is not a common surname and we should probably emphasize the first syllable — creep. This pilot is only mentioned once, so the negative connotations do not refer to any qualities of this very minor character.

Cresap, Daniel (M&D)

Bailey identifies the historical son of Thomas Cresap (164–66).

Cresap, Michael (M&D)

Bailey identifies the historical son of Thomas Cresap (164).

Cresap, Mr. (M&D)

See Cresap, Thomas.

Cresap, Thomas (M&D)

Bailey identifies the pre-revolutionary American frontiersman and patriarch of the Cresap family (passim).

Cromer, Lord [Evelyn Baring] (UR, V)

Grant identifies the historical "British consul general in Egypt" (58).

Cromorne, Rev. (M&D)

Cromorne is a variant of *krummhorn* (corruptly given as *cremona*), meaning "an organ reed stop of 8 ft. pitch, resembling the clarinet in tone" (OED). The specific sound does not seem to have any special application to the character, but given the long and close association between pipe organs and churches, we may read this reverend's name as mildly charactonymic.

Crookes, Sir William (ATD)

"[P]hysicist, chemist, and future President or the Royal Society" who was involved in researching "alleged spiritualist manifestations" in the late nineteenth century (Oppenheim 16).

Crosier, Sister (M&D)

Crosier can mean "cross-bearer," "bearer of a bishop's staff," or "the staff of a bishop or abbot" (OED). It is metonymically appropriate for a nun, but could also refer to a figurative cross to bear, as the nuns at this convent are trained to be sexual servants.

Crouchmas, Clive (ATD)

Crouchmas seems a distortion of Christmas, suggesting debasement. It may also be modelled on the more common Crouchback, recalling the crusader Edmund Crouchback, first earl of Lancaster or Guy Crouchback, the hero of Evelyn Waugh's *Sword of Honour* trilogy. The latter represents the declining aristocracy and premodern values, both of which are ridiculed to some extent by Pynchon through this character. These aristocratic associations are also present in the name Clive, recalling wealthy Clive Mossmoon of GR and Robert Clive of India, the historical nabob in M&D.

Crutchfield or Crouchfield, the westwardman (GR)

One of several enigmatic characters of the novel, Crutchfield's name does not seem to recall or refer to anything.

Crystal (Vine)

Common name.

Crystal (ATD)

Common name.

Cuernacabrón (V)

This portmanteau name derives from two Spanish words: *cuerna* ("horns," "antlers") and *cabrón* ("cuckold"). This is a nice instance of doubling, in which the insult is magnified.

Cufifo, Beto (SI)

Beto is a common Hispanic name and Cufifo is Spanish for "tipsy." If the first name is pronounced with a long e, his full name is "be too tipsy." The name is appropriate for "the town rum-dum" (176). It is ironic, though, that one with a Latino name would be associated with the forces of racism in the story, so the name is simply a joke.

Culpepper, Madge and Mia (ATD)
The most recent Pynchonian feminine duo in a long line (Flip and Flop, Hanky and Panky, Molly and Dolly), these names, too, rely on sound for comic effect. Both given names and the surname are common, with the given names providing alliteration. The joke is in the name of Mia Culpepper, the first four syllables of which approximate the phrase *mea culpa*, Latin for "through my fault."

Curly the waiter (ATD)
Curly is a common nickname, especially for one with especially wavy hair, although we have no physical description of this very minor character who is introduced with an occupational epithet.

Cynthia (GR)
See Girls, Slothrop's.

D'Allesandro, Danny (GR)
See Brennan, Peewee.

D'Amico (Lot 49)
From Italian, the name means "of the friend." The "character" is only mentioned by Bortz in reference to a critical judgment about a text (155). Perhaps the name suggests the cronyism involved in scholarly publishing. It is, however, a common Italian surname.

D'Annunzio (V)
This is a reference to the actual Italian writer and proto-fascist. His political leanings make him an appropriate person with whom Veronica Manganese is intimate (473).

d'Escaubitte, Pépé (M&D)
Ware suggests that the name can be pronounced "peppy disco-beat" ("*Mason & Dixon*").

Da Conho (V)
Grant points out that *conho* means an "isolated rock in a river" in Portuguese (11). The connotations of this meaning are vaguely appropriate for this character who lives in his own Zionist fantasy world (22-3). Note that he is introduced without the occupational epithet Pynchon often uses in similar cases. He is not "Da Conho the chef," but the "chef was one Da Conho" (22). Given that his goal is to fight Arabs in Israel and that he is obsessed with weapons and a violent brand of Zionism, we could read the name as a corruption of the Italian *da conio*, "for hire." He is, after all, a would-be soldier of fortune.

Dahoud (V)
Harder suggests that this name is "chosen at random" (74). Although Dahoud is a fairly common Arabic name, why is it bestowed on a black American? The character is introduced as "a gargantuan Negro named Dahoud." There may be an allusion to jazz trumpeter Clifford Brown by way of his well-known composition "Dahoud" — he was black, but not particularly gargantuan. There is possibly a puerile joke in the name. In the introduction to SL, Pynchon admits that his early works contained "an unacceptable level of racist, sexist and proto-fascist talk" (11). Considering this, we could read the name as a paronomastic encoding of "the hood," short for hoodlum.

Damsel, Anne (M&D)
Charles Mason Sr. married Anne Damsel in 1723 (Robinson "A Note on Charles Mason's Ancestry" 135).

Daniel (M&D)
See Abraham.

Darby, [William] (M&D)
Mentioned in Mason's journal (74). Interestingly, Darby and Cope are always

mentioned together by Mason in the journal, just as Pynchon does in the novel. On only one occasion is one mentioned without the other (Cope on page 191). Danson identifies Darby's first name as William (99). Headlee identifies him as a chain carrier (11).

Dark Hespie, the Pythoness of the Point (M&D)

Hespie is a nickname for Hephzibah ("my delight is in her") (Withycombe 143). As she is apparently a young woman imitating a crone, there may be a sexual connotation intended here. Dark refers to her mystical abilities, Pythoness emphasizes witch-like qualities, while Point (or port) describes her location.

Darlene (GR)

See Girls, Slothrop's.

Darnley, Jill (GR)

Weisenburger identifies the historical Miss Rheingold contestant (185).

Dash, Mayva (ATD)

Mayva is a common name, related to Maeve or Mavis. As Dash is not common, and the meaning of the word has little application to the character, we are invited to see some reference beyond this. There are two possible allusions: Mrs. Dash, a popular brand of salt-free seasoning; and emdash (combining first initial with surname), the double-hyphen used to mark a break in the flow of a sentence.

Dasp, Captain, the notorious Calvert Agent (M&D)

Ware suggests a French origin, *D'asp*, which he translates as "the asp" ("*Mason & Dixon*"). One could derive that sound from the English word and a dialect pronunciation of *the* ("deh"), but the French suggestion is not convincing. "The asp" would likely be rendered as *l'aspic* or more generally as *la vipère*; the *d'* beginning would translate as "of" or "from," not "the." On the other hand, a name suggesting a highly poisonous snake does seem appropriate for this "notorious Calvert Agent" (414), but the English reading is more convincing.

Dave (E)

Common name.

David (V)

See also Maurice. Harder points out that David and Maurice are dismissed as names only (74). Like the name *Maurice*, however, *David* also calls to mind a range of saints. The character may allude to St. David of Bruce (a martyr), St. David of Scotland, or St. David of Wales: all were immensely popular in the British Isles (Farmer 126–8).

Davies, Miss [Marianne] (M&D)

The DNB identifies the "instrumentalist and singer" (Baldwin and Wilson).

Dawes, Linnet (ATD)

Dawes is a fairly common surname, but could be an allusion to Charles Gates Dawes, vice president under Coolidge. Both names also refer to birds: a linnet is a type of finch, and a daw or jackdaw is a crow-like bird.

Dawson, [James] (M&D)

Browne identifies the historical participant in the melee described in the text (155).

De Bosch, Mrs. (M&D)

The surname may be a pun on *debauch*, "to corrupt morally or debase." She is a defender of white Cape Dutch society and its values, including slavery, and she views Dixon with suspicion because of his open admiration for the lifestyle of the blacks and natives.

De Bottle, Dr. Coombs (ATD)

The name is a simple pun whose sound appropriates "comes the bottle," as in "here comes the bottle." It has no particular relevance to this character, but points toward liquor as part of a larger texture of the celebration of all manner of stimulants and depressants throughout the novel. The theme of bilocation is relevant here, too, for there is a connotative link between this character name and that of Heino Vanderjuice (fond o' juice).

De Brutus (GR)
See Salitieri, Poore, Nash, De Brutus, and Short.

De Costa, Min (V)
The name could combine the English *min* ("to remember, think of, or recollect") (OED) with the Spanish *de costa* ("of cost or price"); someone who always thinks of the price. *Min De Costa* also suggests cut-rate, but this fails to have an obvious application to an old practicing witch who keeps orphan mice. It could be a simple play on words with no charactonymic intention. The parts of the name are also an anagram of "mice not sad," appropriate for a character who takes in orphan mice.

de Decker (ATD)
He is Piet Woevre's section officer. Appropriately, de Decker is a common Dutch surname, although the beginning of the name suggests stuttering, so perhaps is meant as comedy as well.

De Forest, Lee (ATD)
Historical radio engineer and inventor of the three-element vacuum tube (Sterling).

de la Luz Blanco, Don José (ATD)
The name comes from El Espinero the shaman. Given the context — he is linked with Madero — the reference seems to be to Don José Maria Pino Suárez (*see* Suárez, Pino). De la Luz Blanco translates to "of the white light" and seems to prefigure Suárez's death by way of the popular notion that the dying are called toward a bright, white light, appropriate since El Espinero sees the future.

de la Tube, Père (M&D)
"Father of the Tube" seems to be an anachronistic reference to our slang word for the television. That the name is a priest's suggests the role television plays in contemporary society — a replacement for the spiritual.

De Profundis, Nick, the company lounge lizard (GR)
As Weisenburger points out *de profundus* is Latin for "of the deep" or "of the profound" (155). The phrase can also be translated "out of the depths," which seems more appropriate for a lounge lizard. Nick is a common name of the devil (OED).

de Sod, Marquis (Vine)
Millard Hobbs's television alter ego is an obvious pun on the name of the transgressive author, the Marquis de Sade. Here sadism is replaced by landscaping, perhaps reflecting the perversion inherent in 1980s values.

De Witt (Lot 49)
De Witt is another fairly common name with no obvious joke or pun that comes to mind. There may be an allusion to Dutch statesman and mathematician (more of Pynchon's math/science arcana?) Johan De Witt (1625–72).

de Wolfe, Elsie (ATD)
Actual New-York-born decorator and actress (Metcalf).

Dean (Lot 49)
Common name.

Declassé, [Theophile] (UR, V)
Grant identifies the historical French foreign minister (44).

Dee, Curly (ATD)
Both common names, but taken together the name is one of Pynchon's math references. As *Thomas Pynchon Wiki* points out, mathematicians call the symbol for a partial derivative a "curly d."

Deeply

Deeply, Dr. Dennis, M.S.W., Ph.D. (Vine)
Besides being delightfully alliterative, the name and the character's involvement in social work and counseling may parody the "touchy-feely" approach popular especially in New Age centers of the 1980s.

Degenkolb (GR)
Fowler identifies the historical industrialist (197).

Degrelle (GR)
Weisenburger identifies the historical French separatist (235).

Delgado (V)
Delgado is a common Hispanic Surname. It seems to serve as an ethnic marker for this very minor character.

Delgado (LL)
Common Hispanic surname.

Delisle, [Joseph-Nicolas] (M&D)
EB identifies the French astronomer ("Delisle, Joseph-Nicolas").

Delores (GR)
See Girls, Slothrop's.

Deltchev, Gotse (ATD)
One of the founders and leaders of IMRO ("Internal Macedonian Revolutionary Organization").

Demivolt (V)
This means, literally, "one half of a volt." Although a very small amount of power for a spy to have, we can read the name two ways: ironically or as an indication of the relatively small role played by spies in a game devised and controlled by larger forces.

Denham, Carl (GR)
Weisenburger identifies this character from the film *King Kong* (290).

Denis (ATD)
Common name.

Derek (Vine)
Common name.

Derek (M&D)
Common name.

Dermy (M&D)
The context suggests that it may be a nickname (perhaps for McDermott or something similar). It has no other clear significance.

Dhimitris (ATD)
Common Greek name.

Di Presso, Manny (Lot 49)
Another pun, the name can be read as "manic depression" or "man, he's depressing."

Díaz, Félix (ATD)
Félix Díaz was the nephew to Mexican dictator Porfirio Díaz (Gonzales 92) as Pynchon states (994).

Diaz, Geronimo (LL)
The name is the unlikely combination of the Apache leader who resisted American governmental policy of consolidating Indians on reservations (Geronimo) (AH4) and the Mexican dictator Porfirio Díaz. The character, Dennis Flanges' analyst, is described as "a crazed and boozy wetback" (57). Certainly his crazed personality is embodied in the name, containing as is does, two completely irreconcilable personalities.

Díaz, Porfirio (ATD)
While not a character as such, this strongly autocratic late nineteenth- and early twentieth-century Mexican president is mentioned throughout the text.

Dieckmann, Dr. (GR)
The name is pronounced the same in German as *dick mann* ("fat man"). He appears with Dr. Gorr ("little boy"). Together the names allude to the two atomic bombs dropped on Japan by the United States.

Dieter (M&D)
Common German name.

Dieter the barkeep (ATD)
One of several characters in the novel introduced with an occupational epithet, Dieter has a common German name.

DiGrandi (SR)
Common Italian surname.

Dimdown, Philip (M&D)
On the surface, the name seems to reflect the dullness of this peevish fop, but it becomes clear that he was merely posing as a fop while "running a clandestine printing Press" and working for the revolution (390). In this context, the name suggests that he has dimmed or dumbed himself down in order to keep suspicion from falling on him.

Dingkopf, Dr. Willi (ATD)
Willi is a common name. Dingkopf is an oddly appropriate name for a psychotherapist, translating to "thing head." We could also reverse it to "head thing," suggesting mental illness. The sound also recalls the popular German term of abuse *Dummkopf* (fool or idiot), reflecting his deranged anti-Semitism (624).

Dipple, Archie (ATD)
Both names are common, but the surname probably relies on the sound of the first syllable for its meaning in the context of the novel. A dip is a stupid person (OED). He is presented as always coming up with crackpot ideas, some of which are characterized as "desperately insane" (358).

Disco, Ellmore (ATD)
When used as a given name, Ellmore is more frequently spelled Elmore. The name is not so common that it does not invite consideration of a couple of well-known examples: Elmore Leonard, the popular mystery novelist, and Elmore James, the blues guitarist and singer. Disco refers to a genre of much maligned mid- to late-seventies dance music. The fact that Pynchon uses the far less common spelling of the given name suggests a joke reading of the name: "Hell, more disco." This is echoed by the character's being referred to as "Ellmore the Evil" (294), connecting Disco to evil. All of these readings rely on Pynchon's well-known interest in pop culture.

Disco, Mrs. (ATD)
See Disco, Ellmore.

Ditters (ATD)
The name of this character from *The Burgher King* operetta is an allusion to classical composer Carl Ditters von Dittersdorf, who composed many comic operas himself. His appearance next to a character named Schleppingsdorff further points to this allusion.

Dixies and Fans and Mignonettes (ATD)
These names of hypothetical girls are all fairly common. Fan may be short for the common name Fanny. The name Mignonette is derived from the name of an herb.

Dixon, Elizabeth (M&D)
One of Dixon's sisters, she is mentioned in Robinson's biographical note (272).

Dixon, George (M&D)
This is the name listed for Dixon's great-uncle. The scant biographical information on Jeremiah Dixon that is easily locatable does not mention a great-uncle, but as Dixon's brother and father were both named George (Robinson "Jeremiah Dixon" 272), it seems that the name was common in the family. Pynchon either had access to more detailed material or extrapolated the name.

Dixon, George, Jr. (M&D)
Identified by Robinson as one of Dixon's brothers ("Jeremiah Dixon" 272).

Dixon, George, Sr. (M&D)
Identified by Robinson as Dixon's father ("Jeremiah Dixon" 272). Hollis

suggests that Dixon's father's name was Ralph (295), but Dixon's brother George is "junior" and his brother Ralph is not.

Dixon, Hannah (M&D)
One of Dixon's, sisters, she is mentioned in Robinson's biographical note (272).

Dixon, Jeremiah (M&D)
There is some confusion about Dixon's dates. *The Encyclopaedia Britannica* (which interestingly, in the 15th edition, has an entry for Dixon, but not Mason) lists only a death date, 1777. Robinson's biographical note on Dixon lists his dates as 1733–1779 (272). As Dixon's will is dated 1778 (Robinson 274), we can safely dismiss the date provided by EB.

Dixon, Ralph (M&D)
Identified by Robinson as one of Dixon's brothers ("Jeremiah Dixon" 272).

Djuro (GR)
As Larsson points out, this is a Slavic name (v732.36). Hereros without native names have either European (especially German) names or Slavic ones, suggesting two external political influences on the native culture.

Dmitri (Vine)
Common Russian name.

Dnubietna (V)
According to Cassola, *Dnubietna* means "our sins" in Maltese (33). Significantly, this is drawn from the Maltese version of the Lord's Prayer. Dnubietna is introduced as an engineer (306) — the sin of progress? — and is both apostate and tempter of Fausto (327–28).

Dobbie, Governor [Sir William] (V)
Maltese governor from 1940 to 1942 (Cassola 327).

Dodd (M&D)
Common name.

Doddling (ATD)
This old school spagyrist (alchemist) has a comic name meaning walking unsteadily or shaking/nodding the head (OED).

(Dodington) Melcombe, George Bubb Dodington (Baron) (M&D)
The DNB identifies this "politician and diarist" (Hanham).

Dodson-Truck, Frank (GR)
Frank is a common name. *See* Dodson-Truck, Sir Stephen for the surname.

Dodson-Truck, Nora (GR)
Nora is a common name. *See* Dodson-Truck, Sir Stephen for the surname.

Dodson-Truck, Sir Stephen (GR)
Weisenburger points to the Datsun truck reference (113). The name is a simple pun on the popular pickup truck produced by Nissan. The mock British hyphenated form of the name makes it plausible enough to mask the pun somewhat. Pynchon's hyphenated names may be modelled in part on those of Evelyn Waugh, such as Mrs. Beste-Chetwynde from *Decline and Fall*, for example.

Dollond, John (M&D)
The DNB identifies this maker "of optical and scientific instruments" (Clifton).

Dolores (V)
One of the two girls Geronimo calls when Angel is upset at the prospect of Fina accompanying them to get "coño," Dolores is categorically defined as a "girl" rather than a source of sex. The name is appropriate as it derives from a title for the Virgin Mary, *Maria de los Dolores* (Mary of Sorrows) (Hanks and Hodges 86).

Domenico (Lot 49)
See also Niccoló. The name of this character from *The Courier's Tragedy*, the Italian form of Domenic(k), may recall the Dominican order. The name literally means "of the Lord" (Withycombe 81).

Domenico (ATD)
This common name is Italian for Dominic.

Dominic (Vine)
Common name.

Doosra, the (ATD)
The term *doosra* refers to a particularly tricky cricket pitch (or bowl, rather), somewhat akin to the curveball in baseball, although the doosra's legality has been widely debated. The character, the Doosra, is a rogue element, a prophet and voracious user of a wide range of drugs, giving his title a figurative appropriateness, as well as tying in to earlier cricket references in the novel.

Dora (ATD)
While a common name, Dora could refer to the concentration camp of that name, which figures in GR (430—32 et al.), or even to Freud's *Dora: An Analysis of a Case of Hysteria* dated 1905 in the standard edition of Freud's works, placing it within the timeframe of ATD. Either one of these allusions would be wholly external, having no descriptive value for this very minor character.

Dorset (GR)
Weisenburger associates the name in its context "Turn off that faucet, Dorset," with other names in rhyming or near-rhyming phrases, such as "Girl in distress, Jess?" and "Got a fag, Mag?" He cites Taylor on the prevalence of these rhymes during World War II (78).

Dorzhieff (ATD)
The reference is to Agvan Dorzhiev, famous Russian Buddhist.

Dotty (Vine)
Common name.

Dou Ya (ATD)
The source for the name of this Chinese character in the Li'l Jailbirds was probably a Chinese menu: it means "bean sprouts."

Doucette (V)
Grant suggest that this character in Gerfaut's novel is reminiscent of Nabokov's Lolita (175). There is no similar connection to the name itself, which is French for "meek" or "mild." This is an ironic name for a girl said to be struggling with unnamable passions.

Douglas (SR)
Common as both a given- and a surname.

Douglas, Captain (M&D)
This is the captain of the vessel that takes Dixon on a journey to the world inside the surface of the hollow earth, as Dixon recounts the story to Mason. Given the story and the name of the vessel (H.M.S. *Emerald*), one seeks an allusion to *The Wizard of Oz* (Oz being the place where the Emerald City is located). The name, however, has no clear link to Oz or any significance that I can see.

Dragsaw, Mrs. (ATD)
A drag-saw is a saw that cuts on the pull rather than the thrust (OED). The character is presented as being somewhat prickly (338), so the name may be mildly charactonymic, or it could be one of many names reflecting Pynchon's interest in relatively obscure terms.

Dragut (V)
Grant identifies the historical pirate (195).

Drave
Drave is the name of a river in central Europe. It is certainly not commonly used as a name, but appears to have little significance for this character who claims he can instruct Lew Basnight in the ways of atonement. He "introduce[s] himself only as Drave" (39), adding to the mystery of this name.

Driblette, Randolph (Lot 49)
Reich sees Driblette as an allusion to *The Wonderful Wizard of Oz* and offers

several interesting parallels (for example, Driblette's head is seen floating in the shower steam backstage like the smoke-wreathed head of the Wizard of Oz [179]; Oedipa is attached to her green sunglasses recalling the green-tinted lenses the denizens of the Emerald city must wear for it to appear green [180]; Driblette directs Oedipa to the script copies kept in a filing cabinet recalling the origin of the name OZ — the letters O to Z on a drawer of author L. Frank Baum's filing cabinet [181]), but there does not seem to be any connection involving the name. Hayles suggests that the surname connects Driblette to his fate and works with the shower scene — "water dribbling down the drain" — to foreshadow his suicide, death by water (108). Hollander reads the complete name as "spot of randy dribble" ("Pynchon, JFK and the CIA" 77), although the significance of this is uncertain. Colvile offers that Driblette can be seen as "having dribbled enough information to frustrate Oedipa" but also emphasizes the liquid aspect of the name, the foreshadowing of his suicide, and the reference to Eliot's "Death by Water" section of *The Waste Land* (30). The literal reading of the surname as a little dribble (a kind of doubling) also suggests his smallness in the greater scheme of things.

Drivelli, Signore (M&D)

The name of this purported manager of Elizabeth LeSpark as a young performer derives from the circus manager Drivelli from a late nineteenth-century Broadway musical called *The Circus Girl*.

Driwelling (GR)

The name of this German engineer does not appear to mean anything in German or to be a common surname, however, the pronunciation — drivelling — suggests drooling or talking idiotically (OED).

Drogo (M&D)

He is described briefly as a half-breed revolutionary. Drogo is a fairly common historical name deriving from the Old German for "bear or carry" (Withycombe 84). Clearly he bears arms. Drogo is also the name of a deformed saint.

Drohne (GR)

Drohne means "drone" in German. He is described as "an assistant." As he is part of the group responsible for Imipolex G and thus connected to the I.G. Farben, the name may suggest also that he and others in the corporate power structure live off the labor of others.

Dromond (GR)

As Larsson points out, a dromond is a large, medieval ship. The name could derive from Pynchon's love of obscure words, or it could be a variant of an old British surname, Dromant or Drummond (Reaney and Wilson 142-3). None of these variants, including the spelling Dromond, is terribly uncommon. In either case, the name has no apparent significance for this minor character about whom we know very little.

Drop, Jimmy (ATD)

Jimmy is a common name. The verb *drop* can mean "to cause to fall, as by hitting or shooting" (AH4), appropriate for a gunman.

Drulov, Jacintha (ATD)

Jacintha is a variant of Jacinth, feminine name and name of a precious stone, ultimately deriving from the Greek for hyacinth (Whitycombe 160). Drulov combines *drool* and *true love*, an apt depiction of Bevis Moistleigh's reaction to seeing her in her "translucent sailor-girl's outfit": "he was instantly and publicly smitten" (822).

Drummer, the (GR)

The "character" is mentioned as an old espionage acquaintance of Katje's; the "name" is probably a meaningless alias. His name has been replaced by an epithet.

Duck, Mock (ATD)

Strange but true, Mock Duck was a Chinese thug in New York's Chinatown at the beginning of the twentieth century:

> Around 1900 a man named Mock Duck appeared on the scene (the transliterations of these Chinese names sound like wild guesses).... He wore chain mail, habitually carried two .45 revolvers and a hatchet, and was very soon known and feared for his favored fighting technique, which consisted of squatting in the middle of the street, shutting his eyes, and firing both guns in a full circle around him [Sante 227].

Pynchon lifted this detail without change: "Mock Duck himself appeared in the street down in his well-known spinning squat, firing two revolvers at a time in all directions" (341). This plausibly Chinese-sounding name is also a term used to describe a vegetarian approximation of duck meat. Mock duck is served at many Chinese restaurants (and can be quite tasty).

Duckworth, Harvey (MMV)

A common name, but somehow it is too pretentious sounding for this swinish character.

Dufay, Kim (SI, GR)

Part of "The Occupation of Mingeborough" scene, Kim Dufay is another character with an ordinary name. The character first appeared in Pynchon's 1964 short story, "The Secret Integration." While the names of the characters in "The Occupation of Mingeborough" scene of GR all have relatively normal names, this is not wholly true of the story SI. The use in GR of only the normal names seems to indicate the life of normalcy from which Slothrop is barred. In the context of her appearance in SI, Hollander suggests that the name "sounds like Morgan le Fay" ("Pynchon's Politics" 44), sorceress of Arthurian legend.

Dufay, Pete (GR)

Part of "The Occupation of Mingeborough" scene, Pete Dufay is another character with an ordinary name. The name Dufay first appeared in Pynchon's 1964 story "The Secret Integration," which takes place in Mingeborough, Massachusetts. *See also* Dufay, Kim.

Dugan, Twinkletoes (SR)

Dugan is a common surname. Twinkletoes is often applied to dancers, originally meaning someone who is "light-footed, nimble" (OED). The name is a charactonym for this character who is heard before he is seen: "a patter of little feet on the porch" (28).

Duke (E)

Common name.

Dulang, Ortho Bob (Vine)

While there is a Mount Dulang-Dulang in the Philippines and the line "dulang, dulang, dulang" occurs repeatedly in the Chiffon's hit "He's So Fine" written by Ronald Mack, there is another reading of the meaning of this name supported by the context of Ortho Bob Dulang's appearance in the novel. *Ortho* is a root meaning "straight" and *dulang* is Indonesian for "food tray"—Straight Bob Food Tray is introduced as devouring Takeshi's "Galaxy of Ribs" platter while he is away from the table for a phone call (170). He appears as an eating machine; D.L. has to translate what he says, as he speaks while his mouth is stuffed with Takeshi's ribs.

Dulles, Allen (GR)

Weisenburger identifies the historical OSS spy and later CIA director (140).

Dunham, Crazy Sue (GR)

Larsson identifies the source for this historical witch as a book called *The Berkshire Hills* (V329.26–27).

Dunkirk, Maggie (GR)

Maggie "Got a fag, Mag?" Dunkirk's first name is connected to the rhyme (*see*

Dorset for more on this phenomenon). Dunkirk was the site of a massive British retreat during the War, but how this may apply to this minor character is unclear.

Dunn (ATD)

A common surname, but Jesse's friend is referred to simply as Dunn, so it might be a given name. Given the financial straits of all the residents of the Ludlow tent colony, the name may be formed on the verb *dun*, "to persistently demand the payment of debts" (W3).

Dupiro the ragman (V)

This is the last (very minor) character introduced into the novel. Like many minor characters, he is never heard to speak. The name could be a paronomastic encoding of "the Pierrot." A Pierrot is a stock character from French pantomime. He was marked by a whitened face and loose white garments (OED). The pantomime communicates without words. The drowned and mutilated corpse of Dupiro sends a message about spying and betrayal, and after having been dragged from the water, Dupiro's face and body must have looked very much like those of the Pierrot.

Duse, Eleonora (V)

Grant identifies the historical actress (127).

Dustuhs, Hudson (ATD)

Not a character, but a parody of Bowery pronunciation. The Hudson Dusters were a gang who controlled the Lower West Side of New York in the late nineteenth century (Sante 225).

Dvindler (ATD)

Not a common name, it seems a Germanic reading of "dwindler" (he uses the German command *komm* [714]), based on the English verb *dwindle* ("to become gradually less") (AH4). It is appropriate for one perfecting a treatment for constipation.

Dwayna (Vine)

As this does not seem to be a common name, it may be a pun on *duenna* ("female chaperon") (OED). Ché's descriptions of Dwayna's maternal skills suggest absolute incompetence, so the name is meant ironically.

Dymphna (ATD)

The name of Crayke's pony lover is Irish, meaning "one fit to be" (Withycombe 87). They were meant to be together.

Dzabajev (GR)

The character is named after the famous Kirghiz aqyn Dzambul Dzabajev (Weisenburger 191).

Dzambul (GR)

Weisenburger identifies the historical bard mentioned in the old aqyn's song (176).

Earp, Wyatt (ATD)

Not technically a character, this wild west figure, while involved in a range of shady activities, is said to have exaggerated his reputation as a gun fighter (O'Neal 100).

Easterling (GR)

Easterling means "a native of the east, especially eastern Germany or the Baltic coasts"; it also refers to a type of German ship (OED). Neither definition seems to apply to the character, but he is associated with Dromond, another character named for a type of ship.

Eberle, Bob (GR)

Weisenburger identifies the historical singer (138).

Echerze, Hanne (V)

Although plausibly German sounding, Echerze is not a common name. The meaning, if any, is unclear.

Eddy, Nelson (GR)

Weisenburger identifies the historical singer and actor (232).

Edelman, Steve (GR)

The surname derives from the German *Edelmann*, meaning "nobleman." Weisenburger claims that the first name comes from the Greek *stephein*, meaning "to encircle" (161), but Steve is common enough that this etymology is uncertain. Weisenburger may support this reading because it fits in with the Mandala imagery he locates throughout the novel. Both Larsson (V315.08) and Fowler (164) suggest that the name may belong to someone Pynchon actually knew, but neither provides any real evidence. Given the character's connection to folk and preterite cultures (315), spiritualism and drug addiction (753), the name may be one of many reversals, where a name with positive attributes is applied to a character who would be held in contempt by "normal" society.

Edgewise, Mr. (M&D)

The surname suggests the idiom "to get a word in edgewise," which does not seem to have any application to this character or his wife. *Edgewise* means "with the edge foremost" (AH4); this could be a reference to his remarkable success at gambling. It could, however, be a simple joke.

Edgewise, Mrs. (M&D)

See Edgewise, Mr.

Edison, [Thomas Alva] (ATD)

The historical inventor, while not a character, is mentioned throughout the text.

Effendi, Karakas (ATD)

The source of Pynchon's spelling is uncertain as most sources give the surname as "Efendi." Karakas Efendi was "the hanende (court singer) to Abdul Hamid II (r. 1876–1909)" (Levy 597).

Effig, Private Rudolf (GR)

This "character" appears only as a name signed to a graffito calling for death to come and take him "like gentle sleep" (733). In this context, "Effig" seems to be a shortened form of "effigy," where the private stands in for or anticipates death, as it ends the war for many participants.

Eggslap, Patience (M&D)

A delightfully Dickensian name, Eggslap somehow captures her role as a culinary extortionist, who manages to raise her cooking fee beyond the agreed amount.

Ehud (M&D)

Given the fact that historical sources, where available, tend to identify the actual crew members by their surnames, *Ehud* is probably contrived. It is one of many biblical names in the text. *Ehud* means "union" (Hamilton 39), but may be taken ironically as this character is introduced as having caused disharmony with at least one fellow crew member by constantly telling "parrot jokes" (453).

Eigenvalue the physician, Dudley (V)

Grant relies on a garbled definition of *eigenvalue* from *Webster's*, where the OED offers the concise and useful "[o]ne of those special values of a parameter in an equation for which the equation has a solution." As the dentist replaces the psychiatrist in V, Eigenvalue does offer "solutions" to his patients. He could also provide the circumstances under which Stencil can fit one more piece of the puzzle together, if the precious metal dentures he created fit the mouth of V. Grant also cites David Milne's claim that *Dudley* suggests "zero" (31). If *Dudley* does mean "zero," we can read the entire name as another instance of doubling: zero is akin to an eigenvalue, for anything multiplied by it drops from the equation, which can then easily be solved. Of course the names together could suggest that his solutions are empty. Regardless of these shades of meaning, the name functions more simply as one of many Pynchon references to mathematical and scientific terminology.

Eileen, the girls named (GR)
The reference is to a line in an Irving Berlin song called "I Left My Heart at the Stage Door Canteen": "I left it there with a girl named Eileen" (Larsson V134.27).

Ekori (GR)
Fowler identifies *ekori* as the Herero word for "cap, hood, cowl" (272). Like most of the purely Herero names, it does not seem to have any special application to the character.

El Ñato (GR)
Weisenburger translates the name as "pugnose" and traces it to a character in *Return of Martín Fierro* (187).

El Ñato (ATD)
Like the El Ñato in GR, this character, too, gets his name from a character in Hernandez's *Return of Martín Fierro*, whose name means "pugnose" (Weisenburger 187).

Elasmo, Dr. Larry, D.D.S. (Vine)
Cowart identifies *elasmo* as a shortened form of "'elasmobranchii,' the order of fish that includes sharks and rays" ("Continuity" 178). The figurative meaning of the word applies here: "Applied to persons, with allusion to the predatory habits and voracity of the shark; one who enriches himself by taking advantage of the necessities of others" (OED). The reference may be to dentistry in general or to the rather unique aspects of Dr. Elasmo's practice, including his extremely persuasive techniques of forcing patients into his office. Diebold and Goodwin see a connection between *Elasmo* and Plasticman, although this seems tenuous.

Elijah the Swamper (M&D)
He is not mentioned in any of the obvious sources, so the name may be contrived. Elijah means "Jehovah is God" (Withycombe 93), but the name has no obvious significance for this character. In the context of his introduction, his epithet *swamper* means simply "helper" (AH4).

Elisa (V)
Common name.

Elizabeth (GR)
Common name.

Elizabeth (M&D)
Dixon provides for Margaret Bland and her two daughters, Elizabeth and Mary, in his will (Robinson "Jeremiah Dixon" 274). The fact that his mother was named Mary and his sister Elizabeth strongly suggests that they were his daughters by Bland, as depicted by Pynchon (751).

Elizabeth, Lady Barnard, the Old Hell-Cat of Raby (M&D)
The lady, if not the ghost, was real ("Darlington and the Tees Vale").

Elizabeths (GR)
See Girls, Slothrop's.

Ellicott, John (M&D)
The DNB identifies this watchmaker and scientist (Thompson).

Ellicott Clock, the (M&D)
The clock is real and was designed by the historical John Ellicott (Cope "A Clock" 265). Its ability to speak is presumably Pynchon's invention.

Elmhurst (Vine)
Common name.

Elroy (M&D)
Common name.

Elsie, One-Tooth (ATD)
One of the women Dally beats out to get the role of Calpurnia in Con McVeety's "Bowery Version" of *Julius Caesar*, she must have presented little competition if the name is an apt description. Besides being unattractive, she would, with only one tooth, have difficulty pronouncing many words.

Elvissa (Vine)
The name is obviously a feminized version of *Elvis*. There could also be a 1980s

popular culture reference to Halloween sex symbol Elvira. There is also a city named Elvissa on the Spanish Island of Ibiza.

Emerson, Mrs. (M&D)
The DNB entry for William Emerson identifies his wife as Elizabeth (Vian).

Emerson, William (M&D)
The DNB identifies this eccentric mathematician (Vian).

Emilio (ATD)
Common name.

Emmett (ATD)
A common name for a "character" only mentioned once.

Encarnación (ATD)
The name is Spanish for "incarnation." It is appropriate. Supposedly killed, she is seen by Jardine Maraca. An incarnation is "a bodily manifestation of a supernatural being" (AH4): a name that could be read as "ghost."

Enrico (ATD)
While Enrico is a common name, it may be an allusion to the famous Italian physicist Enrico Fermi, as the character is described as a "technician" (944).

Enrico, Eddie and his Hong Kong Hotshots (Vine)
The name of this bandleader and band, although a plausible parody of a swing band name, is based on a band from the film *The Adventures of Buckaroo Banzai across the Eighth Dimension*: Buckaroo Banzai and the Hong Kong Cavaliers ("Pynchon-Film"). One of many popular culture references in Pynchon.

Entrevue, Madame (ATD)
The surname is French for "interview" or "discussion," not especially meaningful for this brothel owner who appears in name only.

Enzian, Oberst (GR)
Oberst is a German title equivalent to our Colonel; as an adjective, it means "uppermost" or "chief." We are told that Blicero/Weissmann names "the African boy" Enzian "after Rilke's mountainside gentian" (101). Notice that he has no name until Blicero bestows one, the imposition of a Western image (blue and yellow on this red and brown boy, as Enzian himself points out [101]) on a colonial possession. Fowler also identifies *Enzian* as a Nazi surface-to-air missile (168). Slade claims that the rocket called Enzian lost out, "was 'passed-over' in favor of the V-2" ("Religion" 174). This connects Enzian to the rocket, but also identifies him as preterite.

er-Raisuli, Mulai Ahmed (ATD)
Porch identifies the historical warlord, but gives the name as Sherif Moulai Ahmed Ben Mohammed el Raisuni (107).

Ercole (Lot 49)
See also Niccoló. This *Courier's Tragedy* character name is Italian for Hercules, perhaps suggesting the superiority of the pagan tradition over the corruption of church and state, as presented in the play.

Erdmann, Margherita (Greta, Gretel) (GR)
The character explains that this is not her real name, implying her actual name is identifiably Jewish. The surname is German for "earth man": "anything with Earth in it was politically safe — Earth, Soil, Folk" (395). Fowler suggests that "earthman" makes the character a "perverted Earth Mother" (124). Greta ties her to the Hänsel and Gretel motif that occurs throughout the novel.

Ernö (ATD)
Common Hungarian name.

Ernst (ATD)
See Adolf.

Esberg, Captain (GR)
Common name.

Eskimoff, Madame Natalia (ATD)
The common Russian name Natalia is joined with a plausibly Russian sounding surname, similar to the actual name Ekimoff. The common Russion surname suffix *-off* is attached to *Eskimo* to form a joke.

Espinero, El (ATD)
Not his real name, as he says, Espinero derives from the Spanish noun *espina* (thorn). Just as *caballero* (horseman) derives from *caballo* (horse), Espinero's derivation gives us "The Thorn Man," referring to his shamanic ability to read "a random spill of cactus thorns" just as others would read tea leaves to tell the future (390).

Estelle (GR)
Common name.

Estrella (ATD)
A common Latin-American name, it means "star" in Spanish. It is used largely to recall Estrella Briggs and hint at the theme of bilocation.

Ethelmer (M&D)
There is an Ethelmer mentioned in *The Anglo-Saxon Chronicle*, but there is no obvious connection with our character. Ware cites Thiel, who suggests "2-HydroxyETHYL MERcaptan," a noxious substance that "contributes greatly to the process of entropy" and Sublett who offers "prince of the sea" from *æthel*, "prince" in Old English and *mer*, "sea" in French ("*Mason & Dixon*"). There may be a reference to the Victorian author Ellis Ethelmer who wrote on women's and sexual liberation; our Ethelmer is presented as progressive compared to the other family members.

Eugénie (ATD)
A common name, it may also allude to the wife of Napoleon III.

Eunice (V)
The name derives from Greek roots meaning "good" or "well" and "victory" (Withycombe 105). This is somewhat ironic in that she fails in her attempt to seduce McClintic Sphere.

Euphorbia (ATD)
Kit's made-up name for Dally is actually the name of a genus of plants, but it is similar to the old British name Euphemia.

Euphrenia, Aunt (M&D)
The name seems to be a variant of *Euphemia*, "auspicious speech" (Withycombe 105). Genealogical research suggests that *Euphrenia* was quite common 100–200 years ago. The original etymology of *Euphemia* suggests irony when applied to this garrulous creature.

Eva (V)
Common name.

Evans, Jeremiah ("Merciful") (GR)
The name is another simple pun based on a Cockney or similar pronunciation of "merciful heavens."

Evelyn, Uncle (UR, V)
The character is described along with the Catholic church as forming the foci of young Victoria Wren's "serene orbit" (V 72). Although the name is common enough not to need any particular meaning, it could refer to British Catholic author Evelyn Waugh.

Eventyr, Carrol (GR)
Eventyr is the Danish word for "adventure" (Weisenburger 30). Larsson clarifies this definition by explaining that the word's proper meaning refers to "adventures" in the sense of tales and suggests that "Carrol" may refer to Lewis Carrol or Carrol Righter, a famous astrologist (V31.28). Thus the name might mean "nonsense stories" from Lewis Carrol, or "astrological tales" from Righter. In any event, as a medium, the character Eventyr is responsible for extracting the stories of adventures beyond death.

Everybeet, Jonas, the Quartz-Scryer (M&D)
Everybeet is an amusing parody of "everyman." A quartz scryer would be someone who can see the future or locate something by gazing into quartz — like the well-known crystal ball gazer.

Ewing, Reverend (M&D)
Mentioned in Mason's journal, but spelled Ewen (210), he was one of the line commissioners.

Ezekiel, little (M&D)
Common name.

Fabian (M&D)
The word derives from Fabius Maximus, the Delayer, who was adept at avoiding battles (OED). It is appropriate for a character who suggests a game of quoits in lieu of a duel to the death.

Fabrizio, Signor (ATD)
Fabrizio is a common Italian given name, so this hairdressing character goes by a title and given name, rather than a surname. Although not terribly likely, the name could allude to Fabrizio Sanges, a hairdresser who has won Emmys for his hairstyling of television actors.

Faffner, Hank (GR)
Fowler (239) and Weisenburger (281) both identify the source of the surname as Fafnir, who guards the gold of the Nibelungs. Fowler refers to Wagner's adaptation of the myth. The relevance of the name to this minor character is unclear.

Faggio, Duke of (Lot 49)
Faggio is Italian for "beech," or "beechwood." The immediate connection is unclear. Colvile suggests that the name is a pun on the American slang term *fag* (88).

Fahringer (GR)
The name derives from two German words: the verb *fahren*, meaning "to drive"; the adjective *fahrig*, meaning "nervous." "Nervous driver" is a nice name for an aerodynamics man charged with keeping rockets on course. It is also at odds with his Zen-approach to aerodynamic problem solving.

Fairing, Father Linus, S.J. (V)
Fairing is not an uncommon surname, but the word's semantic richness should cause us to look beneath the surface. The common definition refers to a device placed on a vehicle to reduce drag (AH4). Here is the Pynchon physics reference. Our character Fairing, however, is British, and the word has a different range of meanings in British English. *Fairing* means "a gift of any kind" or "an action allowing something easy passage in its medium" (OED). Father Fairing descends into the sewers of New York during the depression, convinced that the rats will inherit the earth by the end of the year. He hopes to convert them and offer them the gift of salvation, or ease their passage to heaven. He would also become the new "spiritual leader of the inheritors of the earth" (118) much like his namesake St. Linus, who followed St. Peter as Bishop of Rome. Also like Fairing, St. Linus was a shadowy figure, about whom little is known (Farmer 246). His gift of salvation (*fairing*) and role of spiritual leader (St. Linus) make the name a doubling as well as a charactonym, albeit an oblique one.

Falange, Baby Face (V)
While the surname calls to mind *phalange*, one of the bones in the fingers or toes, *Falange* refers to the Spanish fascists under Franco, referred to as Falangists. We may read *Baby Face* as a contradictory name if taken literally, or as a type name for gangsters (like Pretty Boy Floyd and others): thus a doubling of the evil connotations. As the character is only briefly mentioned, the name functions as name only.

Falconer, Captain (M&D)
According to Cope, Falconar (his spelling) was the captain of the ship that took

Mason and Dixon to America ("Charles Mason ..." 544).

Falconière (V)
There does not seem to be a direct link to an identical Romance language word, but the reference seems to be to *falcon* or *falconry*, suggesting, perhaps a predatory nature.

Fallopian, Mike (Lot 49)
Grant cites Watson who suggests the name forms part of a theme of transsexuality in the novel (49). Colvile claims that the name is an allusion to female sterilization (28), referring, presumably, to the tying of these tubes. Hayles offers that Fallopian's name "links him to Oedipa's later intuition that she is pregnant with something the gynecologist has no test for" (105). Although if the name is linked to pregnancy, it might suggest ectopic pregnancy, a dangerous condition where the fertilized egg is lodged in a fallopian tube, rather than the uterus. Another possibility is that the name, like many in the text, is a simple joke with no extensive structure of meaning behind it.

Fame (ATD)
She and Finesse are a pair of prostitutes whose names are chosen for alliteration.

Fangsley (ATD)
It is difficult to tell if this is a purely imagined figure in the context of the growing disorder on the Stupendica, but the name is comic. It could be an allusion to a minor character who appeared in the long-running comic strip Lil' Abner by Al Capp: J.R. Fangsley was a hog breeder, sure to appeal to pig-loving Pynchon.

Fanshawe, Noellyn (ATD)
Noellyn is a fairly common female name. Fanshawe seems a common British surname; there are several Fanshawes listed in the DNB.

Farlow, Robert (M&D)
Mentioned in Mason's journal as "R. Farlow" (191), Headlee identifies him as an instrument bearer (11).

Farnese, Alexander (Lot 49)
Grant cites Delepinne on this historical Dutch governor-general (127).

Farr, Ed (ATD)
Edward Farr was a lawman, killed at Turkey Canyon, New Mexico in 1899 (O'Neal 176).

Fat Clyde, (Harvey) (V)
Harvey was renamed Fat Clyde because of his emaciation (6-foot-1-inch, 145 lbs.). Presumably the name is indicative of the jocular nicknames used by the sailors.

Fatou (ATD)
Not common as a given name, it alludes to the French mathematician Pierre Fatou.

Faun (ATD)
The fauns were rural deities depicted, like the satyrs, as half man and half goat (OED). Overall, an odd name for a female character, although some degree of gender confusion may be intended, given Yashmeen and her friends' lesbian experimentation. It could be meant as a variant of the relatively common name Fawn.

Fauntleroy, Francis X. (SI)
This character appears in a reminiscence of Carl McAfee's, where he steals Carl's last cigarette. The name is surprisingly rich. The surname refers to the children's novel *Little Lord Fauntleroy*, about an American boy who gains wealth and a title in England, written by Frances Hodgson Burnett: surely an ironic reference given the context. Francis X. suggests Francis Xavier, one of the founders of the Jesuits, possibly a sinister reference, given Pynchon's treatment of the Jesuits in M&D.

Fazzo, Harvey (V)
Fazzo may come from the Italian *fazio* ("simpleton or fool"). Or it may approx-

imate the English *Fatso*. We only know that the character is a piano player, so the derision in the name does not seem directed at the character.

Feel, Osbie (GR)

The first name is probably short for Osbert with no particular meaning for this character. The surname suggests a character in search of sensation or stimulation, appropriate for a constant user of a wide variety of drugs.

Feely, Vang (ATD)

This hyper-masculine biker has an odd name. Feely sounds "sensitive" or effeminate, like a person who is touchy-feely, yet it could also be read as a sexual identifier, suggesting his conquests. Stray's hair, disarray, and general appearance after sleeping with Feely (464) support this latter reading. *Vang* is a common Vietnamese surname and the Vietnamese word for "yes," perhaps suggesting the willingness of women to sleep with him, but there is no clear reason why this reference would be couched in Vietnamese. The name may be meant to onomatopoeically suggest the sound of his motorcycle.

Feeny (LL)

This sonarman has a common Irish surname. Given that he appears in a story related by Pig Bodine about his and Feeny's anti-establishment activities in Barcelona, there may be a reference to the fenians, any Irish Americans involved in brotherhoods devoted to revolutionary activity, especially the overthrow of the English government in Ireland (OED).

Feldman, Ditzah Pisk (Vine)

Ditzah is Hebrew for "joy." It is a fairly common name as are the surnames Pisk and Feldman. It is possible there is an allusion here. In an article on the novel, Olster (although she does not make any connection between the names) quotes Dziga Vertov on the role of the film "not as a *mirror* which reflects the historical struggle, but a *weapon* of that struggle" (121). The sentiment is echoed by Ditzah and the other members of the 24 fps film collective.

Feldspath, Roland (GR)

Weisenburger points out the reference to feldspar, a crystalline group of minerals (30). *Feldspar* derives etymologically from the obsolete German word for the same minerals, *feldspath* (AH4). This is another Pynchon name derived from the sciences.

Feldspath, Selena (GR)

Weisenburger links her to the goddess of the moon (30), although that spelling is usually Selene. Withycombe says the name is common in Britain and rejects the connection to the Greek for "moon" in favor of an etymology extending back to French *Céline*, Latin *Coelina* derived from *caelum*, meaning "heaven." In the context of the séance and the general spiritualism in this episode of the novel, the name seems vaguely appropriate. See Feldspath, Roland for the surname.

Felipe (GR)

Common name.

Felipe (Vine)

Common name.

Felix, the clarinet player (GR)

Common name.

Feng, Su (V)

The name of the character played by Mélanie l'Heuremaudit in *The Rape of the Chinese Virgins* combines common Chinese names and need not mean anything special. It is possible that *su* refers to the Chinese for "tell or relate" (Jingrong 653) and *feng* to the Chinese for "the sharp point or cutting edge of a sword" (Jingrong 205). This would describe the ballet she is in: it tells the story of her death by impalement.

Fenice (V)

The word *fenice* is Italian for "phoenix." It is also the name of a famous opera

Feodora

house in Venice. Although there is no compelling reason this name should apply to a defrocked monk who breeds scorpions, it may refer to his abilities of survival or reinvention. We learn almost nothing of him, though. Harder states that the name is "a devoicing of the V in Venice" but does not explain the significance of this (77).

Feodora (ATD)
Common Russian name.

Fepp, Highwayman (M&D)
He is only mentioned as a criminal who was recently executed. The name has no obvious meaning. Mason comments to a fellow execution aficionado that, conventional expectations to the contrary, his "*Membrum virile* was remarkably flaccid" (112). Perhaps *fepp* is meant to onomatopoeically suggest flaccidity.

Ferdinand, Archduke Francis (Franz) (ATD)
The historical Austrian archduke whose assassination started WWI.

Ferguson, Chain (V)
Angel's alias is explained in the text. The name comes from the hero of an unnamed western Profane and the Mendozas had watched on television (140). If this is the name of the character, the film must be obscure (if real). There could be a reference to Al Ferguson who played villains in westerns during the 1930s or Frank Ferguson, a western actor of the 1950s.

Ferguson, Elmer (GR)
See Brennan, Peewee.

Ferrante (V)
The word is an adjective derived from the Italian verb *ferrare*, meaning "to shoe, shackle, or bind with iron." One is tempted to read the name as "shackled," which Pynchon may have intended, but the word for one fitted with irons is *ferrato*; the meaning of *ferrante* is closer to "shoeing" or "shackling." The name may mean, then, "one who binds or shackles others"—an appropriate name for a spy in the service of powerful, unseen forces of political domination. Ferrante is, however, a fairly common Italian surname. There could also be a reference to pop musician Arthur Ferrante of the long-time easy-listening duo, Ferrante and Teicher.

Ferrers, Lady (M&D)
The woman who became Lady Ferrers on marrying Lord Ferrers in 1752 was Mary Meredith (Davenport-Hines, "Shirley, Laurence, fourth Earl Ferrers (1720–1760)).

Ferrers, Lord (M&D)
The DNB identifies the actual historical figure, Laurence Shirley, fourth Earl Ferrers (1720–1760) (Davenport-Hines, "Shirley, Laurence, fourth Earl Ferrers (1720–1760)).

Fétiche (V)
Itague calls Mélanie fétiche (395). This is not metonymic; the character is a fetish. *See also* l'Heuremaudit, Mélanie.

Fiametta (ATD)
The character is only mentioned as a friend of Dally's who is briefly involved with Kit (1077). The name is likely drawn from the Gilbert and Sullivan operetta *The Gondoliers*, which includes a character named Fiametta.

Fibel, Bert (GR)
Fibel is German for "a primer." Weisenburger states that the *A-4 Fibel* was one of Pynchon's sources for rocket information. The name may also suggest inexperience (he is paired with Flaum ["fuzz or down"]).

Fields, Eliza (M&D)
Common name.

Fields, Joseph (M&D)
Common name.

Fife, Melrose (Vine)

Diebold and Goodwin identify a reference to a 1940s and 1950s New York City radio jingle: "Melrose five, five-three-hundred." Given that the character is a law enforcement officer, and knowing Pynchon's usual negative depiction of police, there is also a reference to Barney Fife, the bumbling deputy of *The Andy Griffith Show*.

Filtham (ATD)

The name is reminiscent of GR's Creepham. Again, a plausible sounding name, in this case occasionally seen as an actual surname, that masks a simple joke. The emphasis is on the first syllable, filth. In this case the comic-derisive name is connected to the negative depiction of this much-hated composer.

Finesse (ATD)

She and Fame are a pair of prostitutes whose names are chosen for alliteration. The name Finesse also suggests a great deal of skill, born out by Wren Provenance's appearance after disappearing with the two girls.

Fiona (Vine)

The cocktail waitresses on Kahuna Airlines are "make-believe" Polynesians. Fiona is a Celtic name.

Fiona (M&D)

Common name.

Firelily (V)

The Bondel ridden by Hedwig is given the name Firelily, like the mare, because of his color. Hedwig describes his skin as sorrel, a word typically reserved for horses. The name is meant to be dehumanizing.

Fisk (ATD)

Common name.

Fisk, Jubilee Jim (SI)

Hollander identifies the historical robber baron ("Pynchon's Politics" 46).

Flaco (ATD)

A common name and nickname, it means "skinny" in Spanish. It may also allude to famous Mexican-American accordionist Flaco Jiménez.

Flaff, Gorman ("The Specter") (Vine)

Flaff is a Scottish term for "a fluttering of the wings" or "a puff or gust" (OED). He appears only in a flashback of Vietnam, so it could refer to helicopters, but given the nickname "the Specter" and our knowledge that he is dead, the name Flaff doubles the ghostly description.

Flagg (ATD)

This "cringing weasel" (212) has a common name, but the sound "flag" may also suggest a critique of extreme forms of patriotism, embodied in flag worship.

Flake, the sculptor (V)

According to the OED, one meaning of *flake* is "to break flakes or chips from." The name suits the occupation. Of course the name could also invoke the slang meaning of the noun, "a foolish, slow-witted, or unreliable person" (OED), but there is no description of this character, who, like many others in the text, exists only as a name, so we cannot judge how this meaning would function beyond simple comedy.

Flambo, Wilt (ATD)

Wilt is a common name. Flambo seems a variant spelling of *flambeau*, "a lighted torch" (AH4). He repairs a movie projector, which is operated using acetylene, a flammable gas usually associated with welding torches. The name also suggests *flamboyant* ("given to ostentatious or audacious display") (AH4). After running off with the feed clerk's wife, he sends "everybody picture postals about how much fun he's having" (450).

Flamp, Constance ("Commando Connie") (GR)

Commando Connie seems an appropriate nickname for a war correspondent. Constance derives from the Latin *Constantia*, "constancy" (Withycombe 68), but the name is rather common, so this meaning may not be intentional. *Flamp* does not seem to mean anything, but has a comical sound.

Flamsteed, (John) (M&D)

The DNB identifies the historical astronomer (Willmoth).

Flange, Cindy (LL)

Cindy is a common name, short for Cynthia, which is one of the names of Artemis (Withycombe 73). Artemis, the huntress, was the twin sister of Apollo. Thus in this name the couple's incompatibility is contained: Dionysus (madness, drunkenness) and Apollo (structure, order). The surname seems to apply solely to the husband: *see* Flange, Dennis.

Flange, Dennis (LL)

Dennis is a common name, but deriving from Dionysos "the Areopagite converted by St. Paul at Athens" (Withycombe 77). This Christian reading of the name seems less relevant than the classical source for the name, Dionysus, the Greek god of wine. He is first seen skipping work in order to share a gallon jug of muscatel wine with Rocco Squarcione the garbage man. *Flange* means "a widening or branching out" (OED), applicable to this character who leaves his house and marriage of seven years to enter an Alice-in-wonderlandish world, possibly a product of his own fantasy, but more desirable than the narrow life of respectability from which he escaped.

Flannelette, Dodge (ATD)

On the surface, we have one of many vaguely Dickensian-sounding names, but there may be some charactonymic meaning. He is said to be a bucket shop (fraudulent brokerage house) desperado (130). One meaning of *dodge* is "to practice trickery or cunning" (AH4) and *flannelette* is "a soft cotton fabric with a nap" (AH4). The first name describes his character (in addition to referencing a brand name — the car company) while the second could illustrate his duplicity, suggesting serenity or comfort by way of baby blankets and other soft things made of flannelette.

Flaum (GR)

Weisenburger glosses the name as "fluff or fuzz" (211). It can also mean "down" and may refer to this minor character's youth or inexperience (he is paired with Fibel ["primer or introductory handbook"]).

Flebótomo, César (GR)

The name is a pun on phlebotomy, or blood-letting. As the manager of a casino, he bleeds the gamblers dry. The first name may allude to the famous Las Vegas Casino/Hotel, Caesar's Palace.

Fleische (V)

See also Schwach. He is introduced with Schwach and his name is similar. *Fleisch* is German for "meat," but Pynchon adds a feminine ending, perhaps to deride the soldier as unmasculine, but the reference to meat could be a comment on soldiers in general and how they are perceived by officers and political leaders (canon fodder).

Fleischmann, Sam (MMV)

Fleischmann is a common German, often Jewish, name. In English it would be "flesh man" or "meat man." The name applies to the partygoers in general: Their bodies will all be meat for the cannibal Irving Loon.

Fletcher, Flash (Vine)

The name seems contrived for its alliteration. *Flash* seems vaguely descriptive of this "outlaw leather"-wearing woman chaser (70).

Fletcher, Uncle (ATD)
Context does not specify whether this uncle of Webb's is paternal or maternal, so he may not share the name Traverse, but we are invited to see that this absent character at least shares some qualities of the name (*see* Traverse, Webb): he is mentioned only in the context of his gun, inherited by Webb (88). Fletcher is a common name.

Fleur (Vine)
Meaning "flower" in French, Fleur is another nature name bestowed by 1960s parents on one who is now a teenager in the 1980s.

Flint, [Joseph] (M&D)
Browne identifies the historical "security" given to Justice Price by Catherine Wheat to maintain possession of her child (132).

Flip and Flop (V)
Like other Pynchonian feminine duos, these names should be considered together. In this case the girls are interchangeable and the names are chosen specifically for their compact alliteration. The names also echo McClintic Sphere's theory of social behavior modeled on the two-triode circuit (293-4).

Flores Magón brothers, the (ATD)
Enrique, Jesús, and Ricardo Flores Magón were Mexican anarchists and sometime members of the Partido Liberal Mexicano (Cookcroft passim).

Florinda, Little (M&D)
"[O]ne of the greatest coloratura singers of the nineteenth century ... Adelina Patti made her professional debut in New York on November 24, 1859, as the lead in Donizetti's opera *Lucia di Lammermoor* under the stage name of 'Little Florinda'" (Orr 44).

Floundering Four, the (GR)
With the exception of Slothrop, they all have names beginning with "m," mirroring the alliteration of their joint title. As Weisenburger points out, they are a perversion of the well-known *Fantastic Four* issued by Marvel Comics starting in 1961 (283).

Fong Ding, Charlie (ATD)
Although this sounds like a Pynchon invention, this is the name of the man who laundered the prostitutes' clothing in Telluride; his first name is spelled "Charley" by Barbour (88).

Fop, the Ghastly (M&D)
This eponymous character from the fiction within the fiction seems meant as a parody of gothic novels and serials of the eighteenth century. The comedy of the name stems from the dissonance created by combining the term *fop* (whose foolish vanity suggests a kind of peevish effeminacy) and *ghastly* (suggesting terror). Although *ghastly* might be meant to represent typical fop speech ("How perfectly ghastly ... ") or to recall *ghostly*, appropriate in the gothic context.

Foppl (V)
The name may stem from an obsolete meaning of *fop*—"a fool" (OED). The *Middle English Dictionary* lists *foppe* as "fool" also. It might also refer to the Dutch verb *foppen*, meaning "to fool, cheat, or hoax." The latter seems especially appropriate given Foppl's role as brutal colonizer.

Ford, Bob (ATD)
Another "character" drawn from history, Ford joined the James gang for an opportunity to kill Jesse James and collect the reward; he shot an unarmed Jesse James while James was straightening a picture, an act for which he was widely scorned (O'Neal 111). This accounts for Ewball Oust's comment " that dirty li'l back-shooting Bob Ford" (642).

Förschner, Major (GR)
Förschner is described as the head of a security detail. The name probably derives from the German noun *Forscher*, meaning "inquirer," or "searcher." It seems loosely

appropriate for someone involved in security.

Francesca (Lot 49)
While the names of the characters in *The Courier's Tragedy* seem, for the most part, typical Italianate names, some may point to deeper references. Francesca almost certainly recalls Francesca Da Rimini from the fifth canto of Dante's *Inferno*, where she suffers eternal punishment for incest with her brother (in-law) in the Second Circle of Hell (the lustful). Like her namesake, Lot 49's Francesca is shown engaged in incest with her brother (66–7).

Françoise (GR)
Common French name.

Frangibella (GR)
The name stems from two Italian words, *fràngere* ("to break") and *bella* ("beauty"). A broken beauty, she is described as a drug user with a broken out complexion.

Frank (GR)
Common name.

Franklin, Benjamin (M&D)
The DNB identifies the American revolutionary, writer, and natural philosopher (Lemay).

Fresno, Sloat Eddie (ATD)
The surname is not common and may be modelled on assumed names derived from geographic locations (Fresno, California). Sloat has an undeniably negative sound association, but has no clear meaning. It may combine *slob* and *shoat* (a young pig), doubling the swinish aspect of this repugnant character.

Frieda the pig (GR)
Weisenburger states that the name Frieda comes from Freya, a Teutonic goddess who often appears riding a boar (194–95). The fact that Freya is associated with the Roman Venus also has meaning here, as Slothrop will briefly entertain romantic thoughts toward Frieda.

Friedmann (GR)
Weisenburger identifies the historical mathematician (193).

Friggs (M&D)
This Philadelphia land speculator is not mentioned in Mason's journal or other key sources. The surname is not uncommon. If the character is real, Pynchon's source is uncertain.

Fritz (GR)
The narrator describes him as a Wilhelm Busch original. Weisenburger reads this as "[r]eminiscent of Busch's comic strip characters" (245). In fact, "Hans Huckebein, the Unlucky Raven" contains a young boy named Fritz and a liqueur-quaffing raven, perhaps alluded to by Pynchon in the Haferschleim Fritz gives Slothrop to drink (568–9).

Frobenius (ATD)
German mathematician Georg Ferdinand Frobenius is referred to here ("Georg Ferdinand Frobenius").

Fry, Professor [Joshua] (M&D)
The reference is to surveyor Joshua Fry, who was associated with William Byrd (Bedini).

Fu (V)
The name Fu seems an obvious racial identifier for a character with a large stock of Chinese jokes. The name may have been drawn from the eponymous villain of Sax Rohmer's Fu Manchu novels. There are many Chinese words whose transliterations yield *fu*: "man" or "husband," but also "bend over," and "go down" (Jingrong 206–7). One other possibility is to separate the letters f-u and read the name as an abbreviation of "fuck you." Fu also seems relatively common as a surname. *See also* Charisma and Winsome.

Fuchs, [Lazarus] (ATD)
German mathematician Fuchs was "one of the creators of the modern theory of differential equations" (Bell 540 note).

Fulvio (ATD)
The miners in this section have common ethnic names. Fulvio is a common Italian name.

Fumimota, Takeshi (Vine)
Perhaps this character returns form GR where he appeared as part of the Takeshi and Ichizo show (733). Takeshi is a variant of the Japanese *takeki* ("brave, bold, fearless") (Yoshitaro 1893–4), but spelled Takashi it is a common name (at least four Takashis who were fallen WWII era Japanese soldiers have had their final letters published) (Nihon Senbotsu Gakusei Kinen-Kai 107, 138, 172, 205). Fumimota seems to derive from the Japanese *fumimochi* ("misconduct, loose conduct, fast life, profligacy") (Yoshitaro 307). The surname is especially appropriate for this scotch- and speed-swallowing woman chaser. Taken together, the names suggest a flawed hero — the best kind in Pynchon.

Funch, Caesar (Lot 49)
Hollander claims that Caesar evokes the idea of political assassination (in keeping with his reading of the novel as an allegory of the JFK assassination) ("Pynchon, JFK and the CIA" 88). In general, it is an appropriate name for a boss. Funch is a not-uncommon surname; perhaps Pynchon found the sound of the name amusing.

Fung, Hop (ATD)
Not a common Chinese personal name, but as Luc Sante says of Mock Duck, "the transliterations of these Chinese names sound like wild guesses" (227). Sante does not mention a Hop Fung or similar name in his passages on Chinatown during this period. The first name may be a comic reference to opium, referred to in slang as hop.

Gabika (ATD)
A familiar form of the common Eastern European name Gabi.

Gabrovo Slim (ATD)
The name is pure charactonym. He is "noodle-thin" and from Bulgaria (845). Gabrovo is a town in Bulgaria, so the name is essentially "the thin guy from Gabrovo."

Gadrulfi (V)
This is the name of a florist as well as the identity attributed to Evan Godolphin by the police. Grant offers the following suggestion: "The florist's name is both sufficiently like and sufficiently unlike Godolphin's to signal clearly the comic-opera nature of the confusions and misunderstandings that ensue" (99). It is certainly not a common name and has no obvious meaning.

Gage, General (M&D)
Edgar identifies the historical "commander-in-chief of the British forces in 1775" (61).

Galactica (M&D)
The name is a pun, but also an anachronistic reference. Although *galactic* can mean "relating to a galaxy" it can also mean "causing the secretion of milk" (AH4). This is an appropriate name for a milk maid, but may refer to the film *Battlestar Galactica* (1978), given Pynchon's penchant for popular culture references.

Galina (GR)
Common name.

Garrett, Pat (ATD)
Not properly a character, this wild west legend is perhaps best known for killing Billy the Kid (O'Neal 115).

Garrick, [David] (M&D)
The DNB identifies the historical actor/playwright (Thomson).

Gascoigne (V)
Described only briefly as a Negro helper to Vogt who sometimes brought friends to practice on the instruments in

the shop, Gascoigne is named from an obsolete word meaning *Gascon*, "a native of Gascony in southwest France," or "a braggart or boaster" (OED). Since the character barely exists in the text, there is no reason to assume the name is appropriate or not, although a native of Gascony would not be black. Perhaps the name is an oblique reference to French colonialism in Africa. On the other hand, Gascoigne is a fairly common surname and could refer to Charles Gascoigne, Elizabethan poet and soldier, or Thomas Gascoigne, Jacobite conspirator. While neither of these allusions cast any light on such a minor character, they epitomize the kind of arcana (as regards the common reader at any rate) that Pynchon so delights in weaving into his works.

Gaspereaux, Stilton (ATD)

Like many ridiculous sounding names in the novel, this one has little application to the character. Stilton refers to the popular English blue cheese, and the plausible French ending *-eaux* is added to *gasper*, "one who gasps." The picture is of a corpulent man breathlessly inhaling cheese.

Gates, Frenesi Margaret (Vine)

Only Frenesi seems deliberately determined: Margaret and Gates appear to carry no meaning for this character. According to the narrator, the name refers to a popular song: "her name celebrat[es] the record by Artie Shaw that was all over the jukeboxes and airwaves in the last days of the war, when Hub and Sasha were falling in love" (75). Hite reads the name as a homonym for *frenzy* and concludes that "Frenesi both incites and embodies frenzy" ("Feminist Theory" 150 note 12). Slade reads the character as a version of Proserpine ("Communication" 74), but there does not seem to be a connection with her name. Cowart connects Frenesi to Eve and reads the name as an anagram of "sin free" ("Continuity" 185). Rushdie also spots the anagram: "Frenesi turns out to be an anagram of 'free' and 'sin,' the two sides of her nature, light and dark" (36).

Gates, Hubbell (Vine)

Slade focusses on the nickname Hub and claims that "the wheel image is indicative to his integrity" ("Communication" 81). Given that Gates operates lights for his living, Hubbell could be a reference to Hubbell Lighting Incorporated, an old manufacturer of lights, light fixtures, and other lighting accessories. Gates is a common surname, but it could be a reference to the role he plays as mediator between Sasha and Frenesi. Ware refers to the term *gate* as 1940s slang for a swinger, or one who swings like a gate ("*Gravity's Rainbow*").

Gates, Sasha (Vine)

Sasha's maiden name was Traverse (*see* Traverse, Jess), so any meaning of Gates need not apply to her. Sasha is a Slavic name and may refer obliquely to the character's socialism.

Gatlin, Reverend Moss (ATD)

Given his fiery anti-capitalist rhetoric, the surname must derive from *Gatling gun*, a multi-barreled machine gun. This also ties into his justification for violence against the forces of oppression in the name of freedom. Moss is a common surname, but not frequently used as a given name. It is hard to see how the green plant, often seen growing on trees, could have any application to the character. A Pynchon blog called "The Chumps of Choice" claims that the character is based loosely on anarchist Johann Most ("Will Divide"), which is supported by the name Moss's sound similarity to Most.

Gaucho, the (V)

The name, from the title of the famous cowboys of South America, captures the character's larger-than-life image and his preference for action over planning and subtle maneuvering. Interestingly, Salazar tries to calm Ratón about the Gaucho's presence in Venice by suggesting that the name is a corruption of *gauche* and that he may be left-handed (176). We may also read the *gauche* reference in terms of the character's tactless bluster.

Gauss, [Carl Friedrich] (ATD)
The mathematician Gauss anticipated quaternions 30 years before Hamilton discovered them (Bell 260).

Gavaert, Edouard (ATD)
Both are common Dutch names.

Gaylord (SI)
Common as both a given- and surname, it derives "from the Old French, meaning 'brave'" (Kolatch 94). There is possibly some application to this very minor character who helps smuggle sodium out of the high school chemistry lab with his young girlfriend Kim Dufay (151). Hollander claims that the name "suggest[s] the Arthurian legends" ("Pynchon's Politics" 44).

Gebrail (V)
This is a rare instance of a clever, multifaceted name explained fully by Pynchon in the text:

"[T]he city is only the desert — gebel — in disguise." Gebel, Gebrail. Why should he not call himself by the desert's name? Why not?

The Lord's angel, Gebrail, dictated the Koran to Mohammed the Lord's prophet. What a joke if all that holy book were only twenty-three years of listening to the desert. A desert which has no voice. If the Koran were nothing, then Islam was nothing. Then Allah was a story, and his Paradise wishful thinking [83].

Not only do we have a specific allusion, but a complex pun on similar sounds. Gebrail is also commonly used among Arabs as both a given name and a surname.

Gelsomina (Vine)
A feminized version of *gelsomíno*, the Italian for "jasmine," Gelsomina is also the name of "the childlike heroine of Fellini's *La Strada*" (Diebold and Goodwin).

Gennady (ATD)
Common Russian name.

Gennaro (Lot 49)
This *Courier's Tragedy* character has a name that is a variant form of the Italian *Gennaio*, meaning "January." The CID also lists a jocular use of the word for a person who likes to sit by the fire, "a cold mortal." As the character is described as a "colorless administrator" (75), this reading of the name is mildly charactonymic.

Gennaro (ATD)
Gennaro is a common Italian name, but it echoes the character of the same name from *The Courier's Tragedy* in Lot 49.

Gentleman Bomber of Headingly, The (ATD)
Gentleman refers to this anarchist's method of employing the accoutrements of the civilized game of cricket to dispatch his victims. Headingley (note the slight spelling variation) is the name of a cricket ground near Leeds. He is also referred to as the G. B. of H., suggesting the acronym GBH, which raises two possible references: Grievous Bodily Harm, a British crime classification, and appropriate to a bomb thrower, and GBH as an alternate term for the drug GHB, or ecstasy, popular among those who frequent raves, and a possible reference given Pynchon's penchant for drug allusions.

Gerasimoff, Dr. (ATD)
This *Bol'shaia Igra* crew member is named for one of the co-creators of the video game Tetris: Vadim Gerasimof. *See* Padzhitnoff, Captain Igor.

Gerfaut the writer (V)
Grant defines the name as the French for "gerfalcon" (175), more commonly spelled "gyrfalcon." Given the character's

penchant for underage girls, the name is probably meant to evoke his predatory nature. Perhaps the name is an anagram of "after U G" — "after underage girls."

Gerhard (Vine)

An apparently ordinary name, but the fact that it is German may be significant. His defense of his wretched cooking to the sisters, "'I did what I had to,' the chef blubbered, iron and muffled, 'I was true to the food'" (110), sounds like a distorted excerpt from the transcripts of a Nuremberg trial.

Gerhardt (ATD)

This stoker bears a common German name.

Gerhardt (ATD)

The miners in this section have common ethnic names. Gerhardt is a common German name.

Gerloh, John (M&D)

Browne identifies the historical participant in the melee described in the text (155).

Germain (ATD)

A common name, but given the role of mathematics and mathematicians in the novel, it may allude to Sophie Germain, early nineteenth-century German mathematician.

Geronimo (V)

The character is obviously named for the famous native-American antagonist to white colonization.

Gerry (E)

Not a character, he is mentioned as Meatball Mulligan's namesake. The reference is to famous jazz saxophonist Gerry Mulligan.

Gershom (M&D)

This common Jewish name functions as an ethnic identifier of sorts for this slave who purports to belong to an obscure sect of Judaism (279).

Geschwindig, Hansel (GR)

The German adjective *geschwind* means "fast, agile, or nimble." These are useful qualities for a street urchin. Notice how the first name recalls the Hänsel and Gretel theme that recurs throughout the novel, most overtly in the Blicero-Katje-Gottfried section of episode fourteen in Part One (93–106).

Gessner, [Otto] (GR)

Fowler identifies the historical "wind-tunnel specialist" (198).

Ghislaine (GR)

Common French name.

Ghloix, Otto (ATD)

Otto is a common name; Ghloix is apparently meaningless, if not ridiculous. If one gives it a French pronunciation, it approximates "Gauloise," a popular French cigarette brand.

Giambolognese, Signor (ATD)

The surname sounds plausibly Italian, but seems to combine the name of the Renaissance sculptor Giambologna with that of the famous meat sauce, bolognese. The term *bolognese* can also refer to anything from the city of Bologna.

Giambolognese, Signora (ATD)

See Giambolognese, Signor.

Gibbs, [J.] Willard (ATD)

EB identifies this Yale physicist, chemist, and thermodynamics researcher ("Gibbs, J. Willard").

Gibson, [James] (M&D)

Headlee identifies the historical axman (7).

Gigg, Jack (ATD)

Although Gigg is a common name, the word itself is a variant of *gig* (whirling top) (OED), appropriate to this minor character: "Jack Gigg was unable to sit still. He kept running in and out of Kit's vicinity" (99).

Gilmore, Mr. (ATD)
Common name.

Ginger (ATD)
Frank and Stray's daughter has a common name, often used as "a pet form of Virginia" (Kolatch 332), but it also calls to mind the spicy ginger root. The ginger plant flowers, making one source of this name the same as several other female characters: plants or flowers. Given the time period of this segment of the novel, there could also be a reference to famous dancer and movie star Ginger Rogers, who was born in 1911.

Giou, [Pierre de] (V)
One of the Knights of Malta instrumental in defending Valetta against the Ottoman onslaught of 1565 ("L'Eglise de Giou de Mamou").

Girard, M. (UR)
French consul in Alexandria, Egypt at the time of the story (Baedeker 5).

Girgis the mountebank (V)
Pynchon may have taken this name from his Baedeker on Egypt. A search through an urban telephone book or on the Internet will demonstrate the popularity of this surname, particularly among Egyptians. There is a church named for Saint George (Mari Girgis) in Cairo. The name does not necessarily identify him as a Coptic Christian, but the use of the occupational epithet identifying him as a charlatan and his evening occupation of robbery would seem to place him among the preterite.

Girls, Slothrop's (GR)
All of the names of the women with whom Slothrop has some sexual relationship are rather normal. In no case does there appear to be any special onomastic meaning. We might conclude that these normal names are meant to reflect the normal healthy quality of Slothrop's sexuality (infant conditioning notwithstanding),

especially when foregrounded against the ubiquitous perversion and sadomasochism throughout the novel. Of course, Slothrop is said to have changed the girls' names (302).

Giunghierrace, Anthony, alias Tony Jaguar (Lot 49)
Grant points out that *giunghierrace* is not the Italian word for "jaguar," so there seems to be no connection between the names (56). Of course this is the beauty of the name. On one level, the reader will assume that the surname means "jaguar"; at the next level, the reader will look up the word (and find nothing); finally one can attempt to find some meaning. The name appears to derive from two Italian words, or parts of words: *giúngere* (to arrive) and the root behind *acceleráre* (to accelerate). The name could be read as "to arrive very quickly," as one might do in a Jaguar sports car, one of which appears (the XKE model) in the scene where this character name first occurs (59).

Giuseppina (ATD)
Common Italian name.

Gladys (GR)
See Girls, Slothrop's.

Gland, Dewey (V)
Harder claims that Dewey Gland echoes Dewey Dell from Faulkner's *As I Lay Dying*, but suggests the name has no further implications (71). Given that a gland secretes something, we can read a dewey gland as one that is constantly moist or dripping. Perhaps the name refers to the discharge associated with venereal disease or its prevalence among sailors. There is nothing to indicate that this meaning is particularly relevant to this specific minor character. The name has an undeniably comic sound. When Vladimir Nabokov came across the name, he was reportedly "thr[own] ... into fits of laughter" (Hollander "The Presence" 13).

Glee (ATD)
Like most of the other girls of the Sodality of Aetheronauts who pair up with the Chums of Chance, Glee has a name more useful in characterizing her relationship with Miles than herself: "jubilant delight" (AH4).

Glimpf, Professor (GR)
The "name derives from the German adjective meaning 'lenient' or 'mild'" (Weisenburger 160). The German noun *Glimpf* means "gentleness" or "mildness." As Glimpf is a mathematician, the name may also recall the English *glyph*, meaning "symbol."

Gloaming, Milton (GR)
Gloaming means "twilight" or "shade." The verb *gloam* means "to darken," thus *gloaming* would be read as "darkening." It is not certain whether the connotations apply to his disposition (we really do not see enough to tell) or to the atmosphere of the séance. Perhaps the combined name of Milton Gloaming alludes to the poet John Milton (who eventually went blind) and his "darkness visible" from *Paradise Lost* (Book One, line 63).

Gloobe, Lady Mnemosyne (GR)
As Weisenburger points out, Mnemosyne is the mother of the muses (298). The name combines high and low: Lady Mnemosyne representing her election and, perhaps, her self view; Gloobe, seemingly formed from two vulgar mucous words, *glob* and *goober*, perhaps reflecting her actual appearance.

Gloria (GR)
See Girls, Slothrop's.

Glozing, Ray (Lot 49)
Glozing means "blazing or shining brightly." Taken with Ray (as in a ray of light or sunshine) this produces a doubling. *Glozing* can also mean "the act of glossing or commenting on something, or flattery or cajolery" (OED). We have no textual evidence to support these readings about this old college boyfriend of Oedipa's. The name is probably a simple pun on " a blazing ray of light."

Gnahb, Frau (GR)
Weisenburger points out that Gnahb spelled backward is *bhang*, "the Hindu term for marijuana" (221). Besides being one of several names derived from drug terminology, the name is appropriate for someone heavily involved in the black market.

Gnahb, Otto ("the Silent Otto") (GR)
Friedman suggests a link to Otto Rank, whose psychoanalytic theory of neurosis relied exclusively on the "traumatic experience of birth" and seems to be reflected in Otto's difficult relationship with his mother (112). While there may be a link here, Ware seems to have found the intended allusion: Otto Kretschner was a German U-boat captain whose nighttime surface attacks "earned [him] the moniker 'Silent Otto'" ("*Gravity's Rainbow*"). See Gnahb, Frau for the surname.

Gobbitch, Bartley (GR)
Larsson claims that *gobbitch* comes from *gobbet*, meaning "a fragment or bit, especially of raw flesh" (V9.14–19). The OED adds an "extract from a text, a lump, a mouthful, or a lump of half-digested food." Given Gobbitch's lack of characterization, no one of these meanings seems to apply necessarily. Some connotations suggest grotesque bodily imagery — a fairly common source of names in Pynchon.

Godolphin, Captain Hugh (V)
The first name has no apparent significance. Berressem suggests that the name embodies a complex reference to *The Narrative of Arthur Gordon Pym of Nantucket*, by Edgar Allan Poe. He compares "Godolphin" to "good ol' Pym" (3–17). The surname is actually an old British name (Reaney and Wilson 195). It

is possible that Pynchon took the name from the metaphysical poet Sidney Godolphin.

Godolphin, Evan (V)
Evan is a common name. See Godolphin, Hugh for the surname.

Gollin, Geoffrey (GR)
Fowler identifies the historical "liquid oxygen researcher" (276).

Gómez, Che (ATD)
Presumably the reference is to Arnulfo R. Gómez, who was arrested and executed during a failed rebellion (Gonzales 216). Pynchon says Gómez "was intercepted by Juárez Maza's people, arrested, and shot to death" (988). But Arnulfo Gómez was executed in 1928 (Gonzales 216), later than the time of the novel. Gómez is a common enough name that it might refer to another figure.

Gómez, Eusebio (ATD)
Both are common Latino names. Given that this is an alias, the use of common names makes sense. This is also the name of a character in Vine, one of many instances of Pynchon's earlier works bleeding into this one.

Gomez, Eusebio ("Vato") (Vine)
Eusebio and Gomez are both popular Latino names. The term *vato* is Latino/Pachuco slang, perhaps best translated as "dude" or "brother." *See also* his inseparable partner Bonnifoy, Cleveland ("Blood").

Gongue, Jean-Claude (GR)
Weisenburger speculates that the name might derive from "American underworld slang 'gonga' or 'gongue' (anus)" (130). But since the character is a "notorious white slaver," we could read the French pronunciation of the name, which would nasally approximate the English word *gone*— what happens to women who are abducted by a white slaver. But he is a failure at this occupation and considers taking up drug dealing, an occupation for which the word *gone* also has associations (out of it from the effects of drugs), not to mention the slang *ganga*, "marijuana."

Gongylakis (GR)
This unlikely name is only mentioned briefly; it does not resemble a well-known surname.

González Salas, José (ATD)
General who "resigned as secretary of war to fight Pascual Orozco" and "committed suicide after his defeat at Rellano" (Camp 107).

Gonzi, Archbishop [Michael] (V)
A bishop from 1924, he was appointed archbishop of Malta in 1944 (Cassola 327).

Goodfellow (UR, V)
Any definition of *good fellow* from the OED could work for this character. The primary meaning, "convivial person" or "reveller," fits his description as a "chubby blond man" (V 68). The obsolete sense of "thief or robber" could apply to his role in deflowering Victoria Wren, however, the meaning of "docile or tractable person" could also apply, as Victoria Wren may have chosen him in advance as part of her plan. Grant cites Cowart who identifies *goodfellow* as "Covent Garden slang for a 'vigorous fornication'" (56).

Gophiz, duh (ATD)
Not a character, but a parody of Bowery pronunciation. The Gophers (pronounced "Goofers") were a gang in the Middle West Side of New York in the nineteenth century (Sante 217–18).

Gordon, General [Charles George] (V)
The DNB identifies the historical British army officer (Davenport-Hines, "Gordon, Charles George (1833–1885)").

Gorr, Dr. (GR)
The name derives from the German *Gör* ("brat or little kid"). He is introduced

Gottfried

with Dieckmann as Drs. Dieckmann and Gorr (fat man and the little kid). Clearly we are invited to translate Gorr in this context as "little boy." Thus, they are introduced as "Fat Man and Little Boy," the names of the two atomic bombs dropped on Japan by the United States.

Gottfried (GR)

Weisenburger recalls Pynchon's own gloss of the name (on 465) as "God's peace" and offers a detailed etymology (61). The applicability of the gloss "God's peace" is difficult, unless we read it as peace through utter submission. On the problematic nature of some of the names in the novel, Caeser writes "there is only a name — a joke — where we would expect to find a human presence, a 'god fried' where a Gottfried is" (6). The clever gloss does connect to Gottfried's fate in the rocket launched by Blicero.

Gottlob (ATD)

Gottlob is a common German name, but given that this character is a mathematics student, the name may allude to Gottlob Frege, German mathematician active during the time period covered in ATD (Bell 575).

Gottschalk, Dr. (V)

Common name.

Gould, Jay (ATD)

Hollander identifies the historical robber baron ("Pynchon's Politics" 46).

Governor, the (ATD)

It is unfortunate that such a sinister character is without a proper name. The Governor is "how he likes to be addressed" (210), believing, according to the text, in his sovereign control over the town: "Thinks of this as his little state within a state" (210). He is a satanic character who, upon luring souls into temptations, metes out punishment. Conflating the title "Governor" with the image of Satan suggests the dubious quality of worldly governments.

Grace (Vine)

Common name.

Grace, Angela (ATD)

The name encodes Darby's infatuation with her and her sweet disposition: "Angel O' Grace" or "angel of grace."

Grace, Dr. (ATD)

This figure in Hunter's dream is William Gilbert Grace, famous cricket player and medical practitioner. When WWI broke out, he wrote a letter "urging cricketers to 'come to the help of their country without delay in its hour of need'" (Hewat). This explains the cap and [cricket] whites he is wearing.

Gradenigo, Doge Pietro (ATD)

Late thirteenth-century doge (municipal leader) of Venice.

Graham, "Micro" (GR)

Like many names and allusions in the text, this one stems from drug culture. A microgram is the unit in which dosages of LSD are measured. He is presented in the guise of a drug-dealer, but actually lures "tourists" at the Mittelwerke to secret passages where they can see "what *really* went on in here" (296), perhaps a reference to LSD's ability to allow its users to see beyond the veil of reality.

Grant, Captain (M&D)

The context suggests that this is the actual name of the captain of the Seahorse, but Pynchon's source is uncertain.

Graziana (M&D)

Common name.

Grébaut (UR, V)

Grant identifies the historical "director general of the antiquities service in Egypt" (48).

Grenville, Mr. [George] (M&D)

The DNB identifies the historical British prime minister (Beckett and Thomas).

Gretchen (GR)
Common name.

Gretchen (Vine)
The cocktail waitresses on Kahuna Airlines are "make-believe" Polynesians. Gretchen is a Teutonic name.

Gretchen (ATD)
Common name.

Grey, [Sir Edward] (ATD)
Historical British statesman.

Grincheuse (M&D)
Grincheuse is French for "grumpy" or "grumpy person." Although we see and hear little enough of the sister to determine whether the name is an apt description, it may also be taken as a stereotypical quality of a nun. There may also be an allusion to Dr. Seuss's popular character, the Grinch, whose name is given a feminine ending for "the sister," which also rhymes with the author name, Seuss.

Grisha (ATD)
Grisha is the familiar name for the common Russian name Girgory. He is inseparable from his rhyming partner Misha.

Griswold, Uncle (ATD)
A common surname, but not given name. There is probably a reference to the famous Supreme Court case eliminating a ban on contraception, Griswold v. Connecticut. The case hinged on the right to privacy, an issue central to laws regarding homosexuality. Griswold introduced Cyprian to sodomy, so the allusion to the court case is relevant. Less likely is an allusion to the 1983 comic film *Vacation*, which tracks the antics of the Griswold family on their summer vacation.

Groast, Rollo (GR)
While Rollo is a fairly common name, Groast is not. Groast approximates both *gross* (coarse or disgusting) and *grossed* (earned before deductions are considered). The first reading is comic/derisive, while the second may imply membership in the elect.

Groast the senior, Dr. (GR)
See Groast, Dr. Rollo (his son).

Grodt (M&D)
This fairly common German surname would be appropriate for a neighbor of the German family Redzinger.

Groomsman the quartermaster (V)
Harder suggests that the name is ironic, given the character's constant infestation with crabs. A groomsman is simply "a man who attends the bridegroom at a wedding" (AH4), so it is unclear why such a figure should be endowed with virtue or sexual restraint.

Grosería, Mrs. (V)
The name derives for the Spanish word *grosería*, meaning "grossness," "vulgarity," or "stupidity." She is only mentioned as the owner of a television an unnamed character watches all day, so the reference applies either to the television itself or is a derisive joke not directed at the bearer of the name.

Grossmann (MMV)
A common name, meaning "big man" in German. Like many characters in the story, he has a name commonly held by Jews. Beyond this, there is probably no additional meaning intended, but *see also* Stephen.

Grossmith, George (ATD)
This is presumably a reference to the late-nineteenth/early-twentieth-century comic writer and actor in several Gilbert and Sullivan Operettas.

Grossout, St.-Just (GR)
Larsson identifies the source of St. Just as a French revolutionary figure who advocated the reign of terror and defines *grossout* as "60s slang for 'disgusting,' 'repulsive'" (V540.34). The nickname "Sam

Juiced" is a parody of the French pronunciation of St. Just.

Grundy, Mrs. (Vine)

Lest confusion arise, Mrs. Grundy is not a character, but "an imaginary personage ... who is proverbially referred to as a personification of the tyranny of social opinion in matters of conventional propriety"; she originated as a character in Thomas Morton's 1798 play, *Speed the Plough* (OED).

Grüne the chef (V)

Grüne is a fairly common German surname, but it does mean "green"; since this color is often associated with nausea, it could be a comic derisive reference to his cooking.

Grunt-Gobbinette, Sir Hannibal (GR)

Another hyphenated mock-British name, which may be modelled in part on those of Evelyn Waugh, such as Mrs. Beste-Chetwynde from *Decline and Fall*, for example, its two parts have negative connotations. The sound of a grunt is often associated with hogs (OED). The diminutive ending *ette* is added to *gobbin*, referring to a type of refuse produced in coal mining (OED) making *Gobbinette* mean, "little piece of trash." There is also a likely reference to Joseph-Arthur Gobineau, whose four-volume *Essay on the Inequality of Human Races* made him the father of modern European racism — he is responsible for the term Aryan as a description for Germanic peoples and the concept of the master race ("Gobineau, Joseph-Arthur, comte de"). Hannibal ironically refers to the famous Carthaginian general, but perhaps reflects also the character's elect status.

Gruntling (ATD)

The word means "little grunter" or a young pig, but can also refer to a grumbler or complainer (OED). The first meaning reflects Pynchon's interest in pigs, displayed throughout GR. The second meaning seems appropriate as this accountant was sent out with Professor Sleepcoat's party to prevent "budget overruns" (944). The implication is that previous overruns had resulted in a good deal of grumbling by the university.

Grunton, Myron (GR)

Weisenburger glosses the name of this fictional radio announcer as "sweet grunter," tracing the first name to the Greek *muron*, meaning sweet. An oddly appropriate name for a BBC broadcaster, if somewhat paradoxical. Yet we might view the given name as common and focus on the surname. George Orwell characterized the wartime BBC in the following terms: "the stupidity of its foreign propaganda and the unbearable voices of its announcers" (114). This casts new light on radio announcer as "grunter."

Gus (M&D)

This "character" is mentioned during the passage depicting the marriage of Catherine Wheat and Thomas Hynes, parts of which Pynchon quotes directly from *The Proceedings of the Council of Maryland*. No Gus is mentioned in the original, but the name seems too ordinary to have any significance.

Gutiérrez, Ricky (GR)

See Weisenburger for concise background on the Zoot-Suit Riots (129, 132). Whether Pynchon came across the name in some historical news piece is uncertain. If contrived, it merely indicates Chicano ethnicity and preterition.

Gwenhidwy, Thomas (GR)

The surname seems to derive from Thomas Love Peacock's *The Misfortunes of Elphin*, where the phrase "Beware of the oppression of Gwenhidwy" recurs frequently. In that novel, Gwenhidwy is associated with the sea and its power, but is clearly female. The figure derives from Welsh mythology. Pynchon may wish to recall two Welsh words with the name: *gwyn* (white) and *hud* (magic). Gwenhidwy is one of the more human characters in the novel, so we expect some positive connotation. Despite his association with Pointsman through his co-ownership of the book by Pavlov, he is presented as a positive force. "Thomas" recalls the doubtful apostle and suggests that he has deep doubts about behavioral psychology, especially as practiced by Pointsman.

Hadley, Dr. Edgar (ATD)
He was an actual doctor at the miners' hospital in Telluride (Backus 72).

Hadley, [John] (M&D)
Danson identifies the historical vice president of the Royal Society (66).

Haftung, G.M.B. (GR)
"[T]hat an entrepreneur should be called G.M.B. Haftung (cf. Gesellschaft mit beschränkter Haftung) ... comes as no surprise" (Hohmann 21). The common abbreviation GmbH is used for German companies like our L.L.C. (limited liability corporation).

Haig, [Sir Douglas] (GR)
Weisenburger identifies the WWI "field marshall of the British Expeditionary Force" (53).

Hailstone, Mr. (M&D)
The name is comically improbable, but has no clear reference (cold, hard, wet, etc.) for this character.

Halasz, Lajos (ATD)
This is a common Hungarian name. Lajos is the equivalent of Louis and Halasz is a word for a fisher. Nothing about the name seems especially appropriate to a "local sensitive" (720).

Halfcourt, Lieutenant-Colonel G. Auberon (ATD)
Although Auberon is a fairly common name, there may be an allusion to Auberon Waugh, author, journalist, and son of novelist Evelyn Waugh. *See also* Halfcourt, Yashmeen.

Halfcourt, Yashmeen (ATD)
Yashmeen is a variant of Yasmeen (a common name), meaning jasmine (Ahmed 342). Halfcourt calls to mind sports such as tennis or basketball employing a court divided in half by a line. The name suggests opposition (as between opposing teams or players across the line or net separating the halves of the court). It may apply to her father and his ambiguous role in the military/foreign service, or to her own uncertain role in TWIT. It may have been chosen simply for its comic uncommonness.

Halfpenny, Mr. [William] (M&D)
Despite the seemingly whimsical name, Halfpenny is a real architect and writer. He also used the name Michael Hoare. Flourishing in the mid eighteenth century, he was indeed the author of *Rural Architecture in the Chinese Taste* (1750), mentioned by Lord Pennycomequick (Harris).

Halidom (V)
The name of Evan Godolphin's wartime plastic surgeon means "holiness," "holy thing," "holy relic," or "anything regarded as sacred" (OED). Halidom rejects the accepted practice of using only tissue from the patient for grafts by using inert substances (ivory, silver, paraffin, and celluloid) (100). Grant suggests that the name refers to the fact that Halidom holds his own ideas as sacred (63). The name becomes somewhat ironic in that Schoenmacher enters medicine with noble goals, but falls prey to the same ideas of surgical arrogance that animated Halidom and led to the mutilation of Godolphin.

Haligast, Squire (M&D)
The surname derives from the Old English words *halig* ("holy") and *gæst* ("ghost"); by the middle ages, it was spelled haligast. The name seems appropriate for

an eccentric prophet who seldom speaks, except to offer dire predictions cloaked in opaque, religious phraseology.

Halley, Edmund (Dr.) (M&D)
The DNB identifies the historical astronomer (Cook).

Halliburton, Richard (GR)
Weisenburger identifies the historical writer/adventurer (139).

Halliger, Herr (GR)
Weisenburger cites the source as Dornberger on this historical innkeeper (196).

Hamilton, Maria Bayley (ATD)
Bell identifies this wife of mathematician William Hamilton, giving her name as Helen Maria Bayley (352).

Hamilton, [William Rowan] (ATD)
Bell identifies this historical mathematician and creator of quaternions (355).

Hanenhereyowagh (M&D)
See Abraham.

Hanky and Panky (V)
Like Flip and Flop, and to an extent like Molly and Dolly in M&D, Hanky and Panky function as purely comic names. They are completely interchangeable and function through both sound and sense, rhyme and sexual connotations. Besides comedy, the characters function solely as sexual objects.

Hanna (M&D)
See Abraham.

Hannings, John (M&D)
Headlee identifies the historical instrument bearer (5).

Hardy, G.H. (ATD)
This English mathematician did some work related to Riemann's zeta function (Bell 488), as depicted in ATD (498).

Harland, Bets (M&D)
Possibly the actual name of John Harland's wife, but Pynchon's source is uncertain, as she is not mentioned in Mason's journal.

Harland, John (M&D)
In his journal, Mason mentions this farmer whose home was situated on the same parallel as the "southernmost point of the city of Philadelphia" (38).

Harriman, Brother [Edwin H.] (ATD)
The railroad tycoon is meant here. Vibe's use of the term *brother* to refer to him heightens the sense of collusion between capitalists and reminds the reader that he is modelled on actual robber barons of the period, several of whom are mentioned throughout the text.

Harris (M&D)
This Philadelphia land speculator is not listed in Mason's journal or other key sources. The surname is relatively common. If the character is real, Pynchon's source is uncertain.

Harrison (M&D)
Cope mentions John and William Harrison, father and son clock-makers, one of whom is meant here ("Some Contacts" 234).

Harrold, Captain (M&D)
Common name.

Hart, Dorothy (GR)
Weisenburger identifies the historical Miss Rheingold contestant (185).

Harvitz, Esther (V)
As a whole, the name seems to function as a racial identifier; her Jewishness gets tied to her cosmetic surgery, pregnancy, and abortion. In this light the name Esther becomes ironic. The book of Esther portrays its eponymous heroine as a savior of the Jewish race. The name may have a personal source. Jules Siegel claims that Pynchon accompanied him hitchhiking to Michigan to visit Siegel's then girlfriend Esther Schreier (169).

Hashim, Tariq (ATD)
Both are common Muslim names. Tariq means "morning star" (Ahmed 211) and Hashim, a variant of Haashim, derives from *hashama* (he breaks) (Ahmed 62).

Hassan (ATD)
This Muslim name means "beautifier" (Ahmed 70). A common name, it may also refer to the intended effects on one's perception of the "good-size bale" of marijuana he collects on the journey (772).

Hatch (ATD)
Hatch and similar variants are common as surnames. There is an intriguing possible source however. A Bob Hatch was playing billiards with one of the Earp brothers in Tombstone, Arizona when a gunfight erupted, killing Morgan Earp — it was thought to be a revenge killing for the shooting of a gang including Frank McLawry at the O.K. Corral (O'Neal 97). Our Hatch is mentioned along with his unnamed partner who is whistling "'Daisy, Daisy,' which since Doc Holiday's celebrated rejoinder to Frank McLawry at the O.K. Corral had been sort of telegraphic code among gun-handlers for Boot Hill" (647–8).

Havabananda, Baba (Vine)
Diebold and Goodwin suggest "have a banana," adding "Groucho Marx meets Swami Satchidananda at R. Crumb's." The name is meant more for comic sound than any meaning related to this "saintly night manager" (52), of the Bodhi Dharma Pizza.

Hawasch (GR)
Like Spörri and Wenk, the codename Hawasch is from the name of a character in Fritz Lang's *Dr. Mabuse, der Spieler* (Fowler 198).

Hawke, [Edward] (M&D)
The DNB identifies this British naval officer (Mackay).

Hawkes, Sophrosyne (ATD)
Sophrosyne means "soundness of mind, moderation, prudence, self-control" (OED). The name is somewhat ironic in that she runs off with Ratty McHugh after he kisses her and walks out of his job: "damned if she didn't kiss me back, put down what she was doing, and come along with me. Just let it all go" (932). Hawkes is a common surname, but there may be an allusion to the celebrated American author of the 1950s and 1960s, John Hawkes.

Headless, Hob (M&D)
"A certain 'Hob Headless' haunted the road between Hurworth and Neasham" (Lewis Spence).

Heartsease (ATD)
At first blush, this name would not seem out of place in an allegorical work such as *Pilgrim's Progress*. This charactonymic name, however, is to be taken quite literally, physiologically even: she cures Randolph St. Cosmo of his chronic heartburn (1032).

Heidi (ATD)
Common name.

Heini of Berlin (GR)
The name of this "famous military couturier" derives from the German insult *Heini*, which means "idiot or halfwit." Since there is no other description of the character, the insult may be directed toward the fashion industry and its outspoken characters.

Heinrich (ATD)
Common German name.

Hendricks (M&D)
See Abraham.

Henry (GR)
Common name.

Henryk the Hare (GR)
The epithet *the Hare* derives, according to the text, from a Herero folk tale. See Weisenburger for some background

on the Herero story (302). The given name Henryk reveals the residue of colonial power (Seed, *Fictional Labyrinths* 182). As with similar names, the combination of native and colonial demonstrates an identity conflict felt by many of the Herero characters.

Hermann (GR)
Common name.

Hermann, [Dr. Rudolf] (GR)
Weisenburger identifies the historical researcher (210).

Hernández, Braulio (ATD)
Hernández was a Mexican revolutionary colonel spurned by Pancho Villa for supporting Orozco (Guzman 57).

Herschel, [Sir William] (M&D)
Danson identifies the historical astronomer (197).

Hershel (ATD)
Common name.

Hervé du T. (M&D)
Armand Allègre invents this pseudonym for "a certain well-known Gentleman-*Detective* of the time" (372). The reference is not entirely clear. It could be a strained allusion to Agatha Christie's character Hercule Poirot (certainly a gentleman detective), but this seems too much of a stretch. It would be one of many anachronistic references within the novel.

Hester (M&D)
This younger sister of Charles Mason's is mentioned in the will of Charles Mason, Sr. (Robinson, "A Note on Charles Mason's Ancestry" 135).

Hewat, Mr. [Jas.] (UR)
American consular agent in Alexandria, Egypt at the time of the story (Baedeker 5).

Hickman, Thomas (M&D)
Headlee identifies the historical instrument bearer (11).

Higgs, the Boatswain (M&D)
Millard points out the pun on Higgs-Boson, a concept associated with string theory. The connection is furthered by Higgs's obsession with "knot-work" (54). The pun also demonstrates that Pynchon's interest in contemporary developments in physics continues.

Hilarius, Dr. (Lot 49)
Grant views the name as a simple joke (19). Petillon and Hollander view the character as a thinly veiled Timothy Leary, but surely Pynchon did not associate Leary with Nazism. Seed more reasonably suggests that Hilarius "is a bizarre combination of Timothy Leary and Josef Mengele" (*Fictional Labyrinths* 142). But this is not reflected in the name itself, unless we read hilarity as the prankster spirit advocated by Leary. I suggest that Pynchon came across the name in Helen Waddell's *The Wandering Scholars* (15, 19, 125 [on the saint] and 187 [on the goliard]), which we know from the introduction to SL was a central text for him (7–8). If Pynchon researched the name, he would have come across several options. Hollander suggests [St.] Hilarius of Poitiers [more commonly known as Hilary] and suggests that his connection to the Arian controversy mirrors Dr. Hilarius's involvement in Nazism's ideological basis in a different Aryan concern ("Pynchon, JFK and the CIA" 71). Another intriguing possibility is Hilarius of Sexten (1839–1900), Tyrolean moral theologian thought to be especially gifted at "applying theoretical principles to actual facts"— a possible parallel to psychoanalysis — and who, despite limited approval, gained an immense following in Germany and Austria — another possible connection to Nazism ("Hilarius of Sexten" 348).

Hilbert, [David] (ATD)
One of the greatest German mathematicians, Hilbert spent most of his career at the University of Göttingen ("Hilbert, David").

Hilbert-Spaess, Sammy (GR)
Weisenburger points out the appropriateness of this name for a double agent, as *Hilbert space* is a mathematical term referring to an abstract space in which a point has "a theoretically infinite number of coordinates" (117). This is one of many names Pynchon draws from the terminology of mathematics or science.

Hilde (GR)
Common German name.

Hinckart, Jan (Lot 49)
Grant cites Delepinne on the historical postmaster, spelling the name "Jean Hinchaert" (127).

Hiroshima (V)
It seems ironic that a member of the American Navy would share a name with the first city devastated by atomic attack, carried out by the American military. On the other hand, his only appearance in the novel involves his educating Pig Bodine about "the biological effects of r-f energy" (377), namely that the radiation produced by a radar antenna can render anyone exposed to it temporarily sterile. This could be an oblique reference to the effects of radiation during the aftermath of the bombing of Hiroshima. After all, Bodine is saved from what proves to be the real affect of this energy when the hamburger Profane has stashed near the antenna proves to be cooked by the device (an early microwave, it would seem) (377–78).

Hirsch, Richard (GR)
Leni's old love's surname means "stag" in German. The name suggests virility, especially if we read the two names together as "Dick Stag." Of course a stag is also prey, especially of humans. It is not clear if he dies in the war, but he disappears quickly from the narrative.

Ho (M&D)
According to Woodward, Hsi and Ho are the protagonists of a historical Chinese legend (Ware "Further").

Hobab (M&D)
He is not mentioned in the obvious sources, so the name may be contrived. Hobab is a biblical name meaning "beloved" (Hamilton 57), but this has no apparent significance for this very minor character. Biblical names were quite common among colonial settlers.

Hobbs, Blowden (Vine)
Blowden is a relatively common name with no obvious reference. *See* Hobbs, Millard for the surname.

Hobbs, Millard (Vine)
The surname probably comes from one meaning of *hob*, "to cut the high tufts of grass in a pasture" (OED). Surely this is appropriate for the owner of a lawn-care service. The first name may come from *milord*, "a French designation for an English lord" (OED). This could refer to his impersonation of the Marquis de Sade in his commercials, where he is master of the lawn.

Hod, Pappy (Robert) (V, GR)
Harder points out that Pappy is a "common nickname of all older men who live and work among younger persons" (70). He speculates on the meaning of *hod* as "a device used to carry something," in terms of the character's carrying Paola away from Malta in V. In dialect, *hod* can also be "a vessel for holding liquid" and usage examples refer to liquor (Wright 191). This could be a reference to the character's drinking. The combination of Pappy and the sense of *hod* would yield "old drunk." Only Paola refers to him by the name Robert. In his online guide to GR, Larsson provides an ingenious gloss: Vincent "Pappy" Serio invented a sailboat called the HOD ("Hampton One-Design") in 1934 (v185.22). If the allusion is intentional, it connects the character Pappy Hod to his life as a career sailor. Weisenburger points out that "in Kabbalistic symbolism, *Hod* (majesty or glory) are the thighs on the anthropomorphized tree of life" (298).

Holliday, Doc [John Henry] (ATD)
This historical saloon-keeping dentist and gambler died in Glenwood Springs, Colorado, just prior to the time of the novel (O'Neal 144).

Holt (ATD)
A common name, but it may be a nod to Henry Holt, the publisher of M&D.

Hood, Zachariah (M&D)
Edgar identifies the historical Maryland "distributor of stamps" (209–14).

Hope (ATD)
This sister of Deuce Kindred is married, but no married name is given. The name seems ironic in the context of her brief speech and only appearance: "We went on with our days, children of a captivity some escaped as Deuce did, while others of us never will. For there have to be our kind, too" (473). Her kind sound more like the hopeless kindred than the Hope Kindred.

Höpmann (GR)
This zany toilet ship-fitter has a name with no obvious meaning. The first part may derive from words such as *hopsen* or *hoppeln*, each meaning "to hop." Whether *hop* or *hopping man* has any special significance is unclear, although this etymology seems vaguely appropriate for such a practical joker.

Hopper (GR)
Common name.

Hörlein, [Dr. Heinrich] (GR)
Weisenburger identifies the historical researcher (272).

Houdini, Harry (ATD)
Not a character but a reference to the famous illusionist/escape artist.

Howie (Vine)
Common name.

Hrisoula (GR)
This wife of King Yrjö has a not uncommon Finnish name. Given that the "character" is only mentioned once, it cannot have any particular meaning for her.

Hsi (M&D)
According to Woodward, Hsi and Ho are the protagonists of a historical Chinese legend (Ware "Further").

Hsiang-Chiao (ATD)
This is one of several Chinese terms for the banana (Reynolds 166). While it has no relevance to the character, it recalls, like Chiquita, that sweet fruit that plays such an excessive, Rabalaisian role in the opening of GR.

Huang, Lord (M&D)
This figure is not mentioned in Woodward's historical background on the story of Hsi and Ho (Ware "Further"). If made up, it is appropriate: one English transliteration from the Chinese yielding *huang* means emperor (Jingrong 294).

Huerta, General Victoriano (ATD)
Huerta overthrew Emilio Madero in 1913 (Gonzales 86).

Humfried (ATD)
Common German name.

Hunter, Mary (M&D)
Dixon's mother. Information on her is not readily available in standard reference works. Robinson gives her dates as (1694–1773) ("Jeremiah Dixon" 272).

Hunter, Thomas (M&D)
The name is possibly real, as Dixon's mother's maiden name was Hunter, but biographical information on Dixon is quite scarce, so Pynchon's source is uncertain.

Hunter-Blair, Major-General (V)
Grant identifies the historical lieutenant-governor of Malta (192).

Hupla, Apprentice (GR)
Read as *Hoopla*, the etymology is "from the French *houp-là* (confusing or botched speech)" (Weisenburger 158).

Hutchinson, Governor [Charles] (M&D)
Gosse identifies the historical governor of St. Helena between 1746 and 1764 (186).

Hutton, Mr. [Charles] (M&D)
The DNB identifies this mathematician (Guicciardini).

Hyacinth (LL)
Not a character, but a carefully named pet rat. Hollander suggests that the name is an allusion to the Hyacinth girl from T.S. Eliot's *The Waste Land*, and points out other echoes of the poem throughout the story ("Pynchon's Politics" 30).

Hynes, Tom (M&D)
Browne identifies the historical father of Catherine Wheat's illegitimate child (131).

Hynes, Tom [Jr.] (M&D)
Headlee identifies the historical cook (14).

Hynes, Will (M&D)
Browne identifies the historical father of Tom Hynes (132).

Ibargüengoitia (GR)
This seems to be a not uncommon Hispanic surname and may allude to the well-known Mexican writer Jorge Ibargüengoitia.

Ibargüengoitia, Adolfo "El Reparador" (ATD)
The surname alludes to Mexican novelist Jorge Ibargüengoitia. The nickname is explained in the text, translated as The Repairman. He "solves problems created by revolution" (988). He comes off as a somewhat sinister figure, suggesting that the common name Adolfo may allude to Adolf Hitler. The name also recalls the Ibargüengoitia who appears in GR.

Ibble, Roy (Vine)
The surname is comic sounding, but does not seem to mean anything. Of course it is an anagram of "Bible," a copy of which this character keeps on his desk as a prop to please "born-agains in the Agency" (353).

Ice, Immanuel, the Ferryman (M&D)
The name may be an oblique reference to the play *The Iceman Cometh*, by way of the song "Oh Come, Oh Come, Immanuel." In this way, the character is connected to death, but this new-world Charon does not ferry Mason and Dixon to Hades; instead he tells the chilling (surname Ice) tale of the fate his family met during an Indian massacre.

Ichizo (GR)
Ichizo appears to be a common Japanese name, but also refers to an actual kamikaze pilot, Ichizo Hayashi, whose final letter was published after he died in action (Nihon Senbotsu Gakusei Kinen-Kai 215).

Ictibus, The Phenomenal Dr. (ATD)
This inventor of the phenomenal Safe-Deflector Hat has a charactonymic name describing his invention. The Latin *ictibus* is the ablative plural of the noun *ictus* (strike, blow, hit). So, *ictibus* means "from blows." His hat prevents its wearer from being injured by blows from falling safes.

Ignatius (V)
See also Augustine, Bartholomew, Paul, Teresa, and Veronica. The six named rats in Father Fairing's parish all have appropriate names. It is unlikely that Fairing, a Jesuit, would be referring to Ignatius of Antioch or Laconi: he almost certainly chooses the name to honor Ignatius of Loyola, founder of the Jesuits. Interestingly, after gathering his disciples in Paris, Ignatius of Loyola went to Venice (a central city in the novel) (Farmer 242).

Ilse the hygienist (Vine)
Diebold and Goodwin identify the character as a reference to a 1960s porn

star whose films included such classics as *Ilse, She-Wolf of the SS*. The actual spelling of the film character's name is Ilsa, and *sexploitation* would better describe these films, which were made in the 1970s, but the suggestion is reasonable in the absence of other possibilities.

Imago Portales, Graciela (GR)

Raudaskoski suggests that Imago Portales means "image window," but the Spanish *portal* would be translated more accurately as "gate." We could bend "image gates" into "doors of perception," an allusion to the title of Aldous Huxley's book recounting his experiments with mescaline. Graciela is a common Spanish given name.

Imi (ATD)

Common Slavic name.

Indian, the (GR)

The "character" is mentioned as an old espionage acquaintance of Katje's; the name is probably a meaningless alias. Like the Drummer, the Indian's name has been replaced by an epithet.

Inés Salazar, José (ATD)

Former Madero supporter who ended up denouncing him (Gonzales 88).

Information, Mr. (GR)

Not a character as such, Mr. Information has a name describing his function: he reveals hidden plots and global cabals.

Inga (Vine)

The cocktail waitresses on Kahuna Airlines are "make-believe" Polynesians. Inga is a Scandanavian name.

Ingvarr (M&D)

Clerc points out that Ingvarr suggests Igor, Dr. Frankenstein's assistant in film (*Mason* 77). This also creates a nice parallel between two mad inventors, Franklin and Frankenstein.

Inverarity, Pierce (Lot 49)

Behind Oedipa Maas, this is probably the second most written about name in Lot 49. Kharpertian provides a good gloss, although some of his points have been made by others: "The name Pierce Inverarity ... is paradoxical in its metaphorical implications. Aside from 'inverse rarity'—a misprinted and therefore valuable stamp—and Moriarty, Sherlock Holmes's antagonist, the name puns on 'inveracity' and 'pierce/peers in variety'" (98). "Inverse rarity" is Kharpertian's invention—stamps deemed valuable because they are misprinted (upside down) are properly referred to as "invert errors." Hayles reads *pierce* as both sexual violence and religious illumination (146), but also points out that J.R. Pierce was the author of a popular 1961 book on information theory (164 note 19). Johnston suggests that the name echoes that of C.S. Pierce, American founder of semiotics (56). Tanner offers that the "name itself can suggest either un-truth or in-the-truth" (57). Hollander constructs the (perhaps too) clever combination of *pierce*, meaning "prick" as a verb, *inver* meaning "mouth" in Gaelic, and *rarity*, meaning "unusual or exceptional": "excellent-mouthed, or smart-mouthed prick" ("Pynchon, JFK and the CIA" 69). He also suggests that Pierce could recall Henry Clay Pierce, the unscrupulous oil baron ("Pynchon, JFK and the CIA" 70). Grant examines some of these readings, emphasizing its suggestiveness and fundamentally equivocal nature (citing both Tanner and Kermode on this point) (7–8). He rejects Schaub's suggestion that Inverarity was the birthplace of James Clerk Maxwell (actually born in Edinburgh), but cites his reading of Pierce as a variant of Peter or *petrus*, "rock," as in the rock on which "the profane church of America was built" (7). Brazeau offers an intriguing possibility: the name possibly comes from Joyce's *Portrait of the Artist as a Young Man*, where "Stephen Dedalus's copy of Horace's verse was previously owned by 'John Duncan Inverarity and by his brother, William Malcolm Inverarity'" (186). Brazeau examines some further parallels between the two novels that strengthen this possible source. I suspect the name was drawn from Joyce, but as this is one of several overdetermined names, many of the other readings offered here seem perfectly reasonable.

Invert, Jenny (ATD)
Jenny is a common name. The pertinent meaning of *invert* here is the psychological one, describing "one who takes on the gender role of the opposite sex" (AH4). She is initially described as "three feet taller than" Reginald McHugh, and "a wizard trapshooter" (866). Later, McHugh claims of her "she's more militant than I've ever been, and an even better shot now than she was as a girl" (933).

Ion (GR)
This name of someone Pirate betrayed may be linked to the ionic bond praised by Jamf because electrons are captured rather than shared (577). It could also refer to the Greek *ion*, meaning something that goes (AH4). Either going away or being captured could be linked to betrayal.

Ipsow, Ray (ATD)
The name is clearly a pun on the Latin, *re ipso*, "the thing in itself" or "the real thing." This seems vaguely appropriate for a character who tells off Scarsdale Vibe and proudly acknowledges being a socialist (32).

Irene (GR)
See Girls, Slothrop's.

Irma (Vine)
Common name.

Irving (V)
This is the name Schoenmacher calls his nurse-mistress "by virtue of some associative freak" (45). Grant claims that this association is "far from clear" (23). We are told that Schoenmacher had tattooed thousands of freckles on Irving. The "associative freak" is the song "Pig Tails and Freckles" by Irving Berlin. Although the "present" chapters of V take place in the mid-1950s, the 1963 publication date adds credence to this reference: "Pig Tails and Freckles" appeared on the popular 1962 album *Mr. President* (Irving Berlin).

Isaiah Two Four (Vine)
The name is thoroughly explained in the text. After Zoyd jokes that he named himself after a robot (a reference to R2D2 of *Star Wars* fame), Prairie explains: "After Isaiah Two Four, a verse in the Bible ... which *your* friends his hippie-freak parents laid on him in 1967, about converting from war to peace, beating spears into pruning hooks, other idiot peacenik stuff" (16). Besides highlighting the kinds of names given by the hippie parent generation of the novel, Isaiah Two Four captures the generation gap and rebellion against parents: named for peace, the character is obsessed with violence.

Isvolsky, [Alexander Petrovich] (ATD)
Historical Russian statesman.

Itague (V)
The name is an old French nautical term meaning "tie" (as in a knot). The reference is probably to sexual sadism.

Italo (GR)
Common name.

Ivy (GR)
Common name.

Jabez (M&D)
This biblical name, meaning one "who causes sorrow" (Hamilton 63), is appropriate for a character who acts as guide to Mason and Dixon at the site of a genocidal massacre.

Jade (Vine)
Common name.

James, Major (M&D)
Lossing identifies the historical American revolutionary officer.

James, Yellow the cook (GR)
He is seen briefly operating a sandwich wagon and the name Yellow does not have any obvious connection to the character. Perhaps like the name of the chef Grüne (green), the name Yellow is meant to evoke nausea, not a sensation one wants to associate with any cook.

James the Second (M&D)
The DNB identifies the British monarch (Speck).

Jameson, Dr. [Leander Starr] (UR)
The reference to "Dr. Jameson and the Boers" (109) makes it clear that Leander Starr Jameson is the man in question. He tried to start a rebellion against the Boers, but was outnumbered and had to surrender (Lowry).

Jamf, Laszlo (GR)
"Jamf is an acronym for an American street term, 'Jive-Ass Mother Fucker,' denoting 'the system'" (Slade, "Religion" 174). One could keep the reference to the system and also read the acronym as *Ja, Mein Führer*. In any event, Jamf is a powerful representative of Them, the elect, the system, multinational corporations, the military-industrial complex, or any other not-so-paranoid term for contemporary forces of evil. Although Laszlo is common as both a given name and a surname, there may be a reference to the character Victor Laszlo in *Casablanca*, the freedom fighter played by Paul Henreid. Applied to our Laszlo, such a reference would be highly ironic.

Jarretière (V)
(*See also* l'Heuremaudit, Mélanie) Mélanie's stage name means "garter" — the fetish object par excellence.

Jarri (ATD)
One of several instances of Pynchon's earlier work penetrating this novel, Jarri, or La Jarretière, featured in V, as the stage name of Melanie l'Heuremaudit, who is involved in a relationship with an unnamed manifestation of V. in Paris in 1913, placing her in the time and place of this section of ATD. *See* Jarretière and l'Heuremaudit, Melanie.

Jason (M&D)
McHale glosses this as a "fashionable nineties name" (48). Jason has been a fairly popular "Christian name since the seventeenth century, especially in USA" (Withycombe 165); according to the Social Security Administration, it was among the top ten male baby names from 1971 to 1983 ("Popular Baby Names").

Jeaach (GR)
Larsson cleverly suggests that the name is a joke based on "Pseudo-German phonetic rendering of an expression of disgust" (v703.05), i.e., "yuck."

Jeff (MMV)
Common name.

Jefferson, Thomas (M&D)
Although only referred to as "Tom" in the novel, this reference to the third president of the United States is obvious, from his description as a "tall red-headed youth" to his desire to use Dixon's toast "To the pursuit of Happiness" (395).

Jello, James (GR)
The name combines alliteration with a proprietary name reference (to the sugary gelatin product). It is meant as humor — the character *is* "that year's king of Bohemian clowns" (698).

Jellows, the Fabulous (M&D)
The surname Jellow does not seem to mean anything as a word or to be a common name. It is probably an anachronistic reference to the Jello brand of flavored gelatin products.

Jelly-Belly (M&D)
Standard references do not address this possible nickname for the young Jeremiah Dixon. It is the brand name of miniature jelly beans available in a staggeringly wide

variety of flavors. Created in 1976, they became rather popular when former president Ronald Reagan professed a weakness for their sticky charms.

Jemmy (M&D)
See Abraham.

Jenkins, Robert (M&D)
The DNB identifies the British merchant naval officer formerly attached to the eponymous ear mentioned in the text (Laughton).

Jennifer (GR)
See Girls, Slothrop's.

Jenny (GR)
Probably the Jennifer mentioned on page 23.

Jephthah (M&D)
An ordinary name, Jephthah may be used to show the prevalence of traditional biblical names in the eighteenth century. According to Withycombe, the name was used by English Puritans (166).

Jephthah (Jeff) (ATD)
The biblical name Jephthah means "inconsiderate" (Hamilton 68), appropriate for a preacher who takes the converts of another preacher after "hollering in some agitation" (466).

Jeremiah, Uncle (M&D)
This is Mary Hunter's Uncle, which would make him Jeremiah Dixon's great-uncle. He is possibly real, but biographical information on Dixon's mother's side of the family is quite scarce.

Jeremy (Beaver) (GR)
Larsson claims that the "nickname [Beaver] derives from the 1940s slang for the beard he sports," but also points to the slang use of the word to refer to a woman's vagina (V3627.28). The OED cites both of these slang uses of the word, but offers examples of the word describing a beard used from 1910 through the late 1950s. There may also be an allusion to Lord Beaverbrook, close friend to Winston Churchill: at one point, Jeremy Beaver is seen smoking a pipe whose bowl is a detailed likeness of Churchill's head (707). There is also a probable reference to the character John Beaver from Evelyn Waugh's *A Handful of Dust*; this Beaver, too, is involved in a love triangle, although he is the poor character having an affair with Lady Brenda Last, who is married to Tony Last. GR's triangle of Roger Mexico, Jessica Swanlake, and Jeremy Beaver reverses this situation.

Jewel (GR)
One of two wealthy British women who appear in one short scene, Jewel has a name that may metonymically suggest wealth. Rowena comments in the passage on the Britishness of the name.

Jinx (Vine)
A jinx is any person or thing that causes bad luck. The name seems appropriate given her failed marriage to Weed Atman, although it applies more to the situation than the person.

Joaquín (ATD)
This parrot is given a common name, although common for humans rather than birds.

Jöche, Schutzmann (GR)
A *Schutzmann* is a constable or policeman. Blumberg states that *Joche* (without the umlaut) means "yoke" or "harness" and identifies his role as "brutally keeping the revolutionary activities of German communists in check" (72). Besides this charactonymic reading, Larsson suggests a comic pun by approximating, through pronunciation of the surname, an "expression of disgust ('yuck-ey')" (V220.31).

Johanna (GR)
Common name.

John (M&D)
See Abraham.

Johnson, Barney (M&D)
Browne identifies the historical constable and participant in the melee described in the text (first name given as Barnett) (132).

Johnson, [John] (M&D)
John Johnson was the name of Lord Ferrer's steward (Davenport-Hines, "Shirley, Laurence, fourth Earl Ferrers [1720–1760]").

Johnson, Samuel (M&D)
The DNB identifies the eighteenth-century author (Rogers).

Johnson, Sir William (M&D)
Mason mentions Johnson in his journal as a mediator between the Indians and the line commissioners (172).

Joint, Mr. Dennis (GR)
Seed suggests that Pynchon often uses slang terms, particularly those connected to drug culture, in naming people and places (*Fictional Labyrinths* 7–8). This name seems to be a simple joke referring to a joint (marijuana cigarette).

Jollifox (GR)
He is presented as representing a particular school of thought concerning "mantic archetypes"—a perversion of Jung? The word *mantic* means related to divination or prophecy (AH4). The name suggests a cheery clever rouge, perhaps referring in general to academics or those who traffic in divination.

Joneš, Steve (V)
This policeman's name is an extremely common one, although the diacritical mark over the *s* in Joneš is an enigma.

Jones, Mother (ATD)
Born Mary Harris in Ireland, married George Jones in Memphis, Mother Jones was a "labor agitator" and "miner's angel" (Featherling 1–8).

Juárez Maza, Benito (ATD)
Governor of Oaxaca 1911–12 (Camp 118).

Judy (GR)
See Girls, Slothrop's.

Julius (ATD)
The context—"He worked his eyebrows energetically and pretended to brandish a horsewhip. 'Back! Back, I say!' ... [he] pretended to look around wildly, eyes rolling a mile a minute" (467)—makes clear that this character is Julius Henry Marx, better known by his stage name Groucho Marx.

Jürgen (M&D)
Common name.

Justin (Vine)
According to the Social Security Administration, Justin was among the top ten names for male babies from 1987 to 1990 ("Popular Baby Names"), making the name very common given Vine's 1990 publication date.

Justus (GR)
Justus is seen lighting a taper at the barbecue pit where preterite Roger Mexico and Pig Bodine narrowly escape being transformed into a "surprise roast" at an elect feast. The name Justus is sounded "justice" and is heavily ironic. Or it may reflect the elect worldview: "just us, (not them)."

Jusuf the manager (ATD)
Jusuf is a variant of Yusuf, a Muslim name derived from the name of the biblical prophet Joseph. If any charactonymic meaning is intended, the implied reference to a prophet would be appropriate for a character who warns Kit that he may be in danger, essentially offering a prediction, one of the functions of a prophet. It is, however, a common name.

Kammler, Major-General (GR)
Weisenburger identifies the historical S.S. general (200).

Karel (GR)
Common name.

Karl (ATD)
This common name is the German spelling of Carl.

Katharine (GR)
See Girls, Slothrop's.

Katie (ATD)
See McDivott, Katie.

Katz, Manfred (V)
The combination of Byronic hero (Manfred) with a very common Jewish surname could be read ironically, or it could be a celebration of the preterite (the heroism of the everyday). We do not know enough about this very minor character to determine a clear reading.

Keith (GR)
Common name.

Kellner (ATD)
Although the context should make this clear, *Kellner* is not a name; it is German for "waiter."

Kennedy, Captain (M&D)
Edgar identifies this British regimental commander (173).

Kennedy, Jack (GR)
Future American president, John F. Kennedy.

Kenosha Kid, the (GR)
Weisenburger aptly describes the Kenosha Kid as "[o]ne of the outstanding enigmas in GR" (43). He goes on to point out that the name could refer to Slothrop, the Colonel from Kenosha, or Old Kenosho the radarman (43). The name does not seem to refer to a character, as such, and seems to have been chosen largely for its alliteration.

Kenosho (GR)
Fowler suggests that the name recalls the Colonel from Kenosha, Wisconsin and the Kenosha Kid (246). The name itself does not seem to mean anything.

Kensington Sid (ATD)
Sidney Reilly's nickname, Kensington, is taken from a region in London. It seems meant to highlight the Englishness of this bogus Englishman. See chapter four of Richard Spence's *Trust No One*, titled "The Counterfeit Englishman."

Keuler, Frau (ATD)
This anti-semite has a name derived from the German noun *Keule* (club). The name would be "clubber" or "one who strikes someone with a club," a metaphorical depiction of the effect of Keuler's vicious remarks on Yashmeen.

Khalil (ATD)
This Muslim name means "friend" (Ahmed 98) and is appropriate for a minor character mentioned as a contact who will help Gabrovo Slim in his escape from Salonica.

Khama, King of the Bechunas (GR)
Weisenburger identifies the historical chieftain (163).

Khäutsch, Max (ATD)
This assassin and security agent has a common first name. Khäutsch suggests nothing German or otherwise, but would be pronounced the same as *Keuch* from the verb *Keuchen*, German for "to grasp." It is a comic name but has no clear relevance to the character.

Khevenhüller-Metsch, Count (UR, V)
As Pynchon points out in the introduction to SL, the name of this actual diplomat was lifted from the 1899 Baedeker guide to Egypt (17).

Khlaetsch, Minnie (GR)
Blumberg glosses *Khlaetsch* or *Klatsch* as German for "smack" or "gossip" and *Minne* as Middle High German for "love," reading the whole name as one who "loves both being hit and gossiping" (72). The noun *Klatsche* refers to gossip; the

verb *klatschen* means to smack or clap, but also to gossip or chat. The primary reading of the name is love of gossip, but combining the German surname with the English given name suggests "small talk."

Kholsky (V)

Described as a "huge and homicidal tailor," Kholsky has a name that derives from the Russian *khol*, meaning "linen or canvas." The name and epithet are both related to cloth and as such, achieve a form of doubling.

Kieselguhr Kid, the (ATD)

The name is explained in the passage: "'Kielseguhr' being a kind of fine clay, used to soak up nitroglycerine and stabilize it into dynamite" (171). The nickname for this dynamiting outlaw (Webb Traverse and later applied to Frank Traverse in Mexico) joins one component of dynamite to a common outlaw nickname (Billy the Kid et al.). The *k* alliteration also echoes that enigmatic character in GR, the Kenosha Kid. Perhaps there is also a pop culture reference to Jimmie "J.J." Walker, the dynamite kid, actor popular in the 1970s.

Killogh (M&D)

Three Killoghs acted as packhorse drivers on the survey: John, Ezekiel (both mentioned by Pynchon by name later), and Francis (Headlee 14). It is uncertain which one is referred to here.

Killogh, Ezekiel (M&D)

Headlee identifies the historical packhorse driver (7).

Killogh, John (M&D)

Headlee identifies the historical packhorse driver (7).

Kimura, Mr. Shunkichi (ATD)

Completed his Ph.D. in mathematics at Yale University in 1896 ("Shunkichi Kimura").

Kindred, Deuce (ATD)

Kindred normally describes a family or clan but can also mean "having a similar or related origin, nature, or character" (AH4). *Deuce* primarily means "two" (often referring to a playing card with two of any suit). Taken together, the name is a pun: "two of a kind." It could refer to his relationship with Sloat Fresno or even Lake Traverse, or simply be a pun, two of a kind (a pair) being a hand in poker. But *deuce* is also a substituted name for the devil also meaning something very bad (AH4); these related associations are clearly appropriate to this character. In this sense the full name could be read "coming from the devil" or "of the devil's family."

Kindred, Mother (ATD)

She is only mentioned in the context of a joke (473). Perhaps another instance of doubling, in that both the given- and the surname are related to *family*. For the surname, *see* Kindred, Deuce.

Kit, Mr. (M&D)

Lest confusion arise, this is a reference to Christopher Smart (known as Kit), who is mentioned in this same passage.

Kitchener, Sirdar (UR, V)

Grant identifies the historical "British commander-in-chief of the Egyptian army" (44).

Klein, [Felix] (ATD)

The historical reality of this German mathematician is not surprising. What is more interesting is that Pynchon's zany depictions of mathematicians using knockout drops to sleep and his statement that "Klein himself was a great advocate of" chloral hydrate for this purpose (621) is based in reality: "One of his American students complained that he could not sleep for thinking of his mathematics. 'Can't sleep, eh?' Klein snorted, 'What's chloral for?'" (Bell 548).

Klopski, Vanya (ATD)
Klopski is a common East European surname. Vanya is the familiar form of the common Russian name Ivan.

Knockwood, Mr. (M&D)
The surname clearly derives from the expression "knock wood" or "knock on wood" (a superstitious practice thought to prevent something bad from happening). There is no clear relevance to this character, though, so the name is probably meant to be humorous. There could, on the other hand, be a mild charactonymic reference if we take *knockwood* as a description of knocking on a door — an appropriate action to associate with an inn-keeper.

Knoop (V)
As Harder points out, this name derives from a test measuring hardness, developed by Frederick Knoop (72). An appropriate name for a "hard" graduate of Annapolis who enforces rules gleefully. Knoop eventually befriends the very enlisted men who break most of the rules, suggesting that the name reflects his initial appearance, rather than his true character.

Knott, Professor [Cargill Gliston] (ATD)
British physicist and mathematician who was a professor of engineering and physics in Tokyo in the late nineteenth century ("Cargill Gliston Knott").

Kolchak, Admiral (ATD)
The reference is to the historical Russian naval commander.

Konig (V)
The name is German for "king" and may refer to the ultimate power of the Germans over the Herero in southwest Africa; the character is depicted in the act of arbitrarily killing an elderly African woman (264).

Kosta (ATD)
Common as both a given- and a surname.

Koteks, Stanley (Lot 49)
Grant cites Watson again who reads the name, like Fallopian, as a reference to the theme of transsexuality in the novel (67). Colvile suggests that the image of menstruation connected with the name points toward "potential fertility" (28). Hayles connects the name to waste by viewing it as a reference to "used sanitary napkins" (109). Caesar views it somewhat charactonymically by defining Stanley Koteks as a "functionary" whose sole job is to absorb information (6). All of these meanings derive from the surname's obvious reference to the Kotex brand sanitary napkin introduced in 1920.

Kreuss (GR)
Kreuss seems to combine *Kreutz* ("cross") and *Kreis* ("circle"); it may be meant as a perverted or degenerate mandala. With Höpmann, Kreuss is said to have erected "vaguely turd-shaped monoliths of ice and snow all the way across the Arctic" (451).

Krinkles (E)
Like Slab of V, Krinkles is introduced along with a group of very ordinary names (Duke, Vincent, and Paco), heightening the strangeness of his name. It has no clear meaning for this very minor character and seems chosen solely for its comic sound.

Krishna (Vine)
Another hippie name pointing to Eastern spirituality (Hinduism's handsome flute-playing boy and avatar of Vishnu).

Krodobbly, Missus (GR)
The name does not seem to mean anything, but has a humorous sound emphasized by the spelling of *Missus*. She is described as "drinking her way through the Big Depression" (741).

Kronecker, Leopold (ATD)
This German mathematician was actually Cantor's "archenemy" (Bell 559), as mentioned by Pynchon (593).

Krupp (GR)
Weisenburger identifies the historical financier (151).

Krypton, Albert (GR)
Weisenburger suggests that the surname derives from "the Greek for 'hidden'" and the element Krypton (number 26 on the periodic table) (256). Larsson adds that Krypton is the name of Superman's home planet (V594.31). Perhaps both senses refer to his character — in a constant drug-induced vapor, on another planet, mentally, due to liberal use of intoxicating and mind-altering substances.

Ksenija (ATD)
Common Slavic name.

Kubitschek (Lot 49)
See Warpe, Wistfull, Kubitschek and McMingus.

Kurzweg, Professor Doctor [Herman] (GR)
Fowler identifies the historical "wind-tunnel specialist" (198).

Kutsushita-san (Vine)
This fairly common Japanese name means "stockings or hosiery." If any descriptive meaning is implied it is unclear.

l'Heuremaudit, Mélanie (V)
Grant points out that l'Heuremaudit translates as "the cursed hour" and cites Berressem on the connection to growing decadence and Dugdale on shades of Rilke and Yeats (172). The name could also be translated loosely as the "hour of the damned" or "hour of the devil." Although Mélanie is a common French name, it is said to derive from the Greek word for "black" (Withycombe 206). The name could, then, be another example of doubling. Given the pervasive darkness of the chapter, the role of evil and black masses, and Mélanie's ultimate fate, the name is appropriate.

La Condamine, [Charles Marie de] (M&D)
EB identifies this French naturalist and mathematician ("La Condamine, Charles-Marie de").

La Foam, Happy Jack (ATD)
Happy Jack could refer to a song of that name by The Who, a story of that name by Thornton Burgess, author of Beatrix-Potter-like children's stories, or "Happy Jack" Cheesbro, National Baseball Hall of Famer from the early twentieth century. The original source for the name may be one of Pynchon's Colorado sources. Parkhill's *The Wildest of the West* details a race riot in Denver against the Chinese: "Rioting started when a group of whites, led by a half-wit known as 'Happy Jack,' 'cleaned out' a Chinese saloon" (112). La Foam suggests foaming at the mouth, or lunacy, and he is presented as a mad chemist. "Happy Jack" also reinforces these associations: he is "prescription happy," giving the locals his dubious formulations at every opportunity.

La Habra, Ramón of (Vine)
The name of this famous automobile pinstriper is a parody of a fashion designer, complete with the city of origin. La Habra is in Orange County, California.

La Valette, Grandmaster [Jean Parisot de] (V)
Grant identifies the historical builder of Valletta, Malta (7).

Lacaille, [Nicolas Louis de] (M&D)
EB identifies the French astronomer ("Lacaille, Nicolas Louis de").

Lafrisée, Pléiade (ATD)
Pléiade is the French form of *pleiades*, referring to the constellation, as well as the daughters of Atlas for whom it is named. *Frisée* is French for "curly" or "curly-haired." With the article *La*,

the name would read "the curly-haired" in English. She is at first described primarily through her expression and her eyes (537) and later appears wearing a hat (544), so whether the surname is descriptive is uncertain. *Thomas Pynchon Wiki* reads the singular Pléiade as "sister" and translates *frisée* as "twisted," yielding "twisted sister," which could be charactonymic as well as a pop culture reference to the rock band of that name.

Lalande, J.J. (Joseph-Jérôme) (M&D)

EB identifies the French astronomer ("Lalande, Jérôme").

Lallie just in from Lübeck (GR)

Perhaps from the German *lallen*, "to speak thickly," but probably chosen for alliteration in the phrase in which she is introduced.

Lambert, Joe (ATD)

He was an actual miner shot by Bob Meldrum, as depicted by Pynchon (Backus 76).

Lambton, Henry (M&D)

Henderson identifies the historical Lord of Lambton (252).

Lambton, John (M&D)

Henderson identifies the real/legendary Lord of Lambton and Knight of Rhodes (252).

Lambton, Lord (M&D)

The Lambton family was real, but which of the Lords Lambton meant is unclear from the context of the passage.

Lambton Worm, the (M&D)

This well-known Northern British legend is explored in some detail by Henderson (247–52).

Lamoral II-Claude-Francis (Lot 49)

Sixth generation member of the Thurn and Taxis dynasty (*Thurn und Taxis*).

Lamplighter, Allen (GR)

The surname suggests illumination, but we only know that this inveterate gambler and co-owner of the book by Pavlov ends up dead, "a cold announcement of dead ends" (167).

Landsdowne, Lord (UR)

The reference is to Henry Charles Keith Petty-Fitzmaurice, fifth marquess of Landsdowne, who was British war secretary 1895–1900 (Adonis).

Lanier, Captain (Vine)

The name is an obsolete version of *lanner*, "a species of falcon" (OED). The name and the character's affair with Norleen Chastain may suggest a predatory nature. The surname is, however, fairly common.

Larry, Whilst Ye Tarry, Mister (M&D)

This wig maker's name seems an anachronistic parody of contemporary businesses with clever names.

Latewood, Cyprian (ATD)

The name is tied to his ambiguious sexuality. *Cyprian* was a term used to denote lasciviousness and applied to prostitutes (OED). MacKell claims that one of the terms used to describe prostitutes in the nineteenth century was "fair Cyprian" (5). Cyprian Latewood is presented for some time as a male prostitute. The surname furthers the reference to homosexuality by obliquely alluding to the title of the novel *Nightwood*, by lesbian author Djuna Barnes.

Laureen (ATD)

Common name.

Lazar the deck ape (V)

Lazar means "a poor or diseased person, especially a leper" (OED). Since he scarcely functions as a real character — he is only mentioned in passing in one of the many lists of minor characters — we cannot regard the name as negative description. He is another member of the teeming preterite class.

Le Chisel (M&D)
This mad French frigate captain's name is probably a play on the English verb *chisel* meaning to cheat or defraud (OED).

Le Froyd, Reg (GR)
Weisenburger glosses the name as "Reginald the Cold" (50). Ware offers "King of the Cold" ("*Gravity's Rainbow*"). This significance of cold may be Reg's return to "his ancestor," the sea (rather cold near the White Visitation, one would imagine). Weisenburger also points out that Bert/Bertha (Lord/Goddess of the sea) has a feast celebrated on the Winter Solstice — another connection with cold (50).

Learnèd English Dog (Fang, L.E.D.) (M&D)
Fang (a typical animal's name — Pynchon used it as a name for Mafia Winsome's gray Siamese cat in V) is called the Learnèd English Dog because of his ability to speak and to answer any question put to him. The name was also chosen so as to be abbreviated L.E.D. Millard cites the quote "The L.E.D. blinks" (22) as evidence that the abbreviation is meant as an anachronistic reference to the light emitting diode.

Lefty (GR)
Some of the mice are given archetypical organized-crime names (recall Lefty Ruggiero or Lefty Louie Rosenberg for example), setting the stage for the discussion of their imprisonment in the laboratory and the impossibility of freedom articulated to the mice by Webley Silvernail.

Lefty the drummer (Vine)
Lefty is a common nickname, usually referring to a left-handed person, but there could be a political reference here (lefty meaning liberal); we do not know enough of the character to judge whether it is applicable.

Leman the red-headed water-king (V)
He is briefly presented as a drunk sailor, so the epithet is confusing. The name could be a reference to line 182 of T.S. Eliot's *The Waste Land*: "By the waters of Leman I sat down and wept." In this context, Leman refers to Lake Geneva, but this offers no apparent solution. The word *leman* also means "lover," but this, too, has no clear significance.

Lemay (Vine)
Common name.

Lemonnier (M&D)
Danson identifies the historical astronomer, Pierre–Charles Le Monnier (30).

Leon (Vine)
Common name.

Leon (SI)
Common name.

Leonard (Lot 49)
Common name.

Leonard (Vine)
Common name.

Leonard (ATD)
He is introduced as an oil prospector along with Lyle. These common names seem to have been chosen solely for their alliteration.

Leonard I, Baron of Taxis (Lot 49)
Third generation member of the Thurn and Taxis dynasty (*Thurn und Taxis*).

Leonard II-Francis Count of Thurn and Taxis (Lot 49)
Fifth generation member of the Thurn and Taxis dynasty (*Thurn und Taxis*).

Lepsius (UR, V)
As Grant points out, this name is drawn from an actual Egyptologist, Karl Richard Lepsius (1810–84) (48).

Lepton, Lady (M&D)
See Lepton, Lord.

Lepton, Lord (M&D)
Dewey glosses the surname as a relatively inactive atomic particle (122). Matter is composed of quarks and leptons. Leptons are actually subatomic particles. There is probably no deep meaning beyond the popular Pynchon science reference.

Lerner, Sargeant Howard ("Slow") (GR)
Besides being another simple punname, "Slow" Lerner "anticipat[es] the title of Pynchon's 1984 collection of short stories, *Slow Learner*" (Weisenburger 275).

LeSpark, Depugh (M&D)
Depugh is a common surname, but rarely used as a given name. See LeSpark, J. Wade for the surname.

LeSpark, Elizabeth (M&D)
Elizabeth is a common given name. See LeSpark, J. Wade for the surname.

LeSpark, Ives (M&D)
Like Depugh, Ives is common as a surname, but not as a given name. See LeSpark, J. Wade for the surname.

LeSpark, J. Wade (M&D)
Dewey compares the name LeSpark with other light-related names in the novel (Wicks and Tenebrae) and glosses it as "the brief compensations of a moment's gaudy flashiness" (120). The name may also refer to the character's sometimes bellicose disposition. The surname is shared by Elizabeth, Ives, DePugh, and Lomax.

LeSpark, John (M&D)
See LeSpark, J. Wade.

LeSpark, Uncle Lomax (M&D)
Like Depugh and Ives, Lomax is far more common as a surname than a given one. See LeSpark, J. Wade for the surname.

Lester (Vine)
The name is comically nerdish and ordinary in contradistinction to the names of the other Vomitones (Billy Barf, Meathook, Bad, 187, and Isaiah Two Four). Notice that the ordinary name takes on its own power and meaning when juxtaposed with a set of preposterous names. Thus the ordinary becomes comic.

LeStreet, Chester (ATD)
This house band drummer has a name alluding to the northern English town Chesterlestreet. There may be an allusion to African-American mystery writer Chester Himes, who wrote mysteries taking place in the streets of Harlem. Surely Pynchon might feel affinity for an author who named a recurring character and funeral parlor director H. Exodus Clay.

Leutwein (V)
Grant identifies the historical German administer (131).

Levi (ATD)
The name means "joining" or "attached" (Hamilton 77). It is appropriate in that he functions solely as the husband of Hope, appearing for only a few lines, introduced as "her husband Levi" (473).

Lévi, Éliphaz (ATD)
Eliphas Levi, whose real name was Alphonse Louis Constant, was a nineteenth-century tarot scholar (Kaplan 22).

Levine, Nathan "Lardass" (SR)
Nathan Levine is a common name. There could be an allusion to the famous film producer of that name, but this could have no clear relevance to the character. The name identifies the character as Jewish, as he suggests he is (29). The comic

nickname is partially chosen for alliteration when combined with the surname, but also suggests a softness, characteristic of such later feckless anti-heroes as Benny Profane and Tyrone Slothrop, also military servicemen. Hollander suggests that Nathan recalls the "Old Testament prophet Nathan" who "averted a civil war' by supporting Solomon as king after David's death," and reads Levine as an allusion to the Levites, "the ancient hereditary priest caste" ("Pynchon's Politics" 22, 25). These glosses make sense in the context of his larger reading of Pynchon's short fiction.

Liesele (M&D)
While not as common now, Liesele was a relatively common German name in centuries past.

Liftoff, Sid (Vine)
The comic surname reinforces the character's fondness for the use of cocaine.

Lilli (GR)
Common name.

Lily (GR)
Common name.

Liman von Sanders, [Otto] (ATD)
The reference is to the German general who organized the Ottoman army during World War I; he is best remembered for defeating the allies at Gallipoli ("Liman von Sanders, Otto").

Linda (GR)
Common name.

Linderfelt, [Karl A.] (ATD)
Osur identifies this Colorado National Guard lieutenant (22).

Littlewood (ATD)
The British mathematician John Edison Littlewood is referred to here ("John Edison Littlewood"). Yashmeen recalls this mathematician in part because of his name's similarity to that of Cyprian Latewood, who has just departed.

Ljubica (GR)
As Larsson points out, this is a Slavic name (V732.36). Hereros without native names have either European (especially German) names or Slavic ones, suggesting two external political influences on the native culture.

Ljubica (ATD)
A common Yugoslav name meaning "violet" in Serbo-Croation. Ironically, she is seen in a field of wild lilacs (950) rather than violets, although some lilacs are violet in color.

Lloyd, [Edward] (M&D)
The Honorable Edward Lloyd, Esquire appears in Headlee, but exactly what he did is unclear. He paid a large sum of cash into the account used for the expenses associated with drawing the line, suggesting he was a commissioner or acting on behalf of the commissioners or the state governors whom they represented (29).

Lo Finto, Mrs. (Vine)
Lo finto is Italian for "the false." There is no indication that the name is particularly appropriate to this minor character.

Loaf, H.A. (GR)
Larsson offers the clever "half a loaf," "[a]s in 'Half a loaf is better than none'" (V14.07). The OED lists *loaf* as a slang term for the human head in phrases such as "use your loaf." In this sense, "half a loaf" could mean half-witted. Given the descriptions of the character's constant unthinking actions, such a reading seems appropriate.

Loafsley, "Plug" (ATD)
The name "Plug" suggests *plug-ugly*, a term for a ruffian or gangster derived from a nineteenth century gang called the Plug Uglies (AH4). Pynchon uses the term on 871. It is appropriate for someone whose business interests include child prostitution, opium, and the numbers racket

(398–99). Loafsley recalls the verb *loaf*, "to pass time at leisure" (AH4).

Lobelia (Vine)
Lobelia is "a shrub cultivated for its beautiful and brightly colored flowers" (OED). Perhaps this is a reference to her make-up skills: "purple liner, and at *least* three different eyeshadows" (135).

Lodge, Sir Oliver (ATD)
British Physicist and psychical researcher (Oppenheim 34).

Loïc the bartender (ATD)
Loïc is a common French given name. Even in this most recent novel, Pynchon continues to attach an occupational epithet to the names of some characters.

Lois (ATD)
Common name.

Lolli (Vine)
Lolli seems to be a relatively common Italian name.

Lombroso, Dr. [Cesare] (ATD)
An Italian criminologist of the nineteenth century who claimed, among other things, that criminals were identifiable by facial structure ("Lombroso, Cesare").

Lonsdale, Uncle (M&D)
Given the werewolf theme in this section and the fact that Uncle Lonsdale is said to be the genetic source of Lud Oafery's peculiarity, we can safely assume that the name is an anachronistic reference to the actor Lon Chaney, who portrayed the Wolf Man in film.

Looie (GR)
Some of the mice are given archetypical organized-crime names (recall Lefty Louie Campagna or Lefty Louie Rosenberg for example), setting the stage for the discussion of their imprisonment in the laboratory and the impossibility of freedom articulated to the mice by Webley Silvernail.

Loomis (ATD)
Common surname.

Loon, Irving (MMV)
The name has a comic sound heightened by the juxtaposition of the common Irving with the ridiculous Loon. The name seems wholly inappropriate for an Ojibwa Indian, perhaps reflecting his forced departure from his traditional life: "he was so happy back in Ontario" (207). On the other hand, the name is wholly appropriate. Irving is a variant of Irvin, "beautiful, handsome, fair" (Kolatch 188); Lucy says of him: "Boy, what a hunk" (206). *Loon* means "one who is crazy or deranged" (AH4), linked to such similar words as *loony* and *lunatic*. Siegel notes that Debby Considine uses the clinical term "melancholia" to describe him rather than the more common "melancholy" (208) or simpler still, Siegel's own first impression: "He looks sad" (206). Language pertaining to lunacy peppers the story from this point on, particularly in Siegel's recollection of Professor Mitchell's lecture on "psychopathy among the Ojibwa Indians," the "Windigo psychosis," and even his tone, suggesting "that for him all cultures were equally mad" (208).

López, Don Vicente (M&D)
The context suggests he was a Spanish privateer off Delaware c. 1740, but his historical reality is uncertain. He shares a name with a Spanish artist of roughly the same period, but whether there is any allusion intended is uncertain. Certainly, López is a common surname.

Lorelei (ATD)
Lorelei is "a siren of Germanic legend whose singing lures sailors to shipwreck" (AH4). The name has no clear application to this character, though the name is not uncommon.

Lorraine (GR)
See Girls, Slothrop's.

Lottchen (ATD)
The German diminutive ending, *-chen*, usually means something like "little," in an affectionate sense. Combined with the common German name Lotte, it would be little Lotte, appropriate for a girl described as "a sweet young thing" (621).

Lotte (V)
Common German name.

Lotte (M&D)
Common German name.

Lotus (Vine)
Another hippie name referring to Eastern spirituality (*The Lotus Sutra*, for example, an important Buddhist work).

Louis (GR)
Common name.

Lowry, Nelly (ATD)
As Blinky Morgan is real, one expects Nelly Lowry to be as well. However, available source materials on Morgan do not list a Nelly, Nell, or Nellie Lowry. If she is real, Pynchon's source is uncertain. Both names are common.

Loxley, Benjamin (M&D)
Mason mentions this carpenter in his journal (42).

Luba (GR)
Common name.

Lubbock, Isaac (GR)
Fowler identifies the historical "liquid oxygen researcher" (276).

Lucien the concierge (ATD)
One of several characters in ATD given an occupational epithet, Lucien has a common French name.

Lucille (V)
There is no reason why this common name need have additional meaning, but the name comes from St. Lucilla, a Roman martyr of the third century (Withycombe 191). The scene describing Lucille on the pool table (143) along with her name could be taken as a foreshadowing of Fina's gang rape, which takes place less than ten pages later (151). The look in Fina's eyes is explicitly compared to Lucille's as she lay on the pool table.

Lucky (Vine)
The name of Ché's mother's boyfriend seems to reflect ironically on the women who are in his life — unlucky to be in this abusive relationship.

Lucy (MMV)
A common name, but the character recalls or prefigures another young Lucy, the sexually precocious character Lucille from V (142–45). Like Lucille who offers herself to Profane, Lucy, upon meeting Siegel, says "I want to go to bed with you" (200). Hollander sees this too, reading the name as "Loosie" (28), charactonymically describing her promiscuity.

Ludowick, Master (M&D)
It is no accident that the grunting moron Lud Oafery takes this slightly changed but more refined name after being transformed (in lycanthropic parody) into a peevish fop.

Ludwig (GR)
Fowler states that the character's name derives from Ludwig II of Bavaria, who drowned himself (213) — an appropriate name for a boy who has a pet lemming.

Lueger, Dr. Karl (ATD)
Historical Viennese mayor and anti-semite.

Lupescu, David (MMV)
Lupescu is a common Romanian surname. Hollander suggests that it recalls lycanthropy (where a man imagines he is a wolf) through *canis lupus* (wolf) and ties into the theme of cannibalism, but also that the name alludes to "Magda Lupescu, Jewish mistress, later wife, of King Carol II of Rumania" ("Pynchon's Politics"

27–8). David is a common name but recalls the biblical King David, second king of Israel and father of Solomon. David Lupescu passes the torch of party host to Siegel, linking him to Solomon, though the wisdom of allowing the bloodbath at the end of the story is debatable, although mass slaughter is a predominant Old Testament theme.

Lupita (ATD)

Given Pynchon's interest in horror films, the name may allude to Lupita Tovar, who starred in the 1931 Spanish-language version of *Dracula*. Of course, Lupita is a common Latina name. In fact, there seem to be countless Mexican restaurants called Lupita's.

Lüstig, Lotte (GR)

This character played by Greta has another joke name. Weisenburger defines *Lüstig* as "gaiety and fun, or 'lusty'" (219). *Lustig* (without the umlaut) could be translated as "gay" or "fun," but not "lusty." The pun seems to be on the sound in English: "a lot of lust...."

Luz (GR)

Spanish for "light," *Luz* is a common Hispanic name.

Lych, C. Osric (V)

For a rather minor character, he has an exceedingly rich yet confounding name. Osric is clearly from Hamlet, but why use the name of Claudius's puffed up toady and Laertes's champion? This seems to go against the very little we read of Lych's character. As Harder points out, Osric also means "divine rule," appropriate for the commander of the *Scaffold* (71). Harder also suggests that Lych "could be derived from 'lech,' or 'leech,' or even 'leek'" (71). The significance of these possibilities is not entirely clear. The OED cites *lych* as a variant of *lich*, which can mean either "a living body" or "a dead body." The contradiction within the word itself is interesting, but the name could surely be appropriate for the commander of a ship called the *Scaffold*—a device that turns living bodies into dead ones, but also a symbol of the power of official authority. We may, in fact, read the entire name as "Behold (from C. read as *see*) Divine authority (from Osric): it holds the power of life and death (from the contradictory meanings embodied in Lych as a var. of *lich*)." Of course, since Lych's protection of the ship's greatest malefactors tends to undermine official authority, the meaning of the name retreats to paradox.

Lyle (ATD)

He is introduced as an oil prospector along with Leonard. These common names seem to have been chosen solely for their alliteration.

Lynn, Nathan (M&D)

Browne identifies this participant in the melee described in the text (155).

Maas, Oedipa (Lot 49)

This must be the most studied name in Pynchon. Certainly dozens of critics have offered glosses ranging from the obvious to the outlandish. Clearly the first reference readers see is to the Greek tragic hero and eponymous Freudian psychological complex. Mendelson has pointed out that the relevance to the Oedipus complex cannot be taken as such, since the novel contains no information about Oedipa's relationship with her parents (118). Richwell suggests that the reference is not to *Oedipus Rex*, but to *Oedipus at Colonus*, arguing that both works "open with a journey and end on a note of religious mysticism" and pointing out several verbal links (78). The obvious reference to the Sophocles plays seems to be that Oedipa is given a riddle to solve (Petillon 137). Petillon also suggests that Oedipa's initials, O.M., form the sound of transcendental meditation (127–8). O'Donnell cites Davidson on the meaning of *maas* in Afrikaans—"net" or "web"—signifying either her "ability to connect disparate pieces of information or her entrapment in conspiracy" (18 note 30) and Davis on the meaning of *maas* in Dutch — "loophole" — "connoting her loss of signifying power and activity" (18 note 30). Hollander implies that Maas suggests the Dutch word *maaswerk*, meaning "the underside of a tapestry" ("Pynchon, JFK and the CIA" 63, 69). Colvile extends the reading to gloss the name as "woof" or "background threads through which the warp is woven and which forms the hidden part of the tapestry" (12). She also suggests the similarity to *mass*, or "religious ritual," and the fact that the name Oedipa feminizes Oedipus, thus making the narrative a mock-quest with a heroine rather than a hero (26), and that the name begins with Omega and ends with Alpha, bringing the reader back to the beginning, just as the final words of the text repeat the title (101). Tanner rejects the feminine Oedipus reading and points out the reference of Maas to Newton's Second Law, where "mass denotes inertia," but rejects this as well (60). Herzogenrath claims that Maas derives from an old German text on entropy by Helmholtz, where *Maass* (an archaic spelling of *Maß*) designates measure (particularly of disorganization) allowing the name to "be read as reflecting her precarious and ambiguous position with respect to both order and chaos" (108). Caesar cleverly suggests the name is a pun, where Maas is spoken as "my ass": "this Oedipa is no Oedipus, or only one at the earnest reader's peril" (5). Grant offers an extended look at the name, some glosses, rejections of many glosses, and some initial information on conflicting views of naming in Pynchon (3–6). Obviously one's reading determines which category, if any, the name falls into. Like other overdetermined names, a single, static reading is impossible to fix. The reference to Sophocles' Oedipus is certain, even if it is undercut (deliberately by Pynchon) by other readings. While many interpretations of Maas are reasonable, they are clearly secondary — this is the husband's name and seems to exist primarily for the onomastic joke of which it forms one half (Mucho Maas).

Maas, Wendell ("Mucho") (Lot 49, Vine)

We could refer to some of the glosses for Oedipa Maas, but for the most part they do not seem to work. The joke name is clear: Hollander glosses it as "a pun on the Spanish for 'much more'" but suggests that Wendell is a reference to Wendell Wilkie ("Pynchon, JFK and the CIA" 68). The last part only works well within the context of Hollander's allegorical reading of the novel. Colvile examines the name in detail suggesting that Maas refers to the mass media (his job) and that Mucho points toward the many identities he will take on after his continued use of LSD (25). She also offers a reading of the name as "moo-show" referring to cows and "Ma-a-(s)" imitating the sound of sheep. Together she reads this as an indication of the "imbecilic gregariousness cultivated in people by the mass media" (27). Grant quotes Davidson in reading "Mucho" as "macho" in reference to the character's penchant for young girls (13). The character reappears in Vine, where the name retains only the original pun.

MacBurgess, Ralph (V)

Ironically, Rowley-Bugge's original name was quite ordinary compared to his alias. Although not an anagram, it does share many sounds with the alias Maxwell Rowley-Bugge.

MacClenaghan, Reverend (M&D)

This is not an uncommon surname, but if the character is real, the source is uncertain.

Macclesfield, [Lord George Parker] (M&D)

Danson identifies the historical second Earl of Macclesfield (41).

MacDonald, Ramsay (GR)
Weisenburger identifies the historical British prime minister, but he spells the given name Ramsey (51).

Mackay, Captain [Hugh] (M&D)
Oglethorpe identifies the historical commander of the Highland Rangers.

Madeleine (V)
Common name.

Madelyn (GR)
Common name.

Madero, Francisco (ATD)
Mexican presidential candidate and revolutionary (Gonzales 42).

Magda, the sultry Bavarian (GR)
Common name.

Magdika (ATD)
A familiar form of the common name Magda.

Magyakan (ATD)
The name is an enigma. It is not a common name and does not seem to be a word in any common language. It is similar to the Hungarian *magyarán* (straightforwardly, frankly) and nearly cognate with the English *magician*, both appropriate in a way for a shaman, both in what he may reveal and how he may do so.

Maherero, Samuel (GR)
Weisenburger identifies the historical Herero ruler (163).

Mahmoud (ATD)
This dead rifleman called at a seance has a common Muslim name meaning, like the variant name Muhammad, "praised" or "praiseworthy" (Ahmed 108).

Maijstral, Carla (V)
Carla is, of course, a common name and the associations of Maijstral seem intended for Fausto and Paola, not this very minor character. *See* Maijstral, Fausto and Maijstral, Paola for the surname.

Maijstral, Fausto (V)
Maijstral or *mistral* refers to "the cold north wind," suggesting storminess. Fausto clearly refers to Faust, but this is somewhat ironic, in that Fausto seeks self-knowledge, ultimately. Harder does point out that the character is "marred by too much knowledge of evil and the Twentieth Century [*sic*]" and glosses the name as "master intelligence" (70).

Maijstral, Paola (V)
Harder glosses the name as "small master" (70). *Maijstral* is the Maltese equivalent of "mistral," which derives ultimately from the Latin *magister*, or "master," but the immediate meaning of *mistral* is a "cold northerly wind that blows in squalls toward the Mediterranean coast of Southern France" (AH4). Grant cites Neuman's religious reading centering on Pentecost by stating that the maijstral blows once every three days, "underscoring the relation to the Trinity" (7). In an earlier note, Grant links the name Paola to St. Paul, who was shipwrecked on Malta (7). Fausto points out that properly, Paola's given name is Maijstral-Xemxi (*see* Xemxi, Elena), "a terrible misalliance" (V. 314). *Maijstral* is the Maltese word for northwest wind; *xemxi* is the Maltese word for sunny. Paola seems to contain the opposition of cold and warmth. In this way, the name seems to denote the character's (successful?) ability to exist, in some way, between the either-or, binary opposition evident throughout Pynchon's texts.

Maire, Christopher (M&D)
Referred to also as Le Maire in the novel, this Jesuit mathematician is identified by the DNB (Cooper).

Maledetto, Dr. (GR)
The surname is from the Italian *maledétto*, meaning "cursed" or "damned." Besides the fact that the women love him, we know nothing of this very minor character. It is probably another simple joke.

Mallakastra, the Baron de (GR)

Mallakastra is a region in central Albania; the significance of the name is uncertain.

Manganese, Veronica (V)

One of the many women thought to be V., her name is appropriate. At first glance, the combination consists of an ordinary name and an inanimate object, fusing animate and inanimate according to Harder (69). The name *Veronica* stems from the story of the woman who is said to have wiped the face of Christ with a cloth that retained the image of the face and became a holy relic. According to Withycombe, the name became common in Britain around the end of the nineteenth century (275). Interestingly, the apocryphal Veronica is now widely believed to be a fictional character whose name derives from *vera icon*, which means "true image." Both her name and identity have been questioned by scholars for years (Farmer 477). Manganese is an element (atomic number 25). Harder defines it as "a hard, brittle, grayish-white metallic element" (69). Examples from the OED indicate the usefulness of manganese in the dyestuff industry. This may suggest the character's connection to superficial or exterior transformations. If Pynchon had already done preliminary research or reading that led to GR, the name could also point to the massive German dyestuff conglomerate I.G. Farben, the shadow behind many of Slothrop's nightmares. The I.G. was strong by the beginning of the twentieth century and was responsible for creating all the poison gas used by the Germans in WWI (*see* Borkin, Joseph. *The Crime and Punishment of I.G. Farben*. NY: Barnes and Noble Books, 1997). I.G. Farben was integral to Nazi success and the manganese link to the dyestuff industry may identify the character as a proto-nazi. Grant cites Inglott and glosses the whole name as "True-Icon-In-Dark-Metal" (200).

Mannaro, Sam (V)

Harder suggests this is ironic, as Mannaro has "no manners" (74). Grant says that *mannaro* is Italian for "werewolf." As this is the character's nickname, this meaning is clearly Pynchon's intention, although *mannaro* means "bogey" in Italian — *lupo mannaro* means "werewolf."

Manning, Professor (ATD)

American mathematician Henry Parker Manning is referred to here ("Henry Parker Manning").

Manoel (V)

Common Hispanic name.

Mantissa, Rafael (V)

Harder centers on the definition of *mantissa*, which refers to what follows a decimal in a logarithm, to demonstrate Pynchon's interest in mathematical and scientific terms (76). Grant cites Neuman in showing that the word may come from *mantis*, the Greek word for "seer" (87). He also cites the more appropriate definition of *mantissa*: "an addition of comparatively small importance" (87). This may be misleading; it could refer to the fact that Mantissa is only five feet three. Of course the reference to smallness is balanced by a first name that clearly calls to mind the archangel Raphael. He acts as protector to old Godolphin. The description of his golden hair and mustache also points toward the angelic. When old Godolphin first sees Mantissa, he calls him Raf. This is an obsolete past tense of *riv*, "to rend, split, tear up, put asunder" (OED). Although Raf is obviously meant as a friendly diminutive, the transition from Rafael to Raf may suggest a degeneration — he could be read as a broken angel.

Manuel (Vine)

Common Hispanic name.

Manuela (GR)

A common given name (primarily Hispanic) meant to identify the character's ethnicity in relation to Marvy's desire for dark skin.

Mañuela (ATD)
Common Latina name.

Mara (V)
As the text indicates, the name means "woman" in Maltese.

Maraca, Jardine (ATD)
Jardine is commonly used as a surname and recalls the French for "garden" or "yard" (*jardin*). Lew does meet her at an outdoor party. The surname refers to the Latin-American musical instrument "a hollow gourd-rattle containing pebbles" (AH4). They are used in pairs. She appears at the party with her father: a pair of Maracas.

Maraca, Virgil (ATD)
Virgil is a common name. But there is support for seeing the name as an allusion to the Roman poet Virgil, whose *Aeneid* depicts the foundation of Rome in glorious, mythic terms. Our Virgil says "I like to lose myself in reveries of when the land was free, before it got hijacked by capitalist Christer Republicans for their long-term evil purposes" (1058). Both Virgils see their nations in terms of pure foundations later corrupted. *See* Maraca, Jardine for the surname.

Maratt (V)
The name does not appear to be Maltese and probably refers to famous French revolutionary Jean-Paul Marat. Pynchon's character "was going into politics" (306) and is last known by Maijstral to be "organizing riots among ... the Bantu" (307).

Maratt the welder (V)
Presumably, this is the father of Fausto's friend of the same name. *See* Maratt.

Marcel (GR)
Perhaps a reference, given his description as a French mechanical chess player, to famous artist/chessmaster Marcel Duchamp. *See also* Floundering Four, the.

Marcello (ATD)
Common Italian name.

Marchand, General (UR, V)
Grant identifies the historical French officer, but claims he was only a captain (44).

Marconi, [Guglielmo] (ATD)
The reference is to the Italian inventor popularly credited with the invention of the radio.

Marengo, Jacob (V)
Grant identifies the historical Nama leader (137).

Maria (V)
Common name.

Maria (GR)
Another African with a Western Christian name (Mary), Maria has a name demonstrating the Western influence on the tribe. In this case, the name is also ironic, as Maria (unlike her biblical precursor, the mother of Jesus) wants to abort her child.

Marias (GR)
See Girls, Slothrop's.

Marín, C. (ATD)
As Pynchon later introduces a character whose alias is Chong, we can be certain that the name of this Mexican police officer is a reference to Cheech Marin, who appeared along with Tommy Chong in a series of films, starting with *Up in Smoke* in 1978, that all chronicle the humorous attempts of the duo to smoke as much marijuana as humanly possible.

Marine, Matthew (M&D)
Headlee identifies the historical instrument bearer and overseer (11).

Marjorie (GR)
See Girls, Slothrop's.

Marjorie (GR)
Part of "The Occupation of Mingeborough" scene, Marjorie has one of a few ordinary names within the novel. But all of the names in this scene are relatively normal, reflecting the normal life from which Slothrop is barred irrevocably.

Marthioly, Iron-Mask (M&D)
The reference is to the "man in the iron mask," whose identity is uncertain. At the cemetery where he was buried, the name given is Marchioly, thought to refer to Ercole Matthioli, although others claim, more plausibly, that the man in the iron mask was Eustache Dauger ("Iron Mask").

Marvy, Major Duane (GR)
Marvy is a slang equivalent of *marvelous* and applies ironically to this corpulent racist.

Mary (M&D)
The DNB entry for Charles Mason identifies his second wife as Mary (Howse, "Mason, Charles [1728–1786]").

Mary (M&D)
Robinson identifies the second wife of Charles Mason Sr. as Mary Gardiner ("A Note on Charles Mason's Ancestry" 135).

Mary (M&D)
Dixon provides for Margaret Bland and her two daughters, Elizabeth and Mary, in his will (Robinson "Jeremiah Dixon" 274). The fact that his mother was named Mary and his sister Elizabeth strongly suggests that they were his daughters by Bland, as depicted by Pynchon (751).

Maryam (V)
This figure in Aïeul the libertine's dream has the Muslim version of the name of Mary, the virgin mother of Jesus, ironically bestowed upon her (Ahmed 287).

Mascaregna (ATD)
A common Italian surname. The character is described as "a piratically bearded youth" (738). As the surname contains the letters for "mascara," used to artificially thicken and darken eyelashes, this may suggest that the beard on this youth is not entirely real.

Maskelyne, Edmund (M&D)
The DNB identifies this brother of Nevil Maskelyne (Howse, "Maskelyne, Nevil [1732–1811]").

Maskelyne, Nevil (M&D)
The DNB identifies the Astronomer Royal (Howse, "Maskelyne, Nevil [1732–1811]").

Maskelyne, Peggy (M&D)
The DNB identifies her as Margaret, sister of Nevil Maskelyne and wife of Clive of India (Howse, "Maskelyne, Nevil [1732–1811]").

Mason, Anne (M&D)
This sister of Charles Mason is listed in the will of Charles Mason Sr. (Robinson, "A Note on Charles Mason's Ancestry" 135).

Mason, Charles (M&D)
The DNB identifies the astronomer (Howse, "Mason, Charles [1728–1786]").

Mason, Charles Sr. (M&D)
The DNB identifies the baker, father of Charles Mason (Howse, "Mason, Charles [1728–1786]").

Mason, Doctor Isaac (M&D)
Real name of one of Mason's sons (Cope, "The Astronomical Manuscripts ..." 422).

Mason, Rebekah (M&D)
The DNB identifies her as Mason's first wife (Howse, "Mason, Charles [1728–1786]"). Robinson consistently spells the name Rebecca, but he quotes her tombstone, which gives Rebekah, the spelling used by Pynchon ("A Note on Charles Mason's Ancestry" 134)

Mason, William (M&D)
The name of one of Mason's sons (Cope, "The Astronomical Manuscripts ..." 422).

Matson, Ralph (M&D)
Edgar identifies this owner of one of the homes burned by the Indians (97).

Maureen (M&D)
An ordinary name, but the character who bears it is linked to Pegeen to form one of several pairs in the novel.

Maurice (V)
See also David. Harder points out that David and Maurice are dismissed as names only (74). But surely the names are chosen to some end. Saint Maurice was a martyr who gained immense popularity in England: eight ancient churches were dedicated to him there (Farmer 331-2). Ironically, he was ultimately martyred for refusing to fight, unlike our Maurice, who is on his way to Suez to serve England. The name may be chosen to indicate his impending martyrdom.

Mausmacher (GR)
As Weisenburger points out, the name means "mouse maker" (277). This does not seem to be connected to this Lutheran character "who likes to dress up in Roman regalia" (653). The name is somewhat comic, but does not have any immediately identifiable meaning.

Mauve (M&D)
The name of Fender Belly Bodine's girl for the nonce refers to the color mauve, one of the first synthetic dyes, having been discovered in 1859 (OED). The name may refer metonymically to makeup, a reference to the character as a prostitute perhaps.

Max (GR)
Winston points out that Max and Moritz are the creations of nineteenth century German children's author Wilhelm Busch (73).

Maximilian (GR)
See Floundering Four, the.

Maxixe the drunk (V)
This character is introduced in a list of people living in the same building as Profane's parents. *Maxixe* means "a round dance of Brazilian origin resembling the two-step" (OED). Perhaps the name suggests the character's drunken capering, although he only exists in the novel as a name. With the names of the other neighbors, Maxixe may indicate that the building is occupied largely by immigrants. It certainly demonstrates Pynchon's love of obscure words.

McAdoo, Chevrolette (ATD)
McAdoo is a common surname, shared by an NBA Hall of Fame forward as well as a U.S. Senator. No allusion seems likely regarding this character, however. Chevrolette seems to compress the car name Chevrolet Chevette or Chevrolet Corvette. The spelling might also phonetically suggest the jocular-deliberate mispronunciation of the name Chevrolet itself, that is, voicing the "t." In either case, the brand name allusion is not connected to the character in any meaningful way.

McAfee, Carl (SI)
Both given-and surname are common, making him an everyman and suggesting by virtue of this shared humanity, the folly of racism and segregation. Of course the given name Carl is used as this real man takes the place of the make-believe Carl Barrington in the lives of the boys. There may be an allusion to the African-American physicist and mathematician who first calculated the speed of the moon, Walter S. McAfee, but is not certain if Pynchon would have known of him at the time of the story: "Official news of this scientific breakthrough did not include McAfee's name, nor was there any recognition of the essential role he played" (Gates).

McClean, Alexander (M&D)
Headlee identifies the historical "Tent Keeper" (11).

McClean, Archibald (M&D)
Cope identifies the historical surveyor: "Archibald McClean of York County is a man famous among the surveyors and commissioners of Pennsylvania's boundaries through long years from the 1760's into the 1780's" ("The Jersey Quadrant" 567).

McClean, Moses (M&D)
Although the first reference to the character identifies him as Mr. McClean, we can be certain the reference is to Moses McClean as the context refers to his knowledge of supplies. The historical Moses McClean was "an experienced camp boss" (Danson 118). The accompts record his title as "Steward fulltime" (Headlee 11).

McClean, Nathe (M&D)
There are ten McClean's listed by name in the accompts: not one is Nathe or Nathan. If the character is real, Pynchon's source is uncertain.

McDivott, Katie (ATD)
Common name.

McEntaggart (M&D)
Common Irish and Scottish surname.

McFee, Light-Fingers (M&D)
The character's rummaging through Stig's belongings suggests a predisposition to thievery, captured in the name *Light-Fingers*. McFee is a fairly common surname.

McGonigal, Bridget (ATD)
Both are common Irish names.

McGonigle, Private Paddy ("Electro") (GR)
One of many pun names, nick- and surname are pronounced together as "electromechanical." As the character is described as unconsciously transmitting signals through cranking a generator to power a light bulb, he becomes a sort of machine.

McHugh, Reginald "Ratty" (ATD)
Both given- and surname are common. One expects the nickname to join with the surname to form some joke or pun, but this does not seem to be the case here.

McMingus (Lot 49)
See Warpe, Wistfull, Kubitschek and McMingus.

McNoise, Topman (M&D)
The surname is a pun on "make noise," but seems ironic given that the character is described as tiny and his voice as a mutter.

McNutley, Gwen (M&D)
Gwen is a common name. *See* McNutley, Mr. for the surname.

McNutley, Mr. (M&D)
The character appears with verifiable historical figures, but does not seem to be real. The accompts list Rebekah McNutt (Headlee 24), but no McNutley. The surname seems fairly common.

McTiernan (M&D)
Common name.

McVeety, Con (ATD)
McVeety is a common surname. Con may be short for Conway or Conrad. The meanings of *con* as either noun or verb do not seem to have any clear application to this minor character.

Mead, Mr. (M&D)
Common name.

Meathook (Vine)
See Barf, Billy and the Vomitones.

Meatman, Alonzo (ATD)
Alonzo is a common name. Meatman is a joke name relying on translating a common German name into English: Fleischmann.

Medichevole, Ugo (V)
As Harder points out, *ugo* is Italian for "mind" (although it is a common name

as well) and *medichevole* can be read as "magician" (76), which is the minor character's occupation. We could read the names together as someone who plays tricks on the mind.

Megan (M&D)

The context suggests that she is a granddaughter of Thomas Cresap. Bailey mentions grandchildren, but does not name them. The Cresap family genealogy lists a Megan, but she was born in 1948 (Cresap and Cresap 454).

Mehemet (V)

Mehemet is a form of the name Muhammad (Ahmed 117). This variant is a fairly common name. The name is appropriate for a Muslim character who often uses the oblique language of prophecy and mysticism.

Meknes (V)

Meknes is the name of an important city in northern Morocco, formerly its capitol. Pynchon probably came across the name in his Baedeker.

Meldrum, Bob (ATD)

Pynchon lifted this character straight out of history, keeping his violent temper, his role in the mining conflict between workers and owners, even his extraordinary jealousy regarding his wife (depicted on 290). Meldrum was a gunfighter, marshal, assistant to a Pinkerton detective, strike breaker at Cripple Creek, and had "a tempestuous marriage" (O'Neal 226). Backus mentions him, too, and describes his "extreme deafness" (68), another detail Pynchon includes.

Melpómene (ATD)

Melpómene is the Greek muse of tragedy. The name is appropriate to this character, under whose big tree Frank has a vision of gunfire, blood, and burning flesh (993). What he sees represents a particularly violent period of the Mexican revolution, ten terrible days that became known as the Decena Trágien (994).

Melvin (V)

See also Raoul. Like Raoul, Melvin is a normal name used to foreground Slab as an odd character name.

Mendoza, Angel (V)

Both names are ethnic identifiers. *Ángel* means "angel" in Spanish, but the name is common enough that this meaning may serve no purpose in describing the character.

Mendoza, Cucarachito (Kook) (V)

The surname is an ethnic identifier. *Cucarachito* stems either from the Spanish *cucaracha* ("cockroach") or *cucarachero* ("sly or tricky") with the addition of a diminutive ending. The former might be an affectionate nickname, but the latter, read as "sly, little one" seems appropriate to his character.

Mendoza, José (V)

Both the given name and the surname function as ethnic/preterite identifiers.

Mendoza, Josefina (Fina) (V)

The surname, given name, and nickname are all common Spanish names. They function as ethnic markers. *Fina* also means "fine" in Spanish and might refer to her sexual attractiveness.

Mendoza, Tolito (V)

Both the given name and the surname function as ethnic/preterite identifiers.

Mérode, Cléo de (V)

Grant identifies the historical dancer (127).

Mérode, Cléo de (ATD)

This historical ballet dancer is also mentioned in V and Grant identifies her in his companion (127).

Meroving, Vera (V)

Harder suggests that the name has "Merovingian connotations," referring presumably to that Frankish dynasty's penchant for war (69). The name Vera derives from the Russian Vjera ("faith"), but among Roman Catholics, it is also the equivalent of Veronica (Withycombe 274), linking this incarnation of V. with the later Veronica Manganese. The name may be read as "faith in warfare," appropriate given V.'s appearance during times of strife, violence, and war.

Mescalero (ATD)

The name of Frank's horse is a word of an Apache tribe of the southwest (AH4). Given Pynchon's interests and the description of the horse ("mischief in his eye") (296), one wonders if he does not also intend a reference to the hallucinogenic drug mescaline. One could gloss drug-induced hallucination as "visual mischief."

Metatron (GR)

One of the lunatics "takes the name" of Metatron, an angel from Kabbalistic mythology. *See* Weisenburger for background (121–22).

Metzger (Lot 49)

Metzger is German for "butcher," as numerous critics have pointed out, although there does not seem to be a clear charactonymic reference to the actions of the character. Perhaps it is a derisive reference to lawyers in general. Grant cites Nicholson who explains that butchers in the middle ages often doubled as letter carriers (11). This is a fascinating connection to the novel, although Metzger seems to have no association with W.A.S.T.E. Of course, since Metzger is a common name, it does not work as a very obvious joke or historical allusion.

Mexico, Roger (GR)

The name is something of an enigma. Tololyan offers that the name may have been suggested by "Shell Mex House" (46) or the atomic bomb testing site of New Mexico (67 note 9). It may be, considering the oft-quoted exchange with Pointsman in which Mexico suggests rejecting sterile assumptions and junking cause and effect, that Mexico represents "the South," often thought of as an emotional rejection of the cold rationality of the North. This could tie in with the first name in its sense of "message received." *Roger* is also slang for "to have sexual intercourse with" (AH4); this reading could be supported by the fact that Roger and Jessica's relationship is purely sexual.

Micah (M&D)

Another ordinary name derived from the Bible, Micah has been used "in England and USA since the seventeenth century" (Withycombe 207).

Michele (GR)

One of relatively few ordinary names in the novel. She is described as a friend of Slothrop's, highlighting the normalcy of his desires (for life, pleasure, etc.) against the culture of death, power, and intrigue all around him.

Michelson, [Albert Abraham] (ATD)

American physicist who, along with E.W. Morley, performed experiments measuring the speed of light, eventually discrediting the "ether theories" mentioned throughout ATD ("Michelson-Morley experiment").

Michiko (GR)

Michiko appears to be a common Japanese name. It is the name of a famous survivor of the atomic bomb attack on Hiroshima, Michiko Yamaoka. Michiko Morituri's surname, however, suggests that she does not survive. *See* Morituri, Ensign.

Mickey, Roy (ATD)

Both names are common. There may be an allusion to Roy Williams, big Mousketeer and co-host of the 1950s *Mickey Mouse Club*.

Mifsud, Dr. (V)

Grant identifies the historical secretary of the Maltese National Assembly (200).

Mikimoto, Dr. [Kokichi] (ATD)
"Japanese pearl farmer and merchant who introduced the commercial production of cultured pearls" ("Mikimoto Kokichi").

Miklós the desk clerk (ATD)
One of several characters in the novel given an occupational epithet, but a common name, Miklós has this common Hungarian name, a form of Nicholas.

Miles (Lot 49)
Common name.

Minkowski, Hermann (ATD)
Friend and colleague of David Hilbert ("Hilbert, David").

Minoru (Vine)
Minoru is a fairly common Japanese name, but the word means "to bear fruit, ripen or grow" (Yoshitaro 1231). There is no clear relation between the word and the character. Given that this character is a bomb-squad expert (144), there may be a reference to Minoru Suzuki, a Japanese soldier who was killed by the atomic bomb dropped on Hiroshima (Nihon Senbotsu Gakusei Kinen-Kai 274).

Miraculous, Myrtle (GR)
See Floundering Four, the.

Mirage the unit astrologer (Vine)
The name seems to be consistent with other 1960s names in the novel, but it may suggest a negative attitude toward astrology, a sentiment that the coincidences it reveals are illusion. It could also refer to drug-induced hallucination.

Miriam (MMV)
One of many Jewish names in the story, Miriam means "bitter" or "rebelliously" (Hamilton 86). She dies of cancer, and the name seems to refer to her unnamed husband's bitter grief, crying and cursing. The biblical Miriam is punished with leprosy for speaking against her brother Moses, but healed after Aaron and Moses intercede for her (Num. 12). She does die before reaching the promised land (Num. 20).

Miriam (E)
The Jewish names of the couple Saul and Miriam work together. Saul means "asked for" (Hamilton 102) and Miriam, "bitter" or "rebelliously" (Hamilton 86). Miriam has just left Saul, so her name seems appropriate. We can read Saul one of two ways: he "asked for it" in some way, or he was not the one Miriam asked for. *See also* the entry for the Miriam in MMV for more on the name.

Miserere, Vincenzo (ATD)
Vincenzo is a common name. *Miserere* is Latin for have mercy. It has no clear application to this mirror factory sales rep and probably alludes to the *Agnus Dei* sung in the Catholic mass, where *miserere nobis* (have mercy on us) occurs twice.

Misha (ATD)
Misha is the familiar name for the common Russian name Mikhail. He is inseparable from his rhyming partner Grisha.

Miskolci (ATD)
This vampire has a common Hungarian name.

Mispick, Mr. (M&D)
Mispick is a term for a defective textile machinery pick or the broken pattern in the weave produced by such a device (W3). This does not seem terribly relevant to the character. The name could be a reference to *mispickel*, an obsolete term for the mineral arsenopyrite, which can produce arsenic when heated (OED). This term has some comic relevance to a character who is an apothecary, suggesting the potential toxicity of some of his preparations.

Mitchell, Professor (MMV)
The name is common, but Pynchon's description of the character suggests a parody of one of his Cornell professors.

Given that the story was first published in *Epoch*, a Cornell literary magazine, the name is likely false.

Mitzi (ATD)
Common name.

Mixolydian, Fergus (the Irish Armenian Jew and universal man) (V)
Grant mentions Harder's gloss of the name as "Everyman" and Slade's contention of a possible source in Joyce's *Ulysses* (31). The term *Mixolydian* describes a particular musical mode, associated with dirges according to Plato (197). This seems appropriate for a character described as "the laziest living being in Nueva York" (56). The OED etymology suggests splitting the word into its roots: *mixo* means "mixed," and *Lydian* refers to a people of Asia Minor. Fergus is clearly an Irish reference; although a popular Celtic name, it usually alludes to Fergus the Great, Fergus Mac Leda, or Fergus Mac Roy (see Rolleston passim). Like the Lydians, the Armenians are also of Asia Minor. In addition to being Jewish, the character is Irish and Armenian and identified as such twice.

Mizzi, Enrico (V)
Grant identifies the historical prime minister of Malta (192).

Modestine (ATD)
Modestine is fairly common, both as given- and surname. There could be an allusion to Modestine the donkey from Robert Louis Stevenson's "Travels with a Donkey in the Cevennes." Given that the character is involved in the portrayal of white slavery, there is probably some play on the sound of "modest" or "modesty."

Moe (Vine)
Common name.

Moens, Jean-Baptiste (Lot 49)
Jean-Baptiste Moens was the author of *Bibliothèque des Timbrophiles* (mentioned in the text), a Belgian publication for stamp collectors.

Moffit (V)
Although this is a fairly common surname, it also suggests the word *mofette*, which means "An exhalation of mephitic gas escaping from a fissure" (OED). Thus we can gloss the name suggestively as "fart."

Moïsés (ATD)
This common Hebrew name is a variant of Moses.

Moistleigh, Bevis (ATD)
Bevis is a common surname, but not typically used as a given name. It recalls the astronomer John Bevis, who appeared in M&D. *Thomas Pynchon Wiki* mentions a pop-culture reference to the television show *Beavis and Butthead*, a cartoon highlighting the antics of two cretinous teenage halfwits, one of whom is named Beavis. Our Bevis is depicted as a master of applied idiotics (823), one for whom idiocy came naturally (824). *Bevis* is also a plural of *beef* (OED), which combines with the crude joke embodied in the sound of the surname "moist lay" to give one of many sexual puns in the novel.

Moldweorp (UR)
Pynchon himself glosses this name in the introduction to SL: Porpentine "is an early form of 'porcupine.' The name Moldweorp is old Teutonic for 'mole'—the animal, not the infiltrator. I thought it would be a cute idea for people named after two amiable fuzzy critters to be duking it out over the fate of Europe. Less conscientiously, there is also an echo of the name of the reluctant spy character Wormold, in Graham Greene's *Our Man in Havana*, then recently published" (19–20).

Möllner (GR)
Common name.

Molly and Dolly (M&D)
The names need to be considered together. On the surface, they seem to be a

reprise of Flip and Flop or Hanky and Panky from V, but unlike these characters who are explicitly said to be interchangeable, Molly and Dolly are not. The key to the names, of course, is in the first initials: they represent Mason and Dixon. It is important, too, that, like Mason and Dixon, they are introduced as Molly and Dolly, not Dolly and Molly. Molly is described as melancholic and Dolly as perpetually cheery in a section of the novel that amusingly draws parallels between Molly and Mason, Dolly and Dixon (300).

Molotov (GR)
Weisenburger identifies the historical "Soviet foreign affairs commissar" (258).

Mondaugen, Kurt (V, GR)
Many critics have pointed out the obvious literal meaning of the name ("moon eyes," from the German). In terms of interpretation, a common tactic is to view the meaning of the name in terms of Mondaugen's work with rockets and his romantic views of space exploration (see Blumberg 71 for an example of this view). This works for *Gravity's Rainbow* (although charactonymically, it might be a more appropriate name for Pökler), but the character appeared more than ten years previous in V. Such a reading of the name has far less textual support in V. Seed offers a better reading in which the name identifies the character's function as "a visual register" (*Fictional Labyrinths* 96). Of course this becomes problematic as Mondaugen's voyeurism degenerates to écoutrism (274) and, finally, "preferring at last neither to watch nor to listen," (278) his senses seem completely obstructed. In this sense, moon-eyes could be read as large, blank eyes, like those associated with blindness. Throughout Mondaugen's story, his role is predominantly marked by listening, especially in his official position (not an eye, but a gigantic ear to capture and record atmospheric radio disturbances). Kurt is a typical name and need not be commented on; however, if we accept Grant's reading of Mondaugen's story as "an allegory, much in the tradition of *Heart of Darkness*," (115) we might take Kurt as an allusion to Kurtz, although Grant links Foppl and von Trotha with Kurtz (123).

Monica (MMV)
Common name.

Monika (GR)
Common name.

Monkey Girl, the (GR)
The name of someone Pirate betrayed; the significance is uncertain. Her name has been replaced by an epithet.

Moonpie (Vine)
Moonpie and RC are "taken from Big Bill Liston's fifties hillbilly hit, 'Gimme an RC Cola and a Moonpie'" (Diebold and Goodwin). MoonPie is Chattanooga Bakery's registered trademark name for a snack composed of marshmallow-creme-filled chocolate-covered wafers. *See also* RC.

Moran, [Edmund] (M&D)
Browne identifies this participant in the melee described in the text (155).

Morgan, Blinky (ATD)
The details of Morgan's gang given by Pynchon — robbery of furs, shooting a police detective (59) — are drawn from history. The actual name of this notorious Cleveland criminal is Charles Conklin ("Blinky Morgan Case").

Morgan, John Pierpont (J.P.) (ATD)
The reference is to the historical financier, who is in part a model for the fictional Scarsdale Vibe.

Morituri, Ensign (GR)
Hite points out that *Morituri* is Latin for "we who are about to die" (*Ideas* 110–11), an appropriate name for someone

from Hiroshima. Weisenburger also suggests a 1964 spy thriller by W.J. Lueddecke called *Morituri*. Caesar and Aso trace the Latin surname through the Lueddecke book and subsequent film, seeing in the name a "constitutive Americanness," and an identification of the character as both exile and "hybrid, in a more overarching sense as part of a whole vocabulary for global dispersal and reconfiguration" (383). Indeed, this forms part of a general theme embodied most fully in the discussions of displaced persons, whose dubious status is one of the primary outcomes of war.

Moritz (GR)
Winston points out that Max and Moritz are the creations of nineteenth century German children's author Wilhelm Busch (73).

Morley, Professor Edward (ATD)
American physicist who, along with A.A. Michelson, performed experiments measuring the speed of light, eventually discrediting the "ether theories" mentioned throughout ATD ("Michelson-Morley experiment").

Morning (Vine)
The name is another of vaguely hippie origin pointing, at least tentatively, toward Eastern thought — in the morning the sun rises in the East.

Morris, Abraham (V)
Grant identifies the historical Bondel who returned from South Africa, as depicted by Pynchon (117).

Morrison, Mr. [Herbert] (GR)
Weisenburger identifies the historical "minister of Home Security" (80).

Mortmain (M&D)
The name is French for "dead hand": a good name for a pirate. *Mortmain* is also a legal term describing "perpetual ownership of real estate by institutions such as churches that cannot transfer or sell it," but the word can mean "the often oppressive influence of the past on the present" (AH4). He appears in a list of pirates that are mentioned in terms of the threat they pose to property and tradition. In this sense, both of these definitions give the name a highly ironic cast.

Morton, [Charles] (M&D)
Danson identifies the historical librarian and Royal Society secretary (155).

Mosh, Edna (Lot 49)
This garbled version of Oedipa Maas that comes out of the radio sounding normal is part of Pynchon's theme of (mis)communication central to the novel. Grant offers a detailed analysis (118–19).

Moss Creature, the (GR)
Like the Water Giant, this hallucination from gas huffing is a gross perversion of the natural world, showing the dangers of over-reliance on chemicals. Weisenburger points out that similar fantastic creatures often posed a threat to the comic hero Plasticman (229).

Mossmoon, Clive (GR)
Although it is a common name, Clive may refer to the character's powers and membership in the elect by way of the immensely wealthy Robert Clive of India, who will appear in M&D. See Mossmoon, Scorpia for the surname.

Mossmoon, Scorpia (GR)
The surname seems to be a distortion of the more common name Mossman, although the meaning or symbolism is unclear. Scorpia obviously suggests a poisonous or potentially deadly quality, referring to her ultimate effect on Pirate Prentice (in terms of the necessary end of their relationship because of class differences). The negative qualities of Scorpia may refer to the elect in general.

Mostly, Arnold (SI)
Arnold is a common name. Mostly has a comic sound for a name and may

suggest these brothers are mostly there, but not quite all there: their pastimes are sniffing glue and throwing mouse traps at one another.

Mostly, Kermit (SI)
Kermit is a fairly common name, but may allude to the famous muppet, Kermit the frog, created in 1955. *See* Mostly, Arnold for the surname.

Mostruccio (ATD)
This "small, ill-humored Venetian dog" who delights in "embittered assaults upon the ankles of the unwary" (255) has a name derived from two Italian words: *mostricino* (little monster) and *cuccio* (puppy).

Motley (Lot 49)
According to Grant, Motley was the actual author of one of Pynchon's sources called *Rise of the Dutch Republic*, mentioned in the novel (127).

Moufette (ATD)
From Reef's perspective, the dog is aptly named. Due to his misunderstanding of the term "lap dog" and subsequent, sensitive bite wound, he develops an understandable animosity toward Moufette, whose name is the French word for "skunk."

Mournival, Nick (M&D)
Mournival is an obsolete word from cards referring to four of a kind composed of aces, kings, queens, or jacks (OED). The sense seems to be "winning hand," which becomes clear later when the character wins Jenkins's ear at a game of cards (175). The first name of Nick recalls the familiar name for the devil.

Movay, E. Percy (ATD)
The name is a pun on a famous, if never actually uttered, saying of Galileo. *Thomas Pynchon Wiki* cites the apocryphal saying of Galileo while leaving a courtroom after being forced to recant his assertion that the Earth revolves around the Sun: "And yet it *does* move.... *Eppur si muove*" in Italian. The character is not an astronomer, though, but "a strangely possessed algebraist" (1077).

Mravenko (GR)
The name sounds plausibly Slavic, but does not seem to be a common surname. It could be a variant of the more common Marvenko.

Mucker-Maffick, Lt. Oliver (Tantivy) (GR)
Weisenburger cites Soules on *tantivy*, meaning "gallop" and *maffick*, a word created to describe the celebration of the successful British defense of Mafeking during the Boer War, and adds that a mucker is "one who employs himself in low pursuits, as in the midst of wastes and excrements" (24). *Tantivy* is also an adjective meaning "fast" and an obsolete verb meaning "to hurry away" (OED). The obsolete meaning of *tantivy* (to hurry away) seems to apply to his sudden disappearance from the Riviera. The combination of celebration and low pursuits in the surname suggests at least some affiliation with the preterite, and his orchestrated disappearance and death seems to corroborate this.

Muffage, Dr. (GR)
Muffage may come from the verb *muff*, meaning "to bungle or make some serious mistake." The meaning of the made-up word *Muffage*, then, would be "the act of muffing something up." This clearly applies to apprehending and castrating the wrong person.

Mulciber, Viktor (ATD)
Viktor is a common name. Mulciber is another name for Vulcan, the Roman god of fire; the name means "the smelter" (Harvey 280). Smelter takes on rather dark connotations referring to this arms tycoon attempting to purchase the deadly Q-weapon. His power and position are perhaps implied by a surname deriving from a Roman god.

Müller-Hochleben, Miss (Fräulein) (GR)
Blumberg observes that the English translation of this name reads "Miller High-Life" (popular pilsner beer produced by the Miller Brewing Company in Milwaukee since 1903). He stresses the American origin of the name and identifies this as a "cross-lingual" pun whose "significance becomes accessible only after translation into English" (75).

Mulligan, Meatball (E)
Although Mulligan is a common surname, the mention of this character's namesake, Gerry Mulligan (94) suggests an allusion to the jazz saxophonist. The nickname is alliterative and suggests being overweight. He seems part of the same character genealogy that contains other soft and helpless types such as "Lardass" Levine, Benny Profane, and Tyrone Slothrop.

Murray (M&D)
He is only mentioned as a friend of Nathan McClean. The context does not make clear whether Murray is a surname or a given name: it is common as each.

Musa (V)
This is a common Muslim given name meaning "prophet," referring to the biblical Moses (Ahmed 136). We only know that the character is "the boy who swept floors" at the "German" beer hall in Alexandria (89). While the other employees have Germanic names, it is significant that the lowest worker would come from the local preterite.

Mushtaq (ATD)
This common Muslim name means "longing, desiring, eager" (Ahmed 138).

Mussert, [Anton Adriaan] (GR)
Weisenburger identifies the historical Dutch fascist (but refers to him as "Adrian Mussert") (63).

Mustafa (V)
Schermerhorn identifies the historical Maltese general, whose name she spells "Mustapha" (55).

Mustapha, ("Stuffy") (M&D)
This Muslim name means "chosen, selected, preferred" (Ahmed 138). Perhaps appropriate for a Turkish sultan, but probably only intended to identify this very minor character ethnically. If the sense of chosen is intentional, the nickname Stuffy is a gentle swipe at the aristocracy.

Myers, Kit (M&D)
The official records have the name of this historical instrument bearer as Christopher Myer (Headlee 11).

Myrna (ATD)
Common name.

Nancy (GR)
Jessica Swanlake's sister has a common given name.

Nancy (GR)
Common name.

Närrisch, Klaus (GR)
In German the surname means "crazy or scatterbrained." There is little evidence of its appropriateness for this minor character in any important way. It is probably another comic-derisive name.

Narvik (ATD)
This owner of Narvik's Mush-It-Away Northern Cuisine is appropriately named — Narvik is a town in the northernmost part of Norway.

Nash (GR)
See Salitieri, Poore, Nash, De Brutus, and Short.

Naunt, Arturo (ATD)
Arturo is a common name. *Naunt* is an archaic British term for "aunt." It is another example of Pynchon's love for obscure words.

Nebulay, Barry (ATD)

This Irish mathematician has a common Irish given name with a surname sounded as the plural of *nebula*, usually referring to a cloudlike cluster of stars, but, recalling here, perhaps, a secondary meaning of something ill-defined, insubstantial, or hazy (OED). This would apply more to the atmosphere of the passage (involving exchanges between drunken mathematicians) than the character himself.

Nefastis, John (Lot 49)

Grant cites Nicholson who suggests "*Nefas* means unspeakable and unpleasing to the gods," Palmeri, who claims Nefastis connotes "unholy, unclean, abominable," Abernathy, who sees a link with the word "nefarious," and himself suggests that there may be a connection with the Greek word *nifas* meaning "flake" or "snowflake" (67). Seed echoes Abernathy by suggesting the connotation of "impious or wicked" (*Fictional Labyrinths* 147). Hayes offers the amusing reading of the name as "Johnny Fastest" but also suggests the French word *nefaste*, meaning "unlucky" (36 note 7). The French *nefaste* can also mean "harmful" or "ill-fated." All of these readings seem feasible and the name would appear to be another example of onomastic overdetermination in the novel.

Neil (V)

Common name.

Nemacolin (M&D)

Bailey identifies this assistant to Thomas Cresap while "building a road from Wills' Creek to the Monongahela" (94) and friend to Daniel Cresap (165).

Nerissa (LL)

Hollander recalls that Portia's handmaiden in the *Merchant of Venice* was named Nerissa ("Pynchon's Politics" 33). The name derives from the Nereids, or sea nymphs of Greek mythology: "beautiful, benevolent, but ill-defined creatures" (Harvey 286). The description applies well to Nerissa, as her very reality is not entirely clear.

Nessel, Dr. (M&D)

Nessel is German for "nettle" (the stinging plant, not the act of irritating someone). The name does not refer to any easily identifiable German engineer of the period. One is tempted to look for some comedy or even a charactonymic reference in the name, but Nessel seems to be a fairly common German surname.

Neville (ATD)

He always appears with his sidekick Nigel, partner in chronic drug abuse. Both names are common and chosen for alliteration. There is a chance that the source for the duo's names is one of the following. Famous Welsh cartoonist Grenfell Jones created the pair of "message-bearing sheep" called "Nigel and Neville" ("Welsh Cartoonist Retires"). Twin brothers Nigel and Neville Stronge died in a car crash in Ireland in 2000 ("Twins Killed"). There is a comic theater duo named Ted and Lee who created two characters named Nigel and Neville who are children's literature critics ("Ted and Company").

Niccolò (Lot 49)

Another Italian name for a character in *The Courier's Tragedy*, it could also refer to Nick (a common name for the devil [OED]). Although he is the reputed "good guy" of the play, there is some degree of reversal in the play's character names where the "good" (including Ercole, the pagan hero Hercules) confront the "evil" (Angelo-Angel: faithless Domenico, recalling the Dominicans; Pasquale-Paschal/Easter; Francesca, perhaps recalling the Franciscans). In this reading, the state and religion are aligned with evil, while coup, disruption, and anarchy are aligned with the good.

Nicholas (M&D)
See Abraham.

Nicholas II (Lot 49)
Grant points out that the historical context of this section of the novel would require this figure to be Tsar Alexander II, not Nicholas.

Nigel (ATD)
He always appears with his sidekick Neville, partner in chronic drug abuse. Both names are common and chosen for alliteration. *See also* Neville.

Nikos (ATD)
The miners in this section have common ethnic names. Nikos is a common Greek name.

Nipple, Lloyd (GR)
Here we have another Rabelaisian body-part name. Although we may read names derived from sexual or excretory body parts as transgressive, there is no specific meaning for this minor character.

Nita (V)
Common name.

Noboru (Vine)
Although Noboru seems to be a fairly common Japanese name, the word means "rise, go up, amount to, reach, or be promoted" (Yoshitaro 1378–9). It seems ironic for someone with "the air of a servant."

Nocturna, Domina (GR)
This name of Katje's incarnation as dominatrix literally means "lady night" from the Latin. She is meant to be a figure of death anthropomorphized, but we could also read the title as "lady of the night," as she acts as a kind of prostitute to occupy Pudding while Pointsman pursues his interests without interference. Weisenburger associates the name with witches and offers some background from Grimm (123).

Nookshaft, Nicholas (ATD)
Nicholas is a common name, chosen for alliteration when joined with the surname. Nookshaft is a Dickensian sounding name, but may have sexual connotations. A nook is a hidden spot or small opening and a shaft is a long pole, but as a verb, *shaft* can mean "to have intercourse."

Norma (GR)
See Girls, Slothrop's.

Nosepicker, Neil (GR)
A simple transgressive/Rabelaisian joke-name, whose comedy is emphasized by alliteration.

Noseworth, Lindsay (ATD)
Although Dickensian sounding, Noseworth is a fairly common name, as is Lindsay. At the center of the name is the phrase "say No," which is apt for the ship's disciplinarian.

Nuit, The Reverend Dr. Paul de la (GR)
Larsson offers a fine gloss of this name: "A double pun: '*Pall* [dark and gloomy covering] *of the night*'; also 'Pall *de l'ennui* [of boredom]'" (V81.17) [square bracketed interpretations and emphasis in the original].

O'Brian, Pat (M&D)
Clerc suggests that the character is named for the prolific nautical writer Patrick O'Brian (1914–2000) (120). This seems clear, as the character is portrayed as writing "More Sea Stories" and being the expert on rigging (54).

O'Leary, Peter (V)
Geronimo's alias is self-explanatory in the context of the passage where it occurs. It may also refer to the tendency of Irish families of the time to send a son to the seminary.

O'Rooney, Wolfe Tone (ATD)
O'Rooney is a common Irish name and Wolfe Tone was a famous eighteenth

century Irish revolutionary. The name is quite appropriate to this travelling Irish insurrectionist.

O'Rooty (M&D)
The character is designated as a "Crimp," a deceptive agent who tricks others into doing heavy labor, especially military service (Ware, "*Mason and Dixon*"), or "Body-jobber." He seems a parody of the contemporary parasitical temporary agency, but the name has no clear association with the character.

Oafery, Lud (M&D)
Lud is an obsolete term for "buttocks" and Oafery, from *oaf*, suggests stupidity. We may gloss the name as "Dumb Ass"—a clear charactonym for this character.

Oafery, Ma (M&D)
Given the use of *Ma* rather than mom, mother, mum, etc., a pun on "my ovary" seems likely. *See also* Oafery, Ludd.

Obliterator, The (ATD)
The title of this otherwise nameless character sounds quite sinister, yet he is a benefactor of Reef Traverse, who thinks of him as a "crypto-Anarchist" (1074), suggesting that this customs official obliterates information that could incriminate would-be radicals.

Obrenovich, Alexander (ATD)
Serbian king assassinated in 1903.

Obrenovich, Draga (ATD)
Serbian queen assassinated in 1903.

Octave the barman (ATD)
He is given a common French name and also an occupational epithet. Nothing in this very minor character suggests that the number eight or the musical interval is relevant.

Odo (ATD)
Odo is a male name, albeit not terribly common, meaning "rich" (Kolatch 177). It is appropriate for someone saving up to buy his own dime museum. Of course it also has a primitive sound well matched to his typical speech: "Unnhhrrhhh!" (394).

Oeuillade, Jean-Raoul (ATD)
The given name is common. The surname seems to be a corruption or variant of the French *œillade* (wink), which suggests associatively the titillating nature of his operetta.

Oily Leon (M&D)
The character took part in a revenge massacre, and the derisive nickname is probably meant to characterize him as slippery—note the repetition of the sound *lee* in his name, which sounds vaguely suggestive when spoken.

Okandio (GR)
Fowler identifies *okandio* as a Herero word meaning "little bell" (272). Like most of the purely Herero names, it does not seem to have any special application to the character.

Old Clasher, the (M&D)
The nickname probably refers to the noun *clasher* (one who clashes or collides) (OED), but may also refer to clashing as fighting as he appears in a story told by Dixon presumably involving an altercation between Billy Snowball and the Old Clasher, whose head Mr. Snowball mistook for an ale can (503).

"Old Man," the (ATD)
The commandant receives this nickname from the boys for obvious reasons, but his actual name is never given.

Olga (GR)
Common name.

Ölsch, Etzel (GR)
Fowler believes the character to be historical despite the lack of reference to him in the writings of Albert Speer or other Nazi materials (159). Weisenburger identifies him as fictional and cites

the narrator's gloss of *Etzel* as Attila the Hun and *Öl* as the German for "oil" (157). The name may be read as "oily Hun."

Ombindi, Josef of Hannover (GR)
Both Fowler (271) and Weisenburger (164) explain that the name derives from the Herero word *o-mbinda*, meaning "wild pig." This is not a charactonymic reference, but part of a complex sequence of porcine imagery throughout the novel, whose origin and development are far too complex to be explored here. The "Josef of ..." construction evokes Joseph of Arimathea. There may be a link between the foundation of Christianity, which has developed in modern times, according to Pynchon, in a negative direction with disastrous consequences, and Ombindi's group, the Empty Ones, and their drive toward racial suicide through attempts to complete what the Germans started in southwest Africa at the beginning of the century.

Omnopon, André (GR)
As one of the Zone's drug-using musicians, Omnopon is appropriately named. The OED defines *Omnopon* as "the British proprietary name of a particular mixture of opium alkaloids (known in the U.S. as 'Pantopon')."

Omuzire, Mieczislav (GR)
Like Enzian, whose father was Russian, Mieczislav has a name that reflects the violence of external political forces, though not colonialism as such. Many of the Africans in the novel are portrayed within the context of struggle between traditional/native qualities and Western forces. Africans who were conceived by foreign interlopers and African women became physical manifestations of this conflict. The last name is a Herero word meaning "shadows" (Fowler 272). There does not seem to be special significance in the meaning of *omuzire*, but the linking of African and Western is central to the identity conflict suffered by many of the Herero characters in the novel.

Oneida (ATD)
Oneida is the name of a North American Indian nation. The character is only mentioned in passing, so the name can have no clear relevance to the character.

Onguruve (GR)
According to Fowler (271) and Weisenburger (167), *onguruve* is another Herero word for pig. Again, the pig symbol in GR is complex: the name has no clear significance for this character.

Oof, Scott (Vine)
Oof is a comic onomatopoeic name with no special significance for this character.

Opera singer, the (ATD)
The only miner not given a name, the opera singer goes by this epithet. Presumably he is named for a habit of singing opera snatches in the mines, barring the possibility that he was formerly an opera singer.

Ophir, Mme. (GR)
Ophir was an uncertain location mentioned in the Old Testament where one could obtain fine gold (OED). Blicero's sable merkin manufactured by Mme. Ophir is a treasure of a somewhat different kind. Fowler unaccountably suggests that she may have been an actual historical figure (114), but provides no evidence.

Orozco, Pasqual (ATD)
Mexican rebel leader in the Guerrero District of Chihuahua, Mexico (Gonzales 77).

Orukambe, Andreas (GR)
Orukambe is Herero for "horse" (Gestwicki 151). Notice that the tribal name combines with a German given name, as is the case with may of the Hereros.

Oruni, Dr. (Vine)
The name of this Japanese doctor has no obvious meaning — at least it does not seem to derive from a common Japanese word or to be a common surname.

Oruru (GR)
The name is probably a variant of the Herero *orure*, meaning "long time" or "protracted" (Gestwicki 152). In the novel, Enzian anxiously awaits his arrival, giving the name a charactonymic quality.

Orutyene (GR)
Weisenburger identifies *orutyene* as a Herero word meaning "steep" (302). Like most of the purely Herero names, it does not seem to have any special application to the character.

Osmo, Lord Blatherard (GR)
Osmo refers to the sense of smell, but could be used here to mean smelly. More likely this is a reference to the location of "the giant Adenoid: Lodged as he also is in the pharynx of Lord Blatherard Osmo, the Adenoid satirizes the nasal characteristics of upper-crust British speech; at least, he satirizes how that speech sounds to preterite ears" (Weisenburger 22). Blather, of course, is loud foolish talk, so a "Blather-hard" should be one who continuously spouts nonsense. As a whole, the name should be read as a derisive description of the ruling class. Larsson suggests that *osmo* refers to osmosis, "the process by which the giant Adenoid would absorb its victims" (V14.34).

Otis (Vine)
Common name.

Otis (ATD)
A common name for a minor "character" only mentioned once.

Ottician, Vastroslav (ATD)
Vastroslav is a variant of Vatroslav, a common Slavic name. *See* Ottician, Zlatko for the surname.

Ottician, Zlatko (ATD)
Zlatko is a common Slavic name. The surname, like that of his cousin Vlado Clissan (from Clissa), is tied to a location. It is a variant of Ottocian (from the town of Ottocac). Like Clissan, it is also an Uskok name, referring to refugee families after the Turkish conquest of Bosnia and Herzegovina ("Uskoks").

Otyiyumbu, Jan (GR)
Weisenburger points out that *otyiyumbu* means "firebrand" in Herero and deems it appropriate for a spy in London (273). Notice, too, the Dutch first name, indicating conflict with the native surname as is the case with many of the Herero characters.

Oust, Ewball (ATD)
A ridiculous sounding name on the surface, it does have meaning. To oust means to eject by force, or take the place of (AH4), apt associations for an anarchist revolutionary. On the other hand, the name applies to his situation: he has been ousted from his home by his family (374). Ewball suggests *screwball*, "an eccentric, impulsively whimsical, or irrational person" (AH4), somewhat descriptive of the character, but probably used more for comic effect.

Oust, Ewball Sr. (ATD)
See Oust, Ewball.

Oust, Moline Velma (ATD)
Velma is a common name. She sees herself as a kind of protege of Baby Doe Tabor, who came from Chicago to marry the Tabor money. It is appropriate that she is named Moline, after a smaller city in Illinois, west of Chicago on the opposite side of the state, and she, too, headed west to Leadville to marry her money. *See* Oust, Ewball for the surname.

Oust, Toplady (ATD)
Another outrageous sounding name, it is harder to define as it applies to a male

Overbaby

character. Toplady would connote high social position for a female character. Perhaps it is a comic name suggesting the act of mounting a woman. There may also be an allusion to Augustus Montague Toplady, eighteenth-century minister and poet, author of "Rock of Ages" and many other lesser known hymns. *See* Oust, Ewball for the surname.

Overbaby, Terrence (GR)

Another punning name for a dead airman: "it's over, baby."

Overlunch, Lady (ATD)

See Overlunch, Lord.

Overlunch, Lord (ATD)

While Overlunch suggests the phrase "over lunch," as in meeting over lunch or discussing something over lunch, the sound is undeniably comic, suggesting overeat, perhaps. The Overlunches live in a manor called Bananas, and are associated with the appropriately named T.W.I.T. The excess in the name heightens the description of the surroundings and the comic imbecility of the name furthers the extent to which these idle rich are critiqued for their adherence to fashion, even in the ludicrous case of the gown made of soiled printer's muslin, "enjoying just then a great chic among the bohemian of spirit" (900).

Owlglass, Rachel (V)

A number of critics have identified Owlglass as the English word for Eulenspiegel, the medieval German jester (OED). Grant dismisses any implications of this name (11), but it may have more descriptive value for Rachel's father, Stuyvesant Owlglass (q.v.). The OED also defines Owlglass as "the prototype of roguish fools or any buffoons." Again, this may be more useful for Rachel's father. The name Rachel, of course, begins with the biblical reference. Grant cites Richter in pointing out that Rachel was Benjamin's mother and identifies the maternal aspect of the relationship of Rachel and Benny (11). Interestingly, the biblical Rachel died just after giving birth to Benjamin and naming him (Gen. 35:18–19). Another fascinating reading of the name Rachel may seem far-fetched, but Pynchon's love of obscure words as well as his preface to SL (see page 12) suggest a keen familiarity with the OED. The only definition for the word *rachel* in the OED glosses it as a "light tannish color." A historical example taken from an 1887 advertisement mentions its use in identifying the color of face powder: one color is for fair skin, one for dark skin, and Rachel is for use "by artificial light." Given Rachel's introduction as living wholly in a world of inanimate objects, the first of which is her MG, it seems fair to read the name as an inanimate marker. In this sense, we can read *Owlglass* ("jester") as a marker of the animate.

Owlglass, Stuyvesant (V)

See Owlglass, Rachel especially on Eulenspiegel. His given name recalls the wealthy old New York family, the Stuyvesants. The two names together could be glossed as "rich clown," and as a general poke at the wealthy, but the name is probably meant to reemphasize that Rachel comes from a family of old money.

Oyswharf, Dr. (ATD)

This "mad scientist" has a ridiculous sounding name with no clear meaning. *Thomas Pynchon Wiki* suggests possible echoes of Osbie Feel from GR and August Owsley Stanley III, the king of the LSD trade, but also offers the more appealing "Oyster Wharf," pointing out the role of oyster-related information in the novel (*Thomas Pynchon Wiki*). The latter also recalls Pynchon's home town of Oyster Bay, Long Island.

Ozohande, "Sparks" (GR)

The surname derives from the Herero word *ozohanja*, meaning "reflection"

(Gestwicki 164). The combined name, then, forms the common phrase "sparks reflection." There is no evidence that the name is particularly descriptive of the character.

Paco (E)
Common Hispanic name.

Paco-from-the-Moon (SI)
Paco is a common Mexican name. He is one of three named cellmates of Carl McAfee. Big Knife is a direct charactonym, and Fauntleroy is largely ironic. If Paco is common, "from-the-Moon" may suggest he is crazy, a lunatic from the Spanish for moon, *luna*.

Padzhitnoff, Captain Igor (ATD)
This captain of the Russian balloon *Bol'shaia Igra* ("The Great Game" [123]) is named for the co-creator of the great, and wildly popular computer game Tetris. Alexy Pajitnov (also Pazhitnov) and Vadim Gerasimov developed this game, whose object is to rotate various four-square shapes as they fall, so as to join them together without leaving any gaps (Gerasimov). Lindsay of the Chums of Chance characterizes the *Bol'shaia Igra's* crew's mode of dispatching enemies in terms of the "quadruple brickbats it is your delight to drop on anyone you take a dislike to" (258). Gerasimoff refers to the four-square pieces as "tetraliths," while Pajitnov's term is "tetramino." Should anyone familiar with the game of Tetris have missed the reference up until now, a description of a failed assassination attempt, where the victim ends up standing inside the angle of a right-angled fragment (258), conjures up the image of that very familiar game piece so clearly that the allusion to the game is certain. Perhaps only manically devoted gamers, though, would recognize the names of the creators of Tetris (Pajitnov and Gerasimov) in the *Bol'shaia Igra* crew members Padzhitnoff and Gerasimoff.

Pagano, Patsy (V)
The name can be considered a doubling of sorts, combining function and description. Harder rightly suggests that the character is a "patsy" for the SPs, but cannot find meaning in the connotations of *pagano* (75). *Pagano* is Italian for "pagan" or "heathen." We might interpret this as a preterite marker in a largely Christian society. His role as patsy, being battered in the stomach with a nightstick by the law-enforcing lackeys of the elect, must be connected to his identity as heathen or nonmember. The preterite is always the patsy.

Palladino, Eusapia (ATD)
"[L]usty, illiterate Italian peasant" and "renowned Neopolitan medium" (Oppenheim 149).

Paloverde (ATD)
Palo Verde is a California city. It is not a common surname. *Palo* is Spanish for "stick" or "pole" and can be used for "tree" as well. *Verde* means "green" but also "young." He appears only in a list of friends of young Jesse Traverse, so the associations of youth are appropriate.

Pancho the Bassoon Player (ATD)
Frank's alias when he joins Gastón Villa and His Bughouse Bandoleros is a clear reference to the Mexican revolutionary Pancho Villa, whose actual name was Francisco.

Pankhurst, Sylvia (ATD)
The reference is to the British political activist, artist, and suffragette. While she stayed in Holloway prison and did design logos and icons for various political groups, Pynchon's source on "the brooch of honor designed by Sylvia Pankhurst for veterans of residence in that dismal place [Holloway]" is uncertain. The DNB does not mention it (Hannam).

Parker, "Yardbird" [Charlie] (GR)
Weisenburger identifies the historical jazz saxophonist (46).

Pasarella, Nunzi (SI)
Both are common Italian surnames.

Pascoe (ATD)
A common surname for a very minor character.

Pasha, Fehim (ATD)
Former head of espionage in Turkey who was assassinated when the Young Turks consolidated power in 1908 ("Turkey").

Pasquale (Lot 49)
Another character from *The Courier's Tragedy*, Pasquale has a typical Italianate name. We should note that the name means "paschal," referring to Easter, and may connect to the religious/Pentecostal theme that runs through the novel.

Pasquale (ATD)
Common Italian name.

Passerine, Loren (Lot 49)
Grant cites Watson on the relation of "Passerine" to an order of birds that "includes the passerine ground-dove" and suggests that this is another reference to Pentecost (139). The AH4 defines the order as containing perching and song birds, both appropriate to an auction "crier." If we combine this with *lore*, there may be a suggestion that when the "crying" begins, Passerine will reveal some secret facts or accumulated knowledge. Petillon suggests that he will "pass 'er into the other kingdom" and establishes a link with rights of passage and *The Tibetan Book of the Dead* (138). He also identifies the name as connected to *passerino*, meaning "sparrow" in Italian, but also "a fond nickname for the penis" (165 note 24). Colvile suggests the gloss "initiator" and sees a link with Passover (20).

Patrizia (ATD)
Common Italian name.

Patsy (M&D)
The name is a common Irish one. Given the context and the time period, any Irish name would mark one as preterite. The meaning of the word *patsy* ("someone to be taken advantage of") does not seem to apply here.

Pattison, Jill (SI)
Both the given- and the surname are quite common.

Pauer, Professor (GR)
Weisenburger does not find a reference to this individual. Pynchon may have found him in a source not yet identified, or he could be contrived, but *Pauer* does not seem to exist in German. It could be a variation on *Pauker*, the familiar name for a teacher, or its meaning could be connected to the pronunciation ("power"). Neither of these readings, however, is ultimately convincing.

Paul (V)
See also Augustine, Bartholomew, Ignatius, Teresa, and Veronica. Fairing probably names this rat for St. Paul the epistle writer, who, interestingly, was shipwrecked at Malta (a central location in the novel) on the way to his trial in Rome (Farmer 381).

Pavel (GR)
Another African with a Slavic and Christian name (Paul), Pavel has a name showing the Western influence on the tribe.

Paxtons, the (M&D)
The Paxton boys are quite real. For a wealth of historical information in the form of primary documents regarding the Paxtons and the massacres, see Dunbar, John R. ed. *The Paxton Papers*. The Hague: Martinus Nijhoff, 1957.

Peach, Sam (M&D)
The DNB identifies this son of the Reverend Samuel Peach (Williams, "Bradley, James (bap. 1692, d. 1762)").

Peach, Samuel (M&D)
The DNB identifies the Reverend Samuel Peach as the brother of Susannah

Peach, wife of the astronomer James Bradley (Williams, "Bradley, James (bap. 1692, d. 1762)").

Peach, Susannah (M&D)
The DNB identifies this wife of astronomer James Bradley (Williams, "Bradley, James (bap. 1692, d. 1762)").

Pegeen (M&D)
An ordinary name, but the character who bears it is linked to Maureen to form one of several pairs in the novel.

Pelham, Mr. [Henry] (M&D)
The DNB identifies the historical prime minister (Kulisheck).

Penelope (GR)
Common name.

Penhallow, Constance (ATD)
Both names are common, but *see* Penhallow, Hunter on the surname.

Penhallow, Hunter (ATD)
Hunter is a common name, as is Penhallow. As he is an artist, however, we may read a charactonymic element in the surname. To hallow is to sanctify or make holy (OED). This combined with *pen* suggests the power of art to sanctify, appropriate for an artist.

Penn, [John] (M&D)
The DNB identifies this colonial governor of Pennsylvania (Carter).

Penny (Vine)
Common name.

Pennycomequick, Lord (M&D)
After adjusting for inflation, the surname might be rendered "Fastbuck," an appropriately charactonymic name for a "global-Communications Nabob" (721).

Pensiero, Eddie (GR)
Weisenburger suggests that the surname is related to the Italian for "thought" or the Latin for "thinking" (271). The significance of this is uncertain. The Latin *pensare*, however, also means "to ponder or weigh out" as well as "to requite or to repay." As this section of the novel ends with Pensiero holding the tips of his scissors over the colonel's jugular vein, we can certainly read the name as one who considers (murder) and repays the colonel for his position in the military and the war. Larsson notes that the entire name is a pun on a line from Verdi's *Rigoletto—E di pensiero* (and her thoughts) (V640.30).

Perdoo, Floyd (GR)
As Larsson points out, the surname derives from the French adjective *perdu(e)*, meaning "lost" (V270.16). It is an appropriate name given his success rate at finding Slothrop's girls.

Perkins, Mezzanine (ATD)
Perkins is a common surname. *Mezzanine* means "a partial storey between two main stories of a building" (AH4). Perhaps this reference to being "in between" is an oblique reference to this character's penchant for interracial dating (1042).

Perlimpinpin, Georges "Poudre" de la (GR)
Weisenburger points out that *poudre* is French for "powder" and that *perlimpinpin* is French slang for "dash" or "soupçon." He demonstrates the meaning of the combination of the words with a phrase meaning "that's a bunch of baloney" (128). Since de la Perlimpinpin is a fireworks magnate, we can read the nickname as a reference to *poudre explosif*, that is, gunpowder. The shades of meaning of *de la poudre de perlimpinpin* are also more complex. The *Collins Robert French Dictionary* translates the phrase as "the universal remedy" used ironically, or "a magic cure-all." George's worldview, then, is tied to explosives, or we might read, violence.

Perlimpinpin, Raoul de la (GR)
See Perlimpinpin, Georges "Poudre" de la. We should consider the father's

nickname in connection with the son. Given the role of drugs at Raoul's house and parties, we should remember that *poudre* is also an *argot* term for heroin. Looking again at the phrase *de la poudre de la perlimpinpin* (for Raoul is *le fils de la poudre de perlimpinpin*), we can associate Raoul's worldview with drugs (perhaps as a different panacea). Given the 1973 publication of the novel and Pynchon's use of countercultural slang, the name of a father and son identify a cultural/generational shift from warfare to drugs.

Perril, Nurse Margaret (ATD)
She was an actual nurse at the Miners' Hospital in Telluride (Backus 76).

Pétard (V)
The name is French for "din" or "racket." Harder claims the name "may have the etymological meaning 'to break wind'" (73-4), but *péter* means "to fart." Surely a name meaning "din or racket" is a suitably ironic one for a musicologist.

Peter (M&D)
See Abraham.

Peters, Rev^d [Richard] (M&D)
Mason mentions this line commissioner in his journal (194).

Petitpoint, Robin (V)
As Harder points out, a petitpoint is "a small stitch in embroidery" (77), and his assertion that this seems meaningless is reasonable. Perhaps it comes from the French for a small point or place. This agrees somewhat with his description as a "mild-faced clergy man."

Petrie, Mr. Flinders (V)
Grant identifies the historical Egyptologist (49).

Peychaud, Monsieur (ATD)
Antoine Amédé Peychaud created the Sazerac cocktail.

Pflaumbaum (GR)
The name literally means "plum tree" in German. It is uncertain if the name is meant to suggest his Jewishness or if it has any other significance.

Phantom Filer, the (ATD)
Self-explanatory in context, this supernatural creature (or excuse for poor performance) uses a file on harmonicas "to alter notes and create difficulties" (421).

Philippe (GR)
Common French name.

Philippe (ATD)
The miners in this section have common ethnic names. Philippe is a common French name.

Phoebe (M&D)
Common name.

Piali (V)
Schermerhorn identifies the historical son-in-law of the sultan (55).

Piang, Chu (GR)
Although not introduced with an occupational/descriptive epithet, he is given two: "the comical Chinese swamper" (339) and "the Chinese factotum" (346). The name is plausibly Chinese but may refer to his heavy drug use through two words: *chu*, "cut grass" (Jingrong 101), referring obliquely to marijuana; *pian*, "slanting" or "leaning" (Jingrong 517), referring to his constant tripping over his mop, partly brought about by opium use.

Pierce, Lieutenant (SR)
Pierce is a common surname, but the word as a verb seems to be an intentional allusion. He is linked through intelligence and background to Levine: "Outwardly neither had any use for the other; but each had the vague sense that they were more alike than either would care to admit, brothers, possibly, under the skin" (33). The name seems specially relevant to this last phrase. Hollander suggests that the

name recalls Franklin Pierce, "fourteenth President of the United States, whose term (1853–1857) marked continued attempts to avoid civil war" ("Pynchon's Politics" 26). Part of his (convincing) larger argument is that Pynchon frequently invokes (often quite obliquely) times and places where circumstances foretold imminent civil war.

Pierpont (ATD)
See Morgan, John Pierpont.

Piet (GR)
Common Dutch name.

Pike-Leeming (V)
One of several hyphenated pseudo-British names, which may be modelled in part on those of Evelyn Waugh, such as Mrs. Beste-Chetwynde from *Decline and Fall*, for example, Pike-Leeming combines two obsolete words: the verb *pike* can mean to "make off with oneself, go away quickly ... [or figuratively] to die" (OED); *leeming* is a variant of *lemming*, a creature whose odd migration habits are suicidal. Pike-Leeming was with Godolphin when he saw Vheissu, and has been whisked away to a house in Wales, where he remains incurably mad and incapable of feeling anything (183).

Pilar (V)
One of the two girls Geronimo calls when Angel is upset at the prospect of Fina accompanying them to get "coño," Pilar is categorically defined as a "girl" rather than a source of sex. The name is appropriate as it derives from a title for the Virgin Mary, *Nuestra Señora del Pilar* (Our Lady of the Pillar) (Hanks and Hodges 268).

Pinguez (V)
Harder cites the name as a variant of *pinguid*, "fat, oily, greasy" (74). Given the ending of the name, it is probably from the Spanish cognate *pingüe*, with the same meaning as the English *pinguid*.

Pinguid, Peter (Lot 49)
Grant glosses the name as "greasy prick" citing the OED on *pinguid* meaning greasy or oily and referring to *peter* as slang for penis (49). The derision in the name seems directed at anyone associated with right-wing organizations: Peter Pinguid Society member Mike Fallopian characterizes the John Birch Society as "our more left-leaning friends" (50).

Pinky (ATD)
Given that the blond girls at Girton College, Cambridge view Yashmeen as "the dark rock on our northern shore" (493), Pinky is an ironic nickname to be given to one of dark complexion by those with fair skin.

Pinky, Uncle (Vine)
Pinky is a fairly common male nickname.

Pino (ATD)
Common Italian name.

Piper, Mrs. [Leonora] (ATD)
Late nineteenth-century medium (Oppenheim 147).

Pippo (ATD)
This "Italian kid" character in the Li'l Jailbirds is "played by a negro" (1047). This comic set piece is helped along by the use of this common Italian name.

Piprake, Giles (ATD)
Giles is a common name, but suggests the noun *guile* (cunning): there is "no known problem he can't sort out" (866). The surname is a comic one formed on *pipsqueak*, but with the modified ending *-rake* supplying a note of lasciviousness. He delights in jokes of the that's-not-what-your-wife-said-last-night variety (866).

Pisk, Zipi (Vine)
Pisk is a relatively common surname. Hite suggests that Zipi "has something to do with comic-strip character Zippy ('Are

we having fun yet?') the Pinhead" ("Feminist Theory" 152 note 25). This is not entirely clear.

Pitt (M&D)

The twins are each named for two historical figures (an elder and a younger) so that they might forgo the conflicts of being either the first or second born. Pitt is named for William Pitt (the elder, 1708–1778; the younger 1759–1806).

Pitt, J. Peter (GR)

Another of Slothrop's Harvard classmates, Pitt is probably meant to be a descendant of the powerful British family.

Pityu (ATD)

The name is common in Hungary, but we may be invited to associate the character with the sound of his name in English, "pity you." The conversation between Kit, Dally, and Pityu suggests sympathy on the part of Pityu (914).

Pivoine, Professeur (ATD)

The surname is French for *peony*, a plant with large, usually pink or red flowers. Reef goes to see him after being injured in an explosion. He is described as "a sort of neighborhood couturier of flesh wounds" (851). Perhaps the large, ragged flowers of the peony are meant to suggest flesh wounds by visual association.

Pizzini (GR)

Pizzini is a common Italian surname. Part of "The Occupation of Mingeborough" scene, Pizzini appears among other characters who were first in "The Secret Integration," which takes place in Mingeborough. Although Pizzini does not appear in that story, there are numerous Italian names in "The Secret Integration." *See also* Dufay, Kim.

Plebecula (ATD)

Plebecula is Latin for "rabble," from *plebius*, "plebian" or "common." The name is appropriate for this daughter of anarchist Reef and Yashmeen. There may also be some comic play on the ending of the name, *-cula*, recalling Dracula.

Plechazunga, the Pig-Hero (GR)

The name is connected to lightning and myths related to Thor. Weisenburger offers background on the word and Pynchon's use of Grimm as a source (245).

Pliny (M&D)

Like his twin brother Pitt, Pliny is named for a pair of historical figures: Pliny the Elder (Gaius Plinius Secundus 23–79) and Pliny the Younger (61/2–113). Together the twin's names provide the alliteration often favored by the parents of twins.

Ploce, Lt. Col. Virgil ("Sparky") (Vine)

Ploce is a rhetoric term meaning "the repetition of a word for emphasis" (OED). In the context of his appearance in the novel, it may refer to America's repeated attempts to assassinate Castro, the first of which is said to have been tried by Ploce. Of course, that *ploce* is used solely in rhetoric makes us think of the Roman poet when we see the name Virgil. Sparky Ploce may be a pun on "spark plug," referring to the exploding cigar he is said to have offered Castro.

Ploy (V)

A character wholly reduced to his name. After Navy dentists pull all of his teeth against his will and replace them with artificial ones, his life is reduced to one unchanging ploy: biting the buttocks of people (usually barmaids, but one Marine) with his sharpened dentures. The lack of a first name heightens the degree to which the name acts purely as description.

Plunkitt, Jed (GR)

Common name.

Plush, Fiona (ATD)

Fiona is a common name, but *plush* captures the character rather nicely. The word typically means "luxurious" and the character is presented as "curvaceous" and "presentable" as a model for statuary (894). *Plush* is also historical naval slang for any surplus after rationing (OED), keeping the sense of excess, but also pointing to Pynchon's own nautical past.

Poehlmann (GR)
Weisenburger identifies this historical scientist (199).

Pointsman, Mr. Edward W. A. (GR)
The narrator explains the meaning of the name late in the novel: "He is the pointsman. He is called that because he throws the lever that changes the points.... The lever is very smooth, and easy to push.... He has sent us all the way to Happyville, instead of to Pain City. That is because he knows just where the points and the lever are" (644–45). *Pointsman* is a British term; the American equivalent is *switchman*, "the one who directs rail cars onto the proper tracks." The obvious reference to our Mr. Pointsman immediately concerns his deep commitment to behaviorism as a means of controlling human beings. Hohmann extends this reading by saying "Pointsman ... wants to create a 'happy' mankind by applying Pavlovian conditioning techniques" (355–56). He also connects *pointsman* to determinism and claims that the character is a slave to cause and effect (166). Earle points out that discussions of the pointsman image occur in studies of free will by James Clerk Maxwell, Sir James Jeans, and Sándor Ferenczi, all of whom Pynchon could have read (232), and he points out the ironic aspect of the name concerning "his inability to be his own pointsman, though he tries to be everyone else's" (233).

Pökler, Franz (GR)
The surname derives from the German *pökeln*, "to salt" (as in to preserve or pickle). It may refer to preservation in another sense as all members of the family (although Ilse is not certain) manage to survive the war and the Nazis through various tactics.

Pökler, Ilse (GR)
Ilse is a common German name. *See* Pökler, Franz for the surname.

Pökler, Leni (GR)
Leni is chosen as a first name to allow Franz to call her Lenin (see page 162), referring to her socialism. *See* Pökler, Franz for the surname.

Policarpe (ATD)
A fairly common name, although usually spelled Polycarp, after the saint.

Pomidor, Thetis (ATD)
The juxtaposition of given- and surname creates, on one level, an interesting contrast: Thetis was a Nereid, a greek Goddess, while the name Pomidor derives from the Italian for tomato. But the word *tomato* itself is a slang term in American English, popular in the 1950s, meaning "a very attractive girl or young woman" (Wenthworth and Flexner 549). Reading the first name as equivalent to "goddess" we get a charactonym and a doubling. Thetis provides another possibility in context. The character, though seemingly racist to an extent, is introduced along with Mezzanine Perkins during a conversation about interracial romance. Like Mezzanine, whose name may refer to such relationships, Thetis recalls the goddess who, because it was foretold her son would be more powerful than Zeus, was forced to marry the mortal Peleus (they were the parents of Achilles) (Harvey 309). This classical echo may refer obliquely to the white-black dating issue under discussion.

Ponghill, Brad (ATD)
Ponghill is a parish in Cornwall, so it is conceivable that people from that region might have the name, but it is certainly not common. The brothers — Brad, Buddy, and Burke — all have common names, clearly chosen for their alliteration.

Ponghill, Buddy (ATD)
See Ponghill, Brad.

Ponghill, Burke (ATD)
See Ponghill, Brad.

Ponko, Father (ATD)
Although possibly odd sounding to Western ears, Ponko is a fairly common Slavic surname.

Poore (GR)
See Salitieri, Poore, Nash, De Brutus, and Short.

Pop (GR)
Slothrop first introduces his father, not by name, but by the familiar term *pop* (29). This "name" sets the stage for the later "pernicious Pop" episode (674–81) and the updated oedipal conflict — fathers selling their sons to the system and resulting filial resentment — existing throughout the novel.

Popov, Rear Admiral [Andrei Aleksandrovich] (Lot 49)
Grant identifies the historical Russian fleet commander (50).

Porcaccio (LL)
This plausibly Italian sounding name makes a joke: the name derives from the Italian *porcàio* (swineherd or pigsty) or *porcacciόne* (filthy person). The name seems to link him to another sailor, Pig Bodine, and seems fitting for this drunken would-be mutineer.

Porcépic, Vladimir (V)
The last name means "porcupine" in French, but may be used figuratively to mean "a prickly person." Cowart claims that the character is based on Igor Stravinsky, but Porcépic's decadence, particularly his interest in the black mass, is absent from the original model (75).

Porcino, Krinkles (MMV)
Porcino is a fairly common name. The Italian word refers to a tasty wild mushroom, although its plural *porcini* is more familiar. The meaning of "porcine" or "pig-like" is probably Pynchon's intended reference. So the odd name Krinkles joins with an English rewording of the surname to yield Krinkles the pig, probably used largely for comic effect. Presumably this is the same Krinkles who appears in E (81). He has a friend named Vincent in each story.

Porfirio, Crown Prince (GR)
The surname recalls Mexican dictator Porfirio Diaz, known for his brutal treatment of the poor. Our character, Porfirio, is described as a decadent aristocrat who can "smell the rabble" approaching (698).

Porkyevitch, Dr. (GR)
Presumably the name is meant to reveal a swinish character, but we do not see enough to know if it is applicable, or a pure charactonym. The reference could be a derisive one toward behaviorism. Winston claims that Porky the pig is "certainly ... the inspiration for the name" (74). Certainly, the name is one of numerous references to pigs, cartoon or otherwise, scattered throughout the novel.

Porpentine (UR, V)
Harder suggests, oddly, that the name combines *porcupine* and *turpentine*, but he does not explain the significance of the combination (75). Presumably such a reading would combine prickly and corrosive to create a doubling, but Pynchon himself has commented on the name. Porpentine originally appears in Pynchon's 1961 story "Under the Rose," where his opposite number is Moldweorp. Pynchon acknowledges taking the word *porpentine* from Hamlet and explains his reason: "[porpentine] is an early form of 'porcupine.' The name Moldweorp is Old Teutonic for 'mole' — the animal not the infiltrator. I thought it would be a cute idea for people named after two amiable fuzzy critters to be duking it out over the fate of Europe" (SL 19). Although

this section of V borrows heavily from "Under the Rose," Moldweorp has disappeared and we are left only with Porpentine.

Potamós (V)

Harder suggests that Potamós means Ptomaine (72). There may be a connection here, but the name seems to stem from the Spanish verb *potar*, meaning "to vomit." Ignoring the accent on the ultima, we have the first person plural conjugation of the verb, which translates as "we vomit." Thus, the name describes a cook whose food induces vomiting in the crew members.

Poteet, Sledge (Vine)

The name seems to be a joke combining the sound of *petite* with *sledge*, a hammer that is inherently large and heavy.

Poundstock, Swithin (ATD)

Swithin is a fairly common British name derived from the name of St. Swithun, and, originally, the Old English *swiþ* (strong) (Withycombe 261). Poundstock is a comic name drawn from the way paper thickness is measured, for example: 20-pound stock. The names could be read together as "thick paper."

Poutine (ATD)

This minor character's name is the word for an artery-clogging French-Canadian dish comprising French fries, fresh cheese curds, and gravy.

Pox, DeCoverley (GR)

As Larsson points out, De Coverly derives from Addison and Steele's invented country gentlemen, Sir Roger DeCoverly, appearing in *The Spectator* (V9.14–19). The name may also refer to the 1955 Joseph Heller character, Major — — de Coverly, appearing in *Catch-22*, another novel set during World War II. *Pox*, of course, means "venereal disease" or "any disease accompanied by pock marks or pustules" (OED).

Prance, Lieutenant Dwight

Dwight is a common name. *Prance* typically describes the movements of a horse on its hind legs, but also means to strut (AH4). If the name applies to his arrival ("unannounced, like a sandstorm"), it no longer applies ("filthy, sunbeaten, got up in some tattered wreck of a turnout") (761).

Prandtl, Dr. [Ludwig] (ATD)

German physicist who "did pioneering work in aerodynamics" (Porter 563).

Premulkoff, Namaz (ATD)

One of many fascinating minor historical characters woven by Pynchon into his fiction, he is referred to by first name only by Pierce: "On 2 February a native convict named Namaz led a mass break of fifty inmates from Samarkand oblast prison, and during the week that followed became an almost legendary figure, perpetrating one robbery after another and eluding all pursuit until he was killed on June 1, 1907" (243). Anderson offers more detail and a variant spelling of the surname:

> The most colorful of these [bandit gangs] was that associated with Namaz Pirimkulov. A convict who had escaped from prison in February 1906, Namaz soon acquired a Robin Hood-style reputation in the Samarkand region. Credited by the population with almost miraculous powers, and arousing considerable fear amongst the authorities who suspected he might mobilise a mass following, his activities were followed with considerable excitement by the local press [18].

Prentice, Captain Geoffrey "Pirate" (GR)

Prentice is an archaic form of *apprentice*. With the nickname, we have an apprentice pirate, suggesting his eventual turn to the counterforce, which, like piracy, is a haven for the preterite and a subversion of traditional Western order, power, and rationality. Larsson states that the name actually derives from Gilbert and Sullivan's *The Pirates of Penzance*, "in which the hero's nurse has made a fateful error in carrying out her employer's instructions: Instead of having the boy apprenticed to a (ship's) *pilot*, he was apprenticed to a *pirate*, hence a 'pirate 'prentice'" (V5.06).

Presque Isle, the Boys from (M&D)

Presque Isle ("almost an island" in French) is the name of several towns, bays, etcetera in the United States. In the context describing the battle fought near there, the location is a bay in Pennsylvania, currently part of Presque Isle State Park. While the "boys" are unnamed, the battle was real.

Prettyplace, Mitchell (GR)

Simmon suggests that the character is a "parody of a film scholar" (139 note 10). If so, Prettyplace may suggest superficiality, but this is very ironic in describing the author of the "definitive 18-volume study of *King Kong*" (275).

Price, Captain [Thomas] (M&D)

Browne identifies this Maryland justice (131).

Price, Mrs. (M&D)

Mason does not mention in the journal whether Mr. Price had a wife.

Price, Rhys (M&D)

Mason mentions this farmer and host to Dixon and himself in his journal (81), although he spells the first name "Rice" (92).

Prigsbury (GR)

This is Roger's made up name for one of the police behind them on the road, while Jessica bares her breasts to a lorry full of swarthy mental defectives. The *-bury* ending makes the name sound plausibly British, while *prig* ("someone with a comically heightened sense of propriety") conforms to the physical description of the officers, "English cop-faces pink with rectitude" (123). There could also be a sexual joke on prigs or pricks being buried.

Primula (ATD)

This minor character has a rather rich name. *Primula* is the genus including such flowers as the primrose, but the word *primula* is also Latin for "very first," appropriate for this future mate of Lindsay Noseworth, who is constantly derided for his priggishness and his virginity by Darby Suckling. This suggests, too, the word *prim*, meaning stiffly formal or prudish but also having an obsolete meaning of an attractive young girl (OED). Overall, the name suggests the character's appropriateness as a future wife of Lindsay.

Princess of Plutonia (ATD)

The name of this character of a mentioned Chums of Chance novel within our novel may be read several ways, depending on how one interprets the root of Plutonia: references to the planet Pluto, the radioactive element plutonium, Pluto the ruler of the underworld and god of the dead, and plutocracy, government by the wealthy. They all have relevance, and in context — the character appears in *The Chums of Chance in the Bowels of the Earth*— the underworld reference is undeniable. But plutocracy is invoked. The Princess is said to exert an "all-but-irresistable fascination ... on the crew" (117). The reference suggests the way the forces of capitalism exert control over people by appealing to their own base instincts and their fantasies of acquiring wealth, albeit relative wealth.

Pritchard, Brother (M&D)

Common name.

Privett, Nate (ATD)

One could stretch the nature of charactonym a bit and say *privett* suggests in sound the private detective agency he runs, but both the given name and surname are quite common.

Procalowska, Antoni (GR)

Antoni is a common name. The surname sounds plausibly Polish but does not seem to mean anything. Prokowski and Piorkawska are two similar sounding Polish names, so Procalawska could be a variant. On page 488, the name is spelled Procalowski.

Procalowska, Stefania (GR)

Stefania is a common name. See Procalowska, Antoni for the surname.

Procalowski (GR)

See Procalowska, Antoni.

Prodd, Thunder (GR)

This is a good name for a WWI regiment commander, but we know nothing about him. A prodd is an archaic crossbow designed to shoot stones or bullets (OED). A Thunder Prodd must be a walking weapon, and the name, in the absence of descriptive evidence, acts as pure charactonym, where the name itself defines the character.

Profane, Benny (V)

As one of Pynchon's widely studied character names, Benny Profane is the subject of numerous glosses in a variety of studies of V. Grant comments on Benny as an ironic reference, given his status as "accident-prone schlemihl" to "Benjamin, the lucky 'child of the right hand'" (2). He cites Hite on *bene* ("well-intentioned") and Safer, who sees a reference to the amphetamine Benzedrine (3). The Benzedrine reference would be ironic given our lethargic hero. He cites Chambers on *profane*, suggesting an "estrangement from things sacred," irreverence toward the sacred, and someone "not initiated into the inner mysteries" (2). Looking at the name as a whole, we might discern two primary, although contradictory possibilities:

Benny from the Latin *bene* ("quite or very"), doubling or emphasizing his profanity; Benny from the Italian *bène* ("good"), creating an apparent contradiction. Either reading highlights Profane's membership in the vast preterite class — all those not chosen for salvation. The latter reading, combining goodness and profanity, is consistent with Pynchon's ubiquitous concern, sympathy, and empathy for the preterite.

Profane, Gino (V)

Profane's parents are scarcely mentioned. If anything, his father's name indicates his immigrant background.

Prokladka, Yevgeny Alexandrovitch (ATD)

The general has a common Russian given name and patronymic. The surname means "construction" or "laying" in Russian, but does not seem to be used commonly as a name.

Provecho, Dwayne (ATD)

Dwayne is a common name. *Provecho* is Spanish for "advantage" or "profit." He is initially characterized as a "religious bore" (379), so the surname may be a stone cast at the dubious motivations of many a contemporary religious bore. But there is also an obvious play on the Spanish phrase *buen provecho* (good luck), through the rhyme Dwayne/*buen* joined with the surname Provecho.

Provenance, Wren (ATD)

A wren is a small bird, but the name echoes Victoria Wren in V. Provenance means "place of origin" (AH4) and is appropriate for an anthropologist, one who studies the origin and development of human cultures in all of their facets.

Proximus (ATD)

The name means "next" in Latin, appropriate for a scout, who would be on the lookout for what is coming next.

Prudge, Oleander (ATD)

Like several characters in the novel, Oleander has as her name the name of a flower. But appropriate to one of whom Lake Traverse says, "people like Oleander Prudge, don't care what they say, long as it hurts somebody" (264), Oleander is a poisonous shrub (AH4), albeit one with beautiful flowers. The ugly surname combines *prude* and *grudge*, both appropriate to her character and resentment of Lake.

Pudding, Brigadier Ernest (GR)

Hohmann suggests that the name is somehow symbolically connected to *size*, but offers no explanation; perhaps he reads it as a variant of *piddling*, suggesting small or insignificant. Besides referring to a popular British cake-like dessert, *pudding* is also a slang term for "penis" (OED). We could read Ernest Pudding as "sincere penis." This might suggest that he means well, but is a prick. On the other hand, the name might refer to his sado-masochistic relation with Katje/Domina Nocturna, through which he uses grotesque acts of sexual self-abasement as a kind of penance for seeing most of his men die at Passchendaele (79–80, 235). Indeed, he refers to dying soldiers as having taken Domina Nocturna for their bride, and his sexual relationship with Katje is, in part, the acting out of a desire to die.

Pugliese (ATD)

A common Italian surname, *Pugliese* also refers to things that come from the region of Puglia.

Pugnax (ATD)

This canine character's name stems from the Latin *pugna* (fist fight or battle), suggesting his role in guarding the airship. It also recalls the Latin adverb *pugnaciter*, which can be read as doggedly (having two obvious meanings here). This pun is doubled by the root *pug*, which refers to "a small sturdy dog of an ancient breed" (AH4), although our Pugnax is said to be "a dog of no particular breed" (5).

Pumm (GR)

Pumm is a fairly common German surname; why it is given to this presumably British character is not clear.

Purfle, Avery (GR)

Larsson points out that a purfle is "an ornamental border" (V597.06). The OED extends the definition to any border or outline and defines the verb *purfle* as "to adorn part of a violin with inlaid work." The notion of carving here might be connected to the runcible-spoon fight. The OED lists *avery* as an obscure word referring to "a place where animal feed is kept." There does not seem to be a connection, unless it indirectly suggests preterition. It could also stem from Pynchon's obvious love for very obscure words.

Putyanin (ATD)

Common Russian name.

Putzi (GR)

From the Yiddish *putz* ("penis"), Putzi is an appropriate name for a brothel operator. If the ending is meant as a diminutive, Putzi could be a joke meaning "little penis."

Putzi (ATD)

The name may be a reference to Ernst "Putzi" Hanfstaengl, friend of Hitler's during the twenties, who later wrote *Hitler: The Missing Years*. He also recalls the Putzi in GR and the comic readings of the name in that entry apply here as well.

Qorqyt (GR)

Weisenburger identifies the legendary figure from the aqyn's song (176).

Quall, Delicia (M&D)

Quall is not an uncommon surname. The character is possibly real, although she is not mentioned in the scant biographical information on Mason. Delicia is also used as a name, but would be appropriate for this character who tries to entice the widower Mason to marry her; *delicia* is Latin for "allurements, enticements, or delights."

Quartertone, Margaret (GR)
A quartertone is the fourth of a note or step on the diatonic scale. The character can produce voices on distant recorders without speaking. There is a slight metonymic reference to throwing voices or moving voices in the name, but it seems intended for its comic unusualness.

Quassel, Günther von (ATD)
Günther is a common name, but he is called Günni by Yashmeen, which would be pronounced roughly the same as *goony*. The surname is also comic-derisive, deriving from the German verb *quasseln* (to chatter or talk nonsense).

Quethlock, Lady (ATD)
One of several odd-sounding names derived from actual places in England: Quethlock is located in Cornwall.

Quincke (ATD)
The reference is to German physicist Georg Hermann Quincke.

Quirkel (ATD)
The name must derive from *quirk*: "a peculiarity of behavior" or "an unpredictable act" (AH4). When Lew Basnight is informed that Quirkel is available to be his backup, he shouts "Somebody get Rewrite!," suggesting that Quirkel's doing much of anything is a surprise.

Qulan, Dzaqyp (GR)
Weisenburger glosses the name as "Jacob Wild Horse" (172). The name seems to imply both his preterition and freedom: the biblical Jacob, a trickster stealing Esau's birthright, but fathering the twelve tribes, and the indomitable wild horse.

Quoad, Austin (GR)
Austin is a common given name. *See* Quoad, Mrs. for the surname.

Quoad, Mrs. (GR)
Quoad means "prison" or "to put in prison" (OED). Slothrop is trapped in her living room and forced to ingest a frightening variety of emetic British sweets.

R.C. (M&D)
The name of this local land surveyor does not appear in any of the obvious sources. It does echo the character RC from Vine whose name derives indirectly form the common name for Royal Crown Cola, produced since 1905.

Rachel (MMV)
Common name. The context of the story does not support emphasizing the Jewishness of the name (although she is friends with Siegel) or any biblical parallel. She is, however, described in the same manner as Rachel Owlglass in V: "Rachel who was 4'10" in her stocking feet" (MMV 196); "a girl 4'10" in stocking feet" (V 34).

Radnichny (GR)
The name is a plausibly Russian sounding name, but it does not seem to mean anything.

Rafaello (ATD)
This common name is the Italian for Raphael.

Rahman the barkeep (ATD)
This common Muslim name means "the most gracious" and is "one of the names of Allah" (Ahmed 167).

Rakhman (M&D)
This seems a fairly common Arabic surname, appropriate for a very minor character from Malaysia.

Ramanujan (ATD)
The reference is to the famous British mathematician Srinivas Ramanujan, who completed his Ph.D. at Cambridge in 1916 ("Srinivas Ramanujan").

Ramírez (Lot 49)
The old sailor's friend is certainly one of the preterite. The name Ramírez functions as an ethnic identifier. In the culture of white America, ethnic names almost always mark their bearers as preterite.

Ramiz (ATD)
Although introduced by the descriptive epithet "the Albanian" (653), Ramiz, like the other miners in this section, has a common ethnic name. It is Albanian, still common enough that a late-twentieth-century Albanian leader was named Ramiz Alia, although an allusion to him seems unlikely.

Rao, Dr. V. Ganesh (ATD)
This mathematician has a common Indian name (both given- and surname). Ganesh derives from Ganesha, one of the Hindu deities.

Raoul (V)
See also Melvin. Raoul, Slab and Melvin are introduced together. The names Raoul and Melvin are normal enough to foreground the oddness of the name Slab.

Raoul or Sebastian (ATD)
Not characters, but hypothetical names meant to sound exotic in the context of the passage.

Rapier, Father (GR)
The name seems to parody the sharp rhetorical and logical skills of the Jesuits.

Raquello, Ramón (Vine)
Diebold and Goodwin mention the allusion to the *War of the Worlds* broadcast, which was said to have interrupted a broadcast of Ramón Raquello and his orchestra.

Rathbone, Basil (GR)
Weisenburger identifies the historical actor (232).

Rathenau, Emil (GR)
Weisenburger identifies the historical industrialist (94).

Rathenau, Walter (GR)
Weisenburger identifies the historical statesman and industrialist, son of Emil (94).

Ratón (V)
Ratón is the Spanish word for "mouse." This seems an ironically small name for the Venezuelan Consul-General, especially as he is portrayed screaming and swilling wine.

Rauhandel (GR)
The name comes from two German words: *rauh*, meaning "rough" and *Handel*, meaning "trade." The character merely exists to recount Blicero's athleticism, so we cannot apply the meaning "rough trade" to the character in any useful way. It seems to point toward Blicero, especially in the context of this episode, in which Katje recounts Blicero's deep involvement in sado-masochism. Indeed, *rough trade* is slang for "violent or sadistic sex among male homosexuals" (OED).

Raum, Natasha (GR)
Although *Raum* is German for "space," its use as a surname is not uncommon.

Rautavaara, Veikko (ATD)
Both names are common in Finland. The surname may allude to the prolific contemporary Finnish composer Einojuhani Rautavaara. There could be some intention to play with the Finnish roots of the name: *rauta* (iron), *vara* (reserve), or *väärä* (crooked, bent), or even *vaari* (pay attention to). As he works with Webb Traverse to use force to put the needs of the workers before the capitalists, "pay attention to iron" would be appropriate. And for one who the militia "liked to see how much pounding he could take" (87), "bent iron" would be appropriate.

Ray (GR)
Common name.

RC (Vine)
RC and Moonpie are "taken from Big Bill Liston's fifties hillbilly hit, 'Gimme an RC Cola and a Moonpie'" (Diebold and Goodwin). The name is one of several in Pynchon drawn from popular culture. But the character name and the song derive ultimately from the common name for Royal Crown Cola. Both these character names are assumed as the narrator makes clear: "real names left back along their by now erased-enough trail since the war," but the reason is uncertain as the context suggests, in a description of RC — "mortally cautious bearing, that told of where else he'd been" (36) — that he had served in Vietnam.

Rebecca (GR)
Rebecca is the "token Jewess" in the Pökler commune. Her name is meant to indicate her Jewish ethnicity.

Reclus, [Élisée] (ATD)
Historical French anarchist.

Red (Malcolm) the Negro shoeshine boy (GR)
Identified by Weisenburger as Malcolm X (45).

Redzinger, Frau Luise (M&D)
The name seems ordinary and suggests only that she is of German descent. The surname is shared by husband Peter and daughter Mitzi. There may be a reference to the Red Zinger herbal tea produced by Celestial Seasonings.

Redzinger, Mitzi (M&D)
See Redzinger, Peter.

Redzinger, Peter (M&D)
The surname may be a variation on the more common Rezinger. As it is spelled, it is not as common. Again, there may be a reference to Red Zinger herbal tea.

Reed, Maurice ("Saxophone") (GR)
This is one of many names that function solely as puns.

Reginald (M&D)
Although John Lambton is said to have gone off on a crusade, there is nothing mentioned in available sources of a companion. The character and name are probably Pynchon's invention. The name derives from the "Old English *Regenweald* compound of *regen* and *weald*, both of which mean 'power,' 'force,' 'might'" (Withycombe 241). This etymology could be appropriate for someone heading off to the crusades, more as a description of the church at the time than for this minor character himself, who is a figure of mockery (for the reader), representing the English aristocracy.

Reilly, Sidney (ATD)
Reilly was a famous spy in England, subject of several books and a film. "To some he is the 'Ace-of-Spies,' Britain's greatest secret agent and the real-life model for James Bond. Others have hailed him as an unsung hero of Soviet espionage, the so-called 'First Man' who pioneered the Kremlin's infiltration of Western Intelligence" (Richard Spence x).

Reithinger, Dr. (GR)
Weisenburger identifies the historical statistician (271).

Renata (ATD)
Common Italian name.

René (ATD)
Common French male name.

Renée (Vine)
Common name.

Renfrew, Professor P. Jotham at Cambridge (ATD)
The name Renfrew is a fairly common name, as is Jotham, meaning "God is upright" (Hamilton 73). The surname is chosen as it reverses the letters of Werfner, initially presented as a double, but ultimately revealed as the same person (685). *See* Werfner, Professor Doktor Joachim at Göttingen.

Renzo (ATD)
This is the shortened form of the common name Lorenzo, Italian for Lawrence.

Replevin, Lamont (ATD)
Replevin is a legal term involving the recovery of stolen goods upon promising to return them if the case is lost (OED), appropriate for a character presented as a fence for stolen antiquities. Lamont is fairly common, but more as a surname. There may be an allusion to Lamont Cranston, alter ego of radio's The Shadow, mentioned in Lot 49 (11).

Reyes, Cipriano (GR)
Weisenburger identifies the historical Argentine politician (187).

Rick (Vine)
The name is chosen solely to rhyme with Chick, his twin brother's name. Twins are often given rhyming or alliterative names.

Rideout, Dahlia (Dally) (ATD)
Dahlia is a common name, deriving from the name of a common flower. The nickname Dally is significant: the verb *dally* can mean "to flirt" (OED), appropriate to this character. *See* Rideout, Merle for the surname.

Rideout, Erlys (ATD)
See Snidell, Erlys Mills.

Rideout, Merle (ATD)
Rideout is jazz slang for a final chorus (OED). Knowing Pynchon's interest in jazz, as illustrated throughout V as well as other novels, this allusion is probably deliberate. But Rideout is also a fairly common surname. Pynchon may have come across the name of Walter Rideout, and American literature scholar who published several pieces on Sherwood Anderson as well as the 1956 book *The Radical Novel in the United States, 1900–1954* (Pynchon may have read the book as a literature student at Cornell, whose library has three copies of the book, according to their database). Merle is a common given name.

Riemann, G[eorg] F[riedrich] B[ernhard] (ATD)
Not a character as such (he died decades before the start of the novel), this mathematician did introduce the Reimann hypothesis and zeta function (Bell 488) mentioned throughout sections of ATD as a source of obsession for Yashmeen Halfcourt (589 et al.).

Riickert, Helen (GR)
Weisenburger identifies the historical Miss Rheingold contestant, spelled "Rickert" (185).

Riley (ATD)
Riley is common as both a given name and a surname.

Rinehart, Mr. (ATD)
Not a character, Rinehart is a Harvard legend: "'Rinehart' is a Harvard rallying cry that goes back to the turn of the century. Its eponym was one James B.G. Rinehart '00, who was often hailed by a classmate beneath his window. On a warm June night in 1900, the classmates cry of 'Oh, R-i-i-i-n-e-HART!' was spontaneously taken up by hundreds of inmates of the Harvard Yard" (Liberman). The tradition continued for many years, and Liberman provides very thorough background on it.

Rinpungpa (ATD)
The reference is to the Rimpung (spelled Rinpung) Ngawang Jigdag mentioned earlier. Pynchon's facts are correct:

> The learned Tibetan prince Rinpungpa wrote "The Knowledge-bearing Messenger" in 1557 as a letter to his dead father, whom he believed had been reborn in the earthly paradise of Shambhala. Using meditative visualization, Rinpungpa summoned a Yogi to serve as his messenger. [In part of] the poem, he gives the Yogi directions for reaching Shambhala [Zaleski and Zaleski 349].

Ripov, Nikolai (GR)
Fowler points out the pun on *rip-off* inherent in the name (250). Perhaps he is so named because his organization, the Commissariat for Intelligence Activities, is "ripped off" by Pynchon from the American CIA.

Rippenstoss, Heinz (GR)
The surname comes from the German *Rippen* ("ribs") and *Stoß* ("blow"). Weisenburger glosses Rippenstoss as "kick-in-the-ribs" (97). It appropriately captures the brutality of the Nazis. The name also alludes to the historical Nazi foreign minister Joachim von Ribbentrop, who engineered the Nazi-Soviet Non-Aggression Pact.

Rizzo (SR)
Common Italian surname.

Roaring Dot, Belle of the Harbor (M&D)
She is presented as a colonial gunmoll (she keeps a sap in her stocking). Dot is short for Dorothy, and while Roaring does suggest an aspect of her character, the name is not exceptional.

Robertson, Colonel [James] (M&D)
Alvord identifies this historical "land owner" (169, 369).

Robin (GR)
Common name.

Rocco (ATD)
Common Italian name.

Rochelle, Sister (Vine)
Although a fairly common name, Rochelle may refer to two French words: *roche* ("rock") and *elle* ("woman"). The mother superior of the Sisterhood of Kunoichi Attentives is in many ways a hard woman.

Rocketman (GR)
According to Weisenburger, Slothrop's "superhero" alter ego derives from an actual, albeit short-lived, comic book hero named Rocketman, and developed by Ajax Comics in 1952 (179). The name also connects Slothrop's identity to his quest for the rocket; as he comes to embody his quest, he quite literally becomes the rocket man.

Rodolfo (ATD)
This common name is the Italian for Rudolph or Ralph.

Rodrigo (ATD)
Common Hispanic name.

Rodriguez (V)
Here is another name meant to suggest a member of the preterite through its ethnic associations.

Rohr (GR)
Rohr is German for "reed, cane, tube, pipe, or gun barrel." Perhaps the name is a reference to the massive antenna of which he is the keeper.

Rojas, Sandor (E)
Sandor is a common Hungarian name. Given that he is described as having "the worst chronic case of ... don giovannism in the District of Colombia" (86), there may be an allusion to Hungarian psychoanalyst Sandor Ferenczi. Rojas is a common Spanish surname, but Hollander suggests convincingly that Pynchon may be alluding to two Spanish authors: "Fernando de Rojas (1471–1541), author or *La Celestina*, a graphical account of human passion in classical Renaissance Spanish" and "Francisco de Rojas Zorilla (1607–1648), a dramatist credited with creating the *comedia de gracioso*, or comedy of fools, enlarging the role of the buffoon to include a variety of familiar fools taken from real life" ("Pynchon's Politics" 35). Hollander claims that these two authors and their works embody the two interwoven plotlines of the story: "downstairs, a comedy of fools; upstairs, the passionate realization of the tragic sense of life" ("Pynchon's Politics" 35).

Rollright, Mrs. (M&D)
Although the name sounds delightfully Dickensian and has some amusing sexual connotations, the surname suggests the not-quite-as-famous-as-Stonehenge rock formations of the UK, known as the Rollright Stones.

Romano, Cav. [Cesare] (UR)
Italian consul in Alexandria, Egypt at the time of the story (Baedeker 5).

Romegas (V)
Romegas is the actual nom de guerre of French Knight of Malta, Mathurin de Lescut (Schermerhorn 114–118).

Ron (Vine)
Common name.

Rooney, Mickey (GR)
Weisenburger identifies the historical actor (186).

Roscoe (Vine)
Brock's partner's name is relatively ordinary, but may recall the overzealous, corrupt law-enforcing halfwit of *Dukes of Hazzard* fame, Rosco P. Coltrane. Certainly Pynchon is fond of popular culture references, and the range of television references in this novel makes this allusion plausible. Diebold and Goodwin suggest that *roscoe* is slang for "pistol."

Rose (GR)
Common name.

Roseman (Lot 49)
Hollander reads this as a common Jewish name suggesting, along with other details, that Oedipa is Jewish. It could be an ethnic identifier, but the reason for employing it is unclear.

Rossokovsky, [General] (GR)
Weisenburger identifies the historical Russian general (223).

Rowena (GR)
In the context of the passage, Rowena emphasizes the Britishness of this character. The name became extremely popular in Britain after Scott included a heroine by that name in *Ivanhoe* (Withycombe 247).

Rowley-Bugge, Maxwell (V)
Grant cites Schulz, who identifies the character as a parody of Nabokov's Humbert Humbert from *Lolita* (46), which is plausible, but the name does little to indicate this outside of a shared vowel sound. *Rowley* is an old British surname (Reaney and Wilson 385) and Maxwell has no obvious meaning. *Bugge* may suggest *buggery*, but this would apply better to a pederast than a man who pursues young girls, although it may indicate a general inclination toward pathological sexual practices. The hyphenation and use of an old British name may suggest a desire to use an alias that suggests upper-class British respectability. Pynchon's mock-British hyphenated names may be modelled in part on those of Evelyn Waugh, such as Mrs. Beste-Chetwynde from *Decline and Fall*, for example.

Roxana (ATD)
A variant spelling of Roxanna, a common name.

Rozhdestvenski, Admiral (GR)
Weisenburger identifies the historical Baltic Fleet commander (174).

Rózsavölgyi, Géza (GR)
There appear to be two possible sources for this name: Geza Révèsz, Hungarian psychologist, and Géza Róheim, Hungarian-American psychoanalyst. Our character probably owes nothing beyond his name to either of these figures. The name is also linked to the Hungarian nationality that provides the ostensible excuse for the series of vampire jokes related to the character. The name probably refers to Róheim: see Rózsavölgyi, Sandor for more on this point. Weisenburger suggests that *rózsavölgyi* "signifies an 'evil valley'" in Hungarian (53), however, *Rózsa* means

rose (*Völgyi* does mean valley). Rózsavölgyi is also a common Hungarian surname.

Rózsavölgyi, Sandor (GR)

Géza's father's name indicates the likelihood that "Géza Rózsavölgyi" is taken from Géza Róheim. In 1915, Róheim entered psychoanalysis with Sándor Ferenczi (one of Freud's disciples) ("Róheim, Géza" 141). We may take the use of the names Sandor and Géza Rózsavölgyi as a recondite reference to Géza Róheim's training under Sándor Ferenczi. Beyond this, there is no indication of any significance of this fact for a character who is only mentioned.

Ruby (V)

As a fairly common given name, it is appropriate that Paola Maijstral take it as an alias while hiding out and playing the role of a black prostitute.

Rudi (GR)

Common name.

Rudie (ATD)

He is mentioned as a sidekick of the real Bob Meldrum. O'Neal does not mention any Rudie (or Rudolph) associated with Meldrum (227–8), nor does Backus. Probably fictitious, Rudie has a common name.

Rudolph II (Lot 49)

Holy Roman Emperor, as described in the text.

Rufus (M&D)

At first glance, this seems an odd name for an Irishman, but it stems from the Latin for "red-haired" (Withycombe 248). While we do not have a physical description of the character, the name might refer to an Irish physical type, or common feature.

Rush Brothers, the [George and Henry] (M&D)

Browne identifies this pair of witnesses to the melee described in the text (156).

Russell, Bertie ('Mad Dog') (ATD)

The reference is to philosopher Bertrand Russell.

Ryan (Vine)

The name's popularity has increased over time. According to the Social Security Administration, Ryan has been among the top twenty male baby names since 1976 ("Popular Baby Names").

Sabbarese (LL)

Common Italian name.

Sabine (ATD)

Although Sabine is a common name, a classical reference is likely here. The rape of the Sabine women refers to the abduction of the Sabines: "the wives and daughters of the Sabines were carried off by the subjects of Romulus during a festival. Their menfolk marched against the ravishers, but as the two sides were about to join battle the Sabine women, holding their infants, rushed between the opponents" (Warrington 448). The character Sabine is a member of the doomed tent colony at Ludlow (1007), and the classical reference emphasizes both the victimhood of the women and children, set between husbands and fathers on each side, as well as the valor of the women, qualities mirrored in different ways in the novel.

Sable, Murray (V)

Neither the animal, the fur, nor the color black denoted by *sable* seems to have any significance for this "itinerant race-driver" (300). Although used as a surname, it is not terribly common.

Sachehaandicks (M&D)

See Abraham.

Sachsa, Peter (GR)

Fowler suggests that the name may derive from the town of Bad Sachsa, where V-2 researcher Dornberger hid his technical papers (124), but this connection seems slender. Weisenburger cleverly suggests a connection with the Old High

German *sax*, meaning "a hatchet like tool" and points out that Peter Sachsa's "head was smashed in, as if in fulfillment of the name" (118). The pronunciation of the name is the same as that of the German *Sachse*, meaning "Saxon," although this connection cannot be extended too far.

Sage (ATD)
Not a common name, but the meaning of the word *sage*, wise, has no clear application to the character. Sage is also an herb. Several female characters in the novel are named for plants or flowers.

Sakall, S.Z. ("Cuddles") (GR)
Weisenburger identifies the historical actor (232).

Salazar (V)
Although Salazar is not an uncommon surname, Pynchon may have played with the root for comic effect. *Salaz* is the Spanish word for "salacious or prurient." Although less likely, the ending *-ar* may refer to the Spanish abbreviation for *Alteza Real*, that is, Royal Highness; this would make Salazar the king of prurience. The name could also be an allusion to António de Oliveira Salazar, dictator of Portugal from 1932 to 1968.

Sale, J.K. (Lot 49)
Grant suggests this is a reference to one of Pynchon's Cornell friends.

Salitieri (GR)
See the entry for Salitieri, Poore, Nash, De Brutus, and Short.

Salitieri, Poore, Nash, DeBrutus, and Short (GR)
Fowler points out the pun on Hobbes's description of life (solitary, poor, nasty, brutish, and short) encapsulated in the names of this law firm's partners (222).

Sally (MMV)
Common name.

Sallys, a couple of (GR)
See Girls, Slothrop's.

Sananzolo, Ettore (ATD)
Ettore is a common Italian name, the equivalent of Hector. Sananzolo is not a common name or an Italian word. It seems to be one of Pynchon's masked popular culture references. *San* is short for *santo* (Italian for sacred or holy) and *anzolo* sounds like Han Solo, one of the main characters in the original *Star Wars* film (1977).

Sandra (GR)
Common name.

Sandra (GR)
Probably a different character than the previous, but with the same common name.

Sandra (ATD)
Common name.

Sands, Captain/Inspector (ATD)
The surname is common and seems chosen to allow for his nickname "Sands of Inner Asia" (444), a phrase used later in the novel to refer to the putative location of the mythical Shambhala (628).

Sandwich, Lord (M&D)
The ODEE identifies John Montagu, the fourth earl of Sandwich, politician and gambler, as the noble whose disinclination to leave the gaming table spawned the eponymous convenience food.

Sandys, Duncan (GR)
Weisenburger identifies the historical British MP (121).

Sanktwolke, Edouard (GR)
As Weisenburger points out, *Sanktwolke* translates from the German as "saint cloud" (188). The possible significance of this is unclear.

Sant' Ugo di Tagliapiombo di Sammut (V)
Cassola points out that while this is not a name from Maltese nobility, Samut Tagliaferro is. *Tagliaferro* is Italian for "ironbreaker" and *tagliapiombo* means

"lead breaker." According to Cassola, this character name is meant to parody the real family name (330).

Santora (GR)
Like other characters in "The Occupation of Mingeborough" scene, the Santora family first appears in "The Secret Integration." The name has no clear meaning, but seems to indicate one of the Italian families in Mingeborough (see SI). *See also* Dufay, Kim.

Santora, Tim (SI)
Both given- and surname are common.

Saperstein, Iago (V)
The combination of a common Jewish surname and a given name taken from Shakespeare's embodiment of evil in *Othello* is odd, and probably meant as a purely comic name. Perhaps Iago is meant to reflect on the evil of the insurance industry, where the character is an executive. The surname could also refer to the famous Abe Saperstein, who founded the Harlem Globetrotters.

Sarah (V)
The name of this Herero concubine seems normal enough, but Seed points out the irony of her being named "after the biblical type of conjugal fidelity" (*Fictional Labyrinths* 98). But in some sense, she entertains, perhaps, some bizarre notion of fidelity to Foppl, as she commits suicide after being raped by many members of Foppl's platoon.

Sargner (GR)
This minor character only appears once, flanked by Wimpe of I.G. Farben and Weissman of the S.S. It is unclear whether he is a liaison between the I.G. and the military, but his name signifies in both directions. *Sarg* is the German word for "coffin," so *Sargner* seems to mean "one who entombs (or murders)." The name supports Pynchon's depiction of the I.G. as a willing tool of the war effort and genocide.

Sassoon, Lieutenant [Sir Philip Albert Gustav David] (GR)
Weisenburger identifies the WWI British officer and cousin of the poet Siegfried Sassoon (53).

Satin (V)
The name could refer to the fabric, smooth but inanimate. If we pronounce the *a* long, the name comes out as Satan, referring more to the overwhelming decadence of the chapter than to the character himself.

Saul (E)
A common Jewish name, but *see* Miriam on how these two names work together.

Sawattiss (M&D)
See Abraham.

Scammony, Sir Marcus (Angelique) (GR)
Scammony is "a strong purgative." That his surname means "laxative" could be a metonymic reference to his effeminate homosexuality, but the name is probably a simple, if obscure, joke.

Scantling, Crocker "Bud" (Vine)
"An appropriate name for a logging goon, since a scantling is ... a small wooden beam, or a small timber.... Scantling's first name may be a reference to Charles Crocker, a nineteenth century California tycoon who made a fortune building the Union Pacific Railroad" (Diebold and Goodwin). The primary meaning of *scantling* is "an extremely small amount," so Bud (a slang term for marijuana) Scantling also links the past union repression with the novelistic present in terms of draconian federal programs to eliminate marijuana production in Humboldt County. It could also be read as a joke on the scarcity of marijuana.

Schacht, Hjalmar (GR)
Weisenburger identifies him as the historical head of the Reichsbank (151).

Schess, Frederick (M&D)
Headlee identifies the historical "waggoner" (11).

Schiff, [Jacob Henry] (ATD)
The historical banker and crony of Harriman is referred to here; he was, as Vibe says (131) a Jew (Josephson 438–9).

Schiller, Professor (GR)
Weisenburger does not find a reference to this individual. Pynchon may have found him in a source not yet identified, or he could be contrived. Schiller could be an allusion to the famous German writer, or the name could be based on the German verb *schillern*, "to shimmer," or "to shine in different colors." Schiller is, however, a common German surname.

Schlabone, Gustav (GR)
Schlabone is German for "template." Magda does say of him, "He's so *paranoid*" (367), suggesting, perhaps, that he sees *pattern* (a synonym of template) everywhere.

Schleim, Josef (GR)
As Weisenburger points out, *Schleim* means "slime or mucous" (271) in German. Fowler thinks the name evokes snail slime (280). The name is appropriate for a character said to have engaged in industrial espionage for I.G. Farben. It may also derisively refer to "The System" itself and its slimy tactics.

Schleppingsdorff (ATD)
This comic-sounding name combines two German words: *schleppen* (to drag) and *Dorf* (village). Perhaps it is a derisive name: "the village drag." It recalls the name Max Schlepzig from GR.

Schlepzig, Max (GR)
Seed reads the name in the context of Greta's explanation of her own name as "a Nazi 'folk'-name" (*Fictional Labyrinths* 170). Weisenburger cites the German verb *schleppen*, "to drag or tug in a slow, tedious manner" (92). The same verb in Yiddish is *schlepn*. There may be a quiet reference to *schlemiel*, as well. *Zig* means "umpteen" in German. The original holder of the name has disappeared, probably dragged away by the Nazis (395). It is an appropriate assumed name for Slothrop, whose tedious quest simply drags on with no end in sight and, ultimately, no resolution.

Schmeil (GR)
Schmeil appears to be a fairly common German surname.

Schmitt, Chief [Jacob W.] (ATD)
This Cleveland Chief of Detectives had been appointed Cleveland's Superintendent of Police by 1871 ("Schmitt, Jacob W.").

Schmitz, Carl (GR)
As Weisenburger points out, a Hermann and a Dietrich Schmitz were associated with I.G. Farben, but no Carl Schmitz is easily located (243). If the name is fictional, it is rather common.

Schnorp (GR)
The name derives from the German root *schnor-*: *schnorren* is the verb meaning "to scrounge" and *Schnorrer* the noun meaning "scrounger." The name is appropriate for someone involved in the black market moving such unusual commodities as cream pies. As someone who lives between the nodes of authority and the power structure, rather than on them, he is marked as preterite, and this quality can be associated with his name.

Schoenmaker, Shale, M.D. (V)
The OED offers two especially useful definitions of *shale*: "an outer husk or covering" and "an example of something without value." Schoenmaker comes from the German verb *schönmachen*, meaning to make someone or something look nice. The name is formed on German occupational names: Hutmacher ("hat maker"), Schumacher ("shoe maker"), for example. Thus the name means one who improves

the appearance of the outer husk or one who prettifies that which has little value — appropriate for a cosmetic surgeon.

Schraub, the shoe maker (GR)

The name is based on *Schraube* ("screw" in German), presumably referring to the device used to affix heavy soles on shoes and boots. While the soles of work boots were frequently held in place with screws, the use of improved adhesives has made this practice all but obsolete. Schraub is also a common German surname.

Schrift, C. Morris (Lot 49)

As Grant points out *Schrift* means "writing" in German. He cites Berressem's reading of the name pointing to the dissemination of texts and significations (134). But with a first name given only as the initial C., we are invited to read the name as a phrase: "See Morris Schrift." In English, *shrift* is "confession, penance, or absolution." According to the OED the verb *shrift* is a variant of *shrive*, which means "to impose penance" but also "to absolve." Given the religious theme throughout the novel and Oedipa's presence at the auction with both Schrift and Passerine (who "spread[s] his arms in a gesture that seemed to belong to the priesthood of some remote culture" [183]), Oedipa could be on the verge of penance, absolution, or both.

Schwach (V)

See also Fleische. Introduced with Fleische as the "two good comrades" of a storyteller within Mondaugen's story (possibly Foppl, but it is difficult to be sure — see Grant 132). *Schwach* means "weak or delicate" in German. This can be an ironic description of a brutal German soldier or a commentary on the moral weakness at the heart of colonialism.

Schwartz (V)

That this character in Mafia Winsome's novel is described as "a weak, Jewish psychopath" and given a Jewish name is a reflection of her own anti–Semitism. *Schwartz* is also German for "black," emphasizing another target of her racism.

Schwartzknabe (GR)

This code name for Slothrop literally means "black boy" and is a part of the ubiquitous black/white imagery of the novel.

Schwartzvater (GR)

This code name for Broderick Slothrop literally means "black father" and is a part of the novel's black/white imagery as well as a sinister reminder of the updated Oedipal conflict behind much of Slothrop's activity in the novel.

Schwarz (ATD)

German mathematician Hermann Amandus Schwarz is referred to here ("Hermann Amandus Schwarz").

Schweitar, Mario (GR)

The surname seems to derive from the German noun *Schweiß*, meaning "sweat or perspiration." The notion that he is "one who sweats" connects him to his nervous occupation of industrial espionage.

Schwindel (GR)

Weisenburger claims that this code name for Stinnes means "swindler" and portrays it in charactonymic terms (152). The German for "swindler" is the cognate *Schwindler*. *Schwindel* means "dizziness" or "vertigo," but may also mean a "swindle" or "lie." The charactonymic element does rely on the meaning of the name as "swindle," referring to the circumstances under which Tyrone Slothrop's education is financed. The reference to vertigo, if intentional, may point to Slothrop's ultimate state of almost paralyzed confusion as he tries to sort out his past and apply it to his present situation, despite the fact that the code name applies to Stinnes.

Scuffling, Ian (GR)

The name on Slothrop's fake identification card is a humorously understated charactonym for a war correspondent (World War II could not be thought of as a scuffle).

Scurvham, Robert (Lot 49)

The surname seems to derive from the adjective *scurvy* ("mean or contemptible") and characterizes, not just the man or the Scurvhamites, but all Puritans and their worldview.

Scylla (ATD)

The name has less immediate application to the character than to the context of the brief passage in which she appears. This astrologer laments the odd geometrical situation of Santa Barbara, which requires sunset viewers to be at right angles to others on the coast of Southern California, dooming "the town to reenact endlessly the same cycles of greed and betrayal as in the days of the earliest Barbareños" (1043). This unpleasant fate is mirrored in the name Scylla, referring to the sea monster in Book Twelve of Homer's *The Odyssey* who drowns any sailors who stray too close to her while trying to avoid the whirlpool Charybdis.

Semyavin (GR)

The name of this Russian may derive from two Russian words: *semya* ("semen") and *veen* ("guilt"). He laments the fact that everyone now wishes to buy information: "What's wrong with dope and women" (258). The name can be read as positive, identifying him as preterite (guilt) and a representative of bodily desire (semen). Another transliteration of *semya* yields a Russian word meaning country or nation; thus the name could mean national guilt. We only know that he is involved in the black market through Waxwing, so it is unclear if this reading is charactonymic. The name could be a variant on the common Russian surname Senyavin.

Sensay, Debby (V)

The surname of this "promiscuous" character suggests sensation or sensuality. Given drug references throughout Pynchon's work, the surname could also be a slang reference to sinsemilla, a particularly potent variety of marijuana. There may be an additional reference to the costumes worn by certain carnival revelers in the Caribbean: sensay, from an African word meaning frizzled, are elaborate costumes made entirely of strips of cloth or natural fibers. If the reference is intended, it is to Carnival and the ideas of sensuality with which we began.

Sensei, Inoshiro (Vine)

The last name is actually a title, *Sensei* ("teacher, master") (Yoshitaro 1627). The name *Inoshiro* seems formed from two words: *inō* ("the stomach") (Yoshitaro 619) and *shiro* ("castle, fortress, or stronghold") (Yoshitaro 1705). His castle is his stomach; this chain-smoking, whiskey-swilling, woman chaser is clearly driven by bodily drives, exemplified by the stomach.

Senta (ATD)

Common Slavic name.

Serge (Lot 49)

Common name.

Sergeievitch, Pavel (ATD)

A common Russian name and patronymic, but he shares them with Russian mathematician Pavel Sergeevich Aleksandrov, "who made important contributions to topography" ("Aleksandrov, Pavel Sergeevich"). The character is seen engaged in topology: he "gazed at the horizonless disaster. 'No sign of fire there. No crater, not even a shallow one. It wasn't munitions'"(780).

Seth (M&D)

Common name.

Seymour (M&D)

Common name.

Sfacimento, Benny (V)

Profane's alias is explained in the text; the surname is Italian for "destruction or decay." He originally says *Sfacim*, which offends the girls. *Sfacim* is a slang term for semen. Tim Ware cites Assenza on this word as it occurs in GR: he claims it can best be rendered in English as *spunk*, or even *spunky*, as it is often used as a term of endearment ("*Gravity's Rainbow*").

Sfinciuni, Domenico (ATD)

Domenico is a common Italian name. Sfinciuni is formed from the Italian *sfinge* (sphynx), one of whose definitions is "a puzzling or mysterious person" (AH4), appropriate to this "Shadow-Doge-in-Exile" (247).

Sgherraccio (V)

The name derives from the Italian *sgherro*, meaning "assassin" or "hired ruffian" and the pejorative suffix *-accio*, meaning "bad." A very bad person, one would gather. While a very minor character — serving to move from one manifestation of V. to another — his name is instructive. On one level, the use of the perjorative suffix to amplify the root of the name injects an element of pure moral depravity into the aura surrounding V. and her transformation. But one could read an element of humor into the name as *accio* means "bad" in the sense of not very good at something (CID). Thus, a bumbling thug.

Shalimar (ATD)

Common name.

Sharma (ATD)

Sharma is a common Indian surname.

Sharpe, Governor [Horatio] (M&D)

Mason mentions this governor of Maryland in his journal (31).

Shatsk the notorious Leningrad nose-fetishist (GR)

One expects the name to have something to do with noses, but it does not. Shatsk is a city in Russia, but this has no apparent significance.

Sheaves, Lieutenant Mungo (V)

To *sheave* is to "bring together or collect" and *mungo* can be either "a mongoose, a person of position, or a black slave" (OED). The character gathers together evidence of discontent in Malta and presents it to his superiors. The name is appropriate for this type of bureaucratic functionary. Mungo is also used as a Scots given name; the best known example may be Mungo Park, the Scottish explorer. The name derives from a Saint Mungo (from a Celtic word meaning "my dear friend"), also known as Saint Kentigern, active in Glasgow in the sixth century ("St. Kentigern").

Sheila (GR)

Common name.

Shekhinah (GR)

Greta imagines herself at Bad Karma as this figure of Jewish mythology embodying God's destruction. See Weisenburger on the *Shekhinah's* role in the Kabbalah (218).

Shelby, Captain Evan (M&D)

Host to Mason and Dixon mentioned in Mason's journal (119).

Sheldon (Vine)

Common name.

Sheldon (SI)

McAfee remembers this "Italian kid" who played baritone sax as "Sheldon somebody" (173). Sheldon is a common name, though not Italian, and does not evoke the name of any well-known saxophonist of the era.

Shelton Clock, the (M&D)

The clock is real and was designed by the historical John Shelton (Cope, "A Clock" 262). Its ability to speak is presumably Pynchon's invention.

Shetzline, [David] (GR)

Both Fowler (183) and Weisenburger (191) identify the "character" as a friend of Pynchon's from Cornell.

Shippen, (Edward Jr.) (M&D)

As Mr. Shippen is introduced by Pynchon as "a member of the Governor's Council," we may assume the reference is to Edward Shippen Jr., a signatory on letters from the Baltimore Council sent to Mason and Dixon (Mason 177). A Joseph Shippen, Jr. also sends a note to Mason and Dixon (Mason 139).

Shippen, Peggy (M&D)

Margaret (Peggy) Shippen, "a young woman of loyalist sympathies" married Benedict Arnold ("Arnold, Benedict").

Shirelle, Sister Mary (Vine)

This sister of the Kunoichi Attentives is named for the famous 1950s/1960s girl-group, the Shirelles.

Shirley (GR)

See Girls, Slothrop's.

Shirley (GR)

Common name.

SHOCK (V)

See also SHROUD. Grant points out the source for the mannequins SHOCK and SHROUD, a 1959 NYT piece about two similar devices: "REMAB (Radiation-Equivalent-Man, Absorption) and REMCAL (Radiation-Equivalent-Man, Calibration)" (142). Siegel suggests a different source for the mannequins:

> I ... was working for a public-relations agency. The firm was soliciting an account in the field of atomic research that manufactured plastic mannequins called radiation dummies, made of materials designed to absorb radiation in exactly the same way as the human body. One model had a human skeleton. The other was all plastic. Both had clear skins of something like lucite and were eerily beautiful. I had the literature at home. Tom took some of it with him when he left [170].

SHOCK stands for "synthetic human object, casualty kinematics." Both models show man as dehumanized, an object to be acted on by contemporary forces (SHOCK mimics the effects on humans of traffic accidents). The weird vision of mortality communicated by the models to Profane acts as a "shock." Profane begins to argue against what the models communicate, but he ultimately retreats to indifference, essentially fulfilling the message that humans are moving toward a kind of passive objecthood.

Shockey, Mrs. (M&D)

Mason does not mention in his journal whether Staphel Shockey had a wife.

Shockey, Staphel (M&D)

Mason mentions this owner of a home on the projected path of the line in his journal (111).

Shondra (Vine)

Common name.

Short (GR)

See Salitieri, Poore, Nash, De Brutus and Short.

Short, Coolidge ("Hot") (GR)

Another pun created with an inserted nickname: *hot-short* refers to "brittleness in iron when it is hot" (OED). There is no detail on the character, so the name may be taken as a simple joke.

Short, [James] (M&D)

The DNB identifies this historical "maker of optical instruments" (Clarke).

Shorty (ATD)

This "ship's cook" (506) is only mentioned, but in M&D, Pynchon also named a ship's cook Shorty. Again, the name can have no significance for such a minor character. One wonders if Pynchon came across a Shorty the cook during his own time serving in the navy.

Shorty (the Bad) (Vine)

The name is probably an alias for a petty drug dealer, but has no apparent significance. The epithet is supplied by Hector, and seems ironic in context.

Shorty, the cook (M&D)
Shorty is a common nickname, although we know almost nothing of the character and cannot know if it refers directly or ironically to his height.

Shotton Dobby, the (M&D)
This "local ghost" is mentioned in an 1872 column in *The Newcastle Magazine* ("The Shotton Dobby").

Shovell, Sir Cloudsley (M&D)
The DNB identifies the British naval officer (Hattendorf).

SHROUD (V)
SHROUD stands for synthetic human, radiation output determined. Along with SHOCK, who measures the effect of accidents, SHROUD represents the fate of humanity—radiation and accident. The obvious reference to death in SHROUD's name (a cloth to wrap a corpse) points toward part of his message to Profane, but in a sense, dehumanization seems a fate worse than death. *See also* SHOCK.

Shuja-ud-Daula, the Nabob Wazir of Oudh (M&D)
The source for Pynchon's spelling is uncertain, but he clearly refers to the actual historical figure Siraj-ud-Dawlah (c. 1729–1757), originally named Mirza Muhammad, ruler of Bengal ("Siraj-ud-Dawlah").

Siegel (SR)
Although a common surname, Siegel probably alludes to former Cornell classmate Jules Siegel, who published an article about the reclusive author in the March 1977 issue of *Playboy* called "Who Is Thomas Pynchon ... and Why Did He Take off with My Wife?"

Siegel, Cleanth (MMV)
The surname is drawn from Pynchon's Cornell classmate Jules Siegel: "In *Mortality and Mercy in Vienna*, Pynchon's first published short story, the protagonist is one Cleanth Siegel. My second wife ... tells me that the character represents me. I have noticed the coincidence of name but do not recognize myself" (Siegel 122). Hollander suggests that, given the character's passivity, he is named for Cleanthes, a Greek stoic and disciple of Zeno ("Pynchon's Politics" 27).

Siegel, Mike (MMV)
Mike is a common name, but the Hebrew etymology of the name Michael may be intentional: "like Jehova" or "God like" (Hamilton 85). He is studying to be a doctor and his brother Cleanth fears most the alternative to his being God like, that he "would turn out only to be a doctor, like Zeit, and be cursed some day too by a distraught husband in rent garments, in a twilit bedroom" (196). *See* Siegel, Cleanth for the surname.

Siggi, the Troll (GR)
The shortened name (from Sigmund) and the epithet the Troll both seem to reflect his small stature.

Sigmund (GR)
This one-time companion of Greta's appears only in a reference to the past. The name is probably ordinary, but it may point to Freud as an oblique reference to Greta's perverse sexuality.

Silberschlag, Frau (GR)
Another name formed from two German words. *Silber* means "silver" and *Schlag* means "blow," as in "a punch or strike." The character gives Pökler the message that Leni has left him—a blow to be sure. Whether *silber* represents the hardness of the blow, contradicts the negative meaning of *schlag* with a positive one, or represents the pleasure she will obtain from giving the news is uncertain.

Silvernail, Webley (GR)
Larsson cites the British gun maker Webley for the first name and the Silvernail House as one of the oldest homes in West Stockbridge for the last name, implying that Pynchon would have come

across a reference to the place in his study of the Berkshires (V79.13). These are reasonable suggestions, but they don't seem to have any particular relevance to this character. Like many similar names in Pynchon, these allusions are unmotivated or external to what little we know of the character. See the introduction for the broader implications of this phenomenon.

Sipido, [Jean-Baptiste] (ATD)

Belgian socialist and would-be assassin of the Prince of Wales, as described by Pynchon (528).

Skip (ATD)

This boyish name applied to a talking ball-lightning furthers the personification inherent in Pynchon's description of this natural object.

Skippy (GR)

Ware cites Moore on the source of this name: the eponymous cartoon character of Percy Crosby ("*Gravity's Rainbow*").

Slab (V)

Slab's name, denoting a supremely inanimate object, suggests the inertia of the Whole Sick Crew and the futility of his own art. Seed claims that "Pynchon probably took Slab's name from *Philosophical Investigations* where Wittgenstein hypothesizes a minimal language between a builder and his assistant which would consist of nouns like 'block' or 'slab'" (*Fictional Labyrinths* 75). Seed further suggests how this characterizes the crew's use of "trendy monosyllables."

Slab (E)

While only three years separate the publication of "Entropy" (1960) and V (1963 ... initial copyright listed as 1961), the characters named Slab occurring in these two works are clearly not the same. E's Slab is briefly presented as a boob: "a fat, pimply seaman apprentice who had lost his white hat" shouting about a "hoorhouse" (92). Given this brief characterization, we can see three relevant meanings of the word *slab*: "a flat, thick piece of something solid," "to eat or drink untidily," "to throw aside as useless" (OED). All of these offer at least some description of this thick, useless fellow who has lost his hat.

Sleepcoat, Professor (ATD)

The Dickensian-sounding surname derives from an obscure term for a nightshirt that buttons up the front (OED). It is oddly appropriate, though, as the professor is obsessed with the Lydian mode in music (940), associated in book two of Plato's *Republic* with dirges, relaxing tunes, and drunkenness (197).

Slezak, Leo (ATD)

"Austrian opera singer and film comedian" ("Slezak, Leo").

Slide (Vine)

This minor character appears very briefly, so it is difficult to see how this name could have any significance. Slide is not a common nickname (except for the odd trombonist).

Slime, Kenneth (V)

The name is overheard in a scrap of conversation and meant solely as comedy. It is part of a pattern of comic-derisive names with no particular application to the characters who bear them.

Sloper, Phoebe (ATD)

A common name for a minor character, but there may be some slight charactonymic aspect to the name. Phoebe means "bright, shiny one" (Kolatch 398). She and Tace had spent part of childhood hiding behind a grade near a railroad track, pretending to be train robbers. Sloper refers to the grade, and "bright and shining" refer to the childhood fantasy, long since extinguished.

Slothrop, Broderick (GR)

The name Broderick probably has no intentional meaning, but as Slothrop wryly suggests that T.S. might stand, not for Tyrone Slothrop, but *Tough Shit*, we are invited to read the initials B.S. as *Bull Shit*. The reference would be to the patriarchal structures of control that enslave us all. See Slothrop, Tyrone for the surname.

Slothrop, Constant (GR)

Of the Slothrop ancestor's given names, Constant and Variable form an obvious joke. Besides the mathematical root of the onomastic word play, we can also read the names as an indication of the gap between generations (central throughout the novel, particularly in the oedipal — "pernicious pop" — episode). Another possible reference is to a well-known seventeenth century family — the Mathers. Constant and Variable could be a playful reference to Cotton and Increase Mather. According to Withycombe, however, Constant was a common name in the seventeenth century (69). There may be another literary reference: the character Lord Circumference in Evelyn Waugh's *Decline and Fall* has a son named Tangent. See Slothrop, Tyrone for the surname.

Slothrop, Doctor (SI)

At the time of SI, the later infamous and semantically dense name Slothrop must have been a simple joke, replacing famous early-American John Winthrop's *Win* with *Sloth*, extreme laziness. He is described as Hogan Slothrop's father in SI (151), so must be the Hogan Slothrop who appears in GR (29). See Slothrop, Tyrone for the surname.

Slothrop, Elizabeth (GR)

The first name does not appear to have any significance. See Slothrop, Tyrone for the surname.

Slothrop, Frederick (GR)

The first name does not appear to have any significance. See Slothrop, Tyrone for the surname.

Slothrop, Hogan (GR)

The name is used to explain the existence of Hogan Jr., who first appeared in "The Secret Integration." The name itself does not seem to suggest anything. See Slothrop, Tyrone for the surname. See also Slothrop, Doctor.

Slothrop, Hogan (SI)

This is the Hogan Jr. recalled in GR. See *other* Slothrop entries. Hogan is a common surname, but far less common as a given name (although using old family surnames as given names is common practice among some families). The word *hogan* refers to ceremonial Navajo earth huts with the doors facing east (AH4), perhaps referring obliquely to the ceremonial aspects of Alcoholics Anonymous, of which the young Hogan is a member.

Slothrop, Hogan Jr. (GR)

Part of "The Occupation of Mingeborough" scene, this son of Tyrone Slothrop's brother Hogan first appears as a character in Pynchon's 1964 story "The Secret Integration." See the above entry.

Slothrop, Lt. Isaiah (GR)

There may be a reference to the book of Isaiah, which recounts times of strife and warfare; conjoined with the military rank of lieutenant, the name is appropriate. Lieutenant and Isaiah could be read together as "soldier of God." See Slothrop, Tyrone for the surname.

Slothrop, Lt. Tyrone (GR)

Of the hundreds of names in GR, Slothrop's is the most commented upon. The primary reference relies on a perversion of Winthrop (*see also* Slothrop, William on this connection). As John Winthrop founded the Massachusetts Bay Colony and became the forefather of the elect and those who would embody the Protestant work ethic, the Slothrops represent the preterite masses, the great losers and schlemiels. Indeed, Tyrone Slothrop is part of an unbroken chain of loser-heroes in Pynchon, beginning with Benny Profane and in less obvious ways Oedipa Maas, continuing through Zoyd

Wheeler and, one could argue, even the fictionalized Mason and Dixon. Reading any members of the Traverse clan in ATD in this way is more problematic, but the picaresque quality of the brothers' wanderings, though they have a quest too, is reminiscent of Tyrone Slothrop's wanderings through the Zone in GR. But the name offers much more. Kharpertian suggests the obvious connection to the deadly sin of sloth, but adds the gloss of "sleuth" so that the name "echo[es] both the family's 'reasoned inertia' that keeps it and its paper business in Massachusetts when opportunity lies elsewhere and Slothrop's own mysterious quest of the rocket" (35). We might also combine *sloth* and its implications with the abbreviation *R.O.P.*, meaning "run of paper," an appropriate connection to the family business. Hohmann cites Simberloff's assertion that the surname contains the abbreviation of "Second Law of Thermodynamics," which he describes as the physical law that might be responsible for his disintegration (21). Clerc cites the same gloss, which "indicates the reason for Slothrop's failure as a messiah ... : he is too slow" ("Film" 174). Rushdie reads the name as an anagram of "Sloth or entropy," a revelation of the character's essence (36). The "surname could possibly link him with the allegorical personifications of Puritan writing. *Sloth* would be appropriate in the sense that he receives experiences rather than initiating them, and from a very early stage in the novel Pynchon indicates that he has an inherited Puritan sensibility" (Seed, "Pynchon's Names" 42). Friedman and Puetz suggest that Slothrop "might be an allusion to Thomas Love Peacock's rambunctious, love-starved hero of *Nightmare Abbey*, Scythrop" (78). Less attention has been paid to the first name, Tyrone. Clerc suggests a connection to Tyrone Power the actor, pointing out that Slothrop can be a "swashbuckling lady's man" in the scenes lacking paranoia. The name certainly suggests *tyro*, meaning "a beginner or learner in anything ... a novice" (OED), with relevance to paranoia, rocketry, systems of power, even his own past and his family. Finally, there may be a connection to the amino acid tyrosine. It is mentioned on 147 in relation to its role in melanin production and skin pigmentation. Besides being referred to in the records as Schwartzknabe ("black boy") (286), he is forced to discuss American race relations and his experiences with blacks in Roxbury (62–66), and Scammony states that Slothrop was "sent ... out to destroy the blacks" (615). We should recall, though, that the Slothrop family name was created in the 1964 story, "The Secret Integration." Presumably, Pynchon began to play with some of the connotations of the name well after he created it. While the name is another overdetermined one, the primary readings are clear enough: the genealogy of preterition embodied in the name's perversion of Winthrop and its combination of the terms sloth and entropy.

Slothrop, Nalline (GR)

As Weisenburger notes, Nalline is the proprietary name of Nalorphine, "once widely employed in police work as a diagnostic test for the presence of opiates, especially heroin, in a suspect's blood" (24). This places her on the side of the authorities who have "sold out" her son. According to the OED, Nalline is derived from morphine and has some morphine-like effects. This suggests that she is narcotized or numbed into submission to a system that controls the preterite. During the scene with her letter to Joseph Kennedy in which she bemoans the role of labor unions in the breakdown of society, she is numbed by three socially acceptable martinis (682). *See* Slothrop, Tyrone for the surname.

Slothrop, Variable (GR)

Variable and Constant Slothrop's names combine to form a reference to two components of many mathematical equations. *See* Slothrop, Constant. *See* Slothrop, Tyrone for the surname.

Slothrop, William (GR)
Weisenburger points out that this character and his description echo Pynchon's own ancestor William, who wrote *The Meritorious Price of Our Redemption*, a tract somewhat similar to the fictional *On Preterition*; both the real and the fictional books were publicly burned in Boston (237–38). In the case of William Slothrop, another note on the surname is in order. Given the much-quoted passage about "the fork in the road America never took" (556) (essentially Slothropian heresy over Winthropian orthodoxy), we should also read Slothrop as a deliberate contrast to or corruption of Winthrop.

Slough, Mr. (M&D)
The character brings to mind snakes through the sloughing (casting off of their skin) which they undergo. It seems meant to call to mind sinister connotations, as this character was involved in the massacre described in the text. It may also call to mind the "Slough of Despond" from *Pilgrim's Progress*, a melancholy-inducing place near the City of Destruction, a pitfall for Christians. Either Slough of Despond or City of Destruction could refer to the massacre site visited by Mason and Dixon in the section where Mr. Slough appears.

Slowcombe (M&D)
The name is a fairly common surname, but the context (especially the character's ability to charm women with his fife) suggests some reference to the Pied Piper of Hamelin. *See* Ulrich, Johann for more on this connection.

Smaragd, Generaldirektor (GR)
As Weisenburger points out, *Smaragd* is the German word for "emerald" (95). Perhaps the name refers to the color and connects the character onomastically to the dyestuff industry central to the I.G., of which he is a part. Or he may be linked to the Wizard of Oz, who exercises autocratic control over the denizens of the Emerald City.

Smareglia, Antonio (ATD)
Not a character, but not as well known as the other composers along with whom he is mentioned, Smareglia was a late nineteenth- early twentieth-century Italian opera composer.

Smart, Christopher (M&D)
The DNB identifies the poet (Williamson).

Smile, Murray (GR)
More a figment of Slothrop's imagination than a character, Murray Smile has a comic sounding name, but with no obvious meaning.

Smith, Captain (M&D)
According to Cope, Smith was the name of the Captain of H.M.S. *Seahorse* ("Some Contacts ..." 233).

Smith, Sheriff Samuel (M&D)
Mason mentions this former (at the time of his writing) sheriff of Lancaster County, Pennsylvania in his journal (67).

Smuggler, the (ATD)
Lest confusion arise, this is not the name of a character, but an actual mine in Telluride, Colorado.

Snade, Mrs. (GR)
A snade is "a piece cut from the tail of a mackerel for use as bait" (OED). Certainly there can be no significance for this "character" who only appears as an author of a letter to the *Times*. It is probably simply another opportunity to use a very obscure word, although it is not a terribly uncommon surname.

Snarb, Arnold (Lot 49)
While the name sounds vaguely comic, it has no obvious meaning. The repetition

of the *ar* sound approximates mocking laughter, but the character to whom the name is attached disappears as soon as he is introduced, rendering the name at least charactonymically meaningless. However, the mocking laughter in the sound of the name is appropriate to this section of the text where Oedipa begins to feel as if she is the victim of a cruel joke.

Snazzbury, Dr. (ATD)

The comic name is built on *snazzy* (fashionable) and appropriate to the creator of the silent frock: "Every girl must have one" (500).

Snežana (ATD)

Common Slavic name.

Snidell, Bert (ATD)

Both names are fairly common and Snidell does not appear to have any meaning in English or by sound association.

Snodd, Grover (SI)

Snodd is fairly common as a surname, but also Swedish for cord, braid or lace. In the context of the story's depiction of innocent youth's natural yearning for integration, despite adult society's fears, the sense of being inextricably twined together, as in a braid, may be intended here. Grover, too, is common, but Hollander suggests that, by invoking the name of losing 1884 presidential candidate James Blaine, Pynchon reveals that election's winner, Grover Cleveland, as the source for the boy's name ("Pynchon's Politics" 46). See also Snodd, Mr.

Snodd, Mr. (SI)

While Snodd is a fairly common name, the Swedish word *snodd* means cord, braid, or lace. We are invited to look for a different implication here, for while the son embraces integration, the father is part of the adult culture that supports the continuation of de facto segregation. So, "cord" calls to mind the ropes used by white bigots to lynch blacks. The sound of the word also calls to mind *snot*, "an arrogant person," in this context suggesting the adult society's perception of racial superiority and the "rightful places" of whites and blacks. *See also* Snodd, Grover.

Snodd, Mrs. (GR)

Part of "The Occupation of Mingeborough" scene, the Snodd name first appears in Pynchon's 1964 story "The Secret Integration." The name may derive from the adjective *snod*, meaning "neat," "tidy," or "comfortable." The significance of the name can be argued for "The Secret Integration" (the conclusion highlighting Grover's comfortable life so distinct from that of blacks at the time), but this onomastic derivation does not seem to serve any purpose within GR. *See also* Dufay, Kim, Snodd, Mr., and Snodd, Grover.

Snow, Mr. (M&D)

Christine Karatnytsky suggests this character is named for Enoch Snow from the musical *Carousel*; he pilots a "round-bottomed boat" unlike our Mr. Snow, the pilot of a keel, which has a flat bottom (Ware "Etymologies").

Snowball, Billy (M&D)

This putative drinking companion of Dixon's has a comical name with no clear meaning applicable to his character.

Snuvvle, Rex (Vine)

Rex suggests king, recalling the character's ambition for power, but Snuvvle is rather enigmatic. It may suggest *snoffa*, Anglo Saxon for "nausea" or *snivel*, "mucous dripping from the nose" or "to affect emotion by sniffing" (OED). Together the names yield "King Snot" or "Snivelling King."

Soames (M&D)

Typically a surname, it seems out of place as one of the names of the slave driver's children; Tiffany and Jason are the others. That the slave driver hesitates before offering this name of an additional child suggests that he is fabricating both child and name on the spot out of fear of the thrashing with which Dixon is threatening him (699).

Soames, Jack "Fingers" (M&D)
The first- and surnames are ordinary. The nickname is explained right after he is introduced: to all overtures, he employs his "eponymous Gesture," not out of hostility, but a desire "to be left alone" (53). He gives everyone the finger.

Soceena (M&D)
See Abraham.

Solange (GR)
This alias used by Leni in Putzi's brothel is probably an ordinary name, but it could stem from two French words: *sol* ("ground") and *ange* ("angel"). We could read it as "earthly or earthy angel," a rather pleasing term for a prostitute.

Soltera, E.B. (ATD)
This alias of Estrella Briggs, or "Business name," as she calls it (644), is quite rich. It is a near anagram of Estrella Briggs. But *Soltera* is Spanish for "spinster" or "unmarried woman." This combines with her initials to yield, "Estrella Briggs, Spinster," capturing the solitude of her life during this period after Reef's disappearance. She discusses it, as well as her past and her and Reef's son in this section where the alias appears (644–6).

Somble, Strool, and Fleshway (ATD)
Pynchon's most recently invented law firm has a Dickensian sound with no very obvious meaning. Strool is the only name that is also an actual word, a Scotts term meaning "a stream of water" (OED), but this meaning may not be intended. Somble suggests somber, Strool rhymes with cruel, and Fleshway has a kind of double gravity through sound association (flesh and weigh), suggesting girth on a large scale. So, we have a corporate name suggesting a somber, cruel giant, appropriate for Scarsdale Vibe's legal staff.

Spears, Mr. (M&D)
Mason claims in his journal that Spears allowed the sector to be stored at his home when not in use (179).

Spectro, Dr. Kevin (GR)
The surname is the prefix form of *spectrum* used in such words as *spectroscope* and *spectrochemistry*. In many cases, such words refer to situations where light is viewed through a prism as separate bands of color. The name is appropriate for Spectro (and the other students of Pavlov's book) for it has to do with breaking into parts and analyzing. There may also be a reference to *specter*, foreshadowing the character's death.

Speed, Harvey (GR)
Given Speed's abysmal failure as a detective, the name seems ironically to reflect his mental slowness.

Sphere, McClintic (V)
Grant points out that the character seems to be based on Ornette Coleman (based on a description of the music and Sphere's unique saxophone), and mentions that Sphere was Thelonius Monk's middle name (33). This connection was already established by Charles Hollander ("Does McClintic" 4–7). Although McClintic is a common surname, it is uncertain why Pynchon chose it as Sphere's given name. It could be a reference to Broadway and theatre producer Guthrie McClintic, who died the year V was published.

Spielmacher, Herr (ATD)
The name is not uncommon and literally translates from the German as "play maker." It is used as a term to describe scorers in soccer, but certainly "play maker" takes on greater resonance when describing this international manager of the Bank of Prussia—his name places

him among other capitalist power brokers in the novel, such as Scarsdale Vibe.

Spinney, Mr. (M&D)

The context and the proximity to the real Mr. Sweet suggest that this character, too, may be real, but he is not listed in the official accompts of all those who worked on the line (Headlee). Pynchon may be playing on an obsolete meaning of the word *spinney* ("thorn hedge") (OED). The character is seen complaining that the cooks have not milled the oats to his specification, and that the salt, too, does not meet his criteria. He is a very prickly person. Spinney is also a fairly common surname, so no additional meaning need be intended.

Spit, Bully Guy (M&D)

Also called Guy Spit, the Pass-bank Bully (542), his name captures the qualities of a bully in each of its parts.

Splanchnick, Dr. Hugo (Vine)

The surname derives from the word *splanchnic*, meaning "situated in, connected with the viscera or intestines" (OED). It seems an odd name for a rhinologist, but seems to refer to his preaching against drugs and the unorthodox methods he uses to manipulate Mucho into quitting his drug use. For the most part in Pynchon, drug use is treated positively as transgressive and anti-authoritarian, so the reference may be to anti-drug propaganda, comparing it to what is most frequently found in the intestines.

Spokeshave, Doggo (ATD)

A spokeshave is a tool used for planing and to lay doggo means "to wait." There is nothing relevant to the character here, just another example of Pynchon's love for obscure words.

Spongiatosta, Prince (ATD)

The reading of the surname as "milquetoast" may refer to the Prince's inability to do anything about his wife's frequent extramarital affairs. *See also* Spongiatosta, Principessa.

Spongiatosta, Principessa (ATD)

Spongia tosta is a homeopathic remedy made from toasted sea sponge. The name is probably a play on two Italian words: the prefix *spongi* (sponge) and the verb *tostáre* (to toast), together suggesting soggy toast, or by association the English milquetoast.

Spontoon, Dr. (GR)

Fowler offers the following comment on the word *spontoon*: "a short pike carried by eighteenth century French infantry officers, just the sort of arcana that always delights Pynchon" (223). The instrument may also represent the blunt violence inherent in the decision to castrate Slothrop as well as the scalpel used by Muffage and Spontoon to carry out the procedure.

Spooninger, Mouthorganman Apprentice Bing (ATD)

The title captures his youth and role as "Band Mascotte." Mouthorganman, while describing a harmonica player, has obvious sexual connotations, suggesting fellatio, and the surname is built on "spooning" (two people nesting like spoons), a homoerotic reference in this all-male group. Bing probably alludes to singer/actor Bing Crosby. When the character arrives among his classmates, they quickly break into song, reminiscent of any Hollywood musical, even when presented as parody.

Spörri (GR)

As Achtfaden points out, the code names (Spörri, Hawasch, and Wenk) were drawn from a movie. Fowler identifies the film as *Dr. Mabuse, the Gambler [Dr. Mabuse, der Spieler]* (198).

Springer, der (GR)

Von Göll's underworld name refers to the chess knight and literally means "jumper." The name obviously signifies his ability to leap throughout the Zone, unimpeded in his criminal activities. Weisenburger also suggests there may be a reference to Ludwig "Der Springer," a king who erected churches near Nordhausen in the eleventh century (183).

Sprue, Amy (GR)

Weisenburger suggests that the surname derives from "an archaic term for a type of throat infection" (169). *Sprue* also refers to a tropical disease caused when nutrients are poorly absorbed, resulting in diarrhea, emaciation, and anemia (AH4). In either case, this antinomian's surname suggests that she is viewed by the elect as an irritant or social infection.

Spugo, V.A. ("Brushhook") (V)

The surname seems to derive from the Russian root *spug-* ("terror"). In the context of the description, his brushhook inspired terror in the rats he slew with it.

Squalidozzi, Francisco (GR)

The surname derives from the Italian *squalidezza*, "dreariness or gloom." He is referred to as "the sad Argentine" (263). There may also be a reference to *squalid*, "filthy, repulsive, or miserable," referring to his preterition. Francisco recalls St. Francis of Assisi, patron of the poor and dispossessed, an appropriate saint for an anarchist.

Squarcione, Rocco (LL)

Rocco is a common Italian name. Squarcione alludes to the Italian Renaissance painter, Francesco Squarcione. Hollander offers the joke name "square chin" ("Pynchon's Politics" 31). There is also an Italian word *squarcione*, meaning "a swaggering or blustering person."

Squasimodeo (V)

The word is Italian for simpleton. A humorous name for a character with no particular function. He is introduced in a rapid list of characters at a party.

Ssagen (ATD)

This talking white reindeer has a charactonymic name explained in the text: "That's a Buriat pronounciation of *tsagan*, which is Mongol for 'white'" (785).

St. Blaise, Group Captain ("Basher") (GR)

As Ware points out, the name St. Blaise derives from an early Catholic martyr who was beheaded — he was depicted in Germany holding a pig's head ("*Gravity's Rainbow*"). Despite numerous pig references in the novel, there is little relevance to our character. The nickname Basher does seem appropriate for a group captain.

St. Cosmo, Randolph (ATD)

The surname derives from the name of St. Cosmos who was martyred along with his twin brother Damian, but this allusion has no clear application to the character. As beleaguered commander of the crew, he could be read as a kind of martyr. The common name Randolph suggests the familiar Randy, or *randy* (lacivious), an ironic name for this character.

St. Emilion, Solange (ATD)

The given name is common, and the surname is the name of a city in Bordeaux France, an important wine producing area.

St. Foux (M&D)

This mad French frigate captain's name may play on the French *foutre* yielding "damned," "fucked," "buggered," or similar vulgar expressions of unpleasant outcomes.

Stead, W.T. (ATD)

Journalist and "editor of the *Pall Mall Gazette* during the 1880s" (Oppenheim 33).

Steed, [Peter] (M&D)

Browne identifies this witness to the melee described in the text (156).

Steele (SR)

Common surname.

Stencil, Herbert (V)

Numerous critics have pointed out the obvious association here: a stencil is a pattern, or a device used to create a pattern. "Stencil's name, of course, is entirely appropriate for someone who seeks to impose structure on the potential chaos of experience. Stencil is what he does" (Grant 25). This is an example of almost pure charactonym; the name Herbert does not seem to offer any similar associations, although Withycombe claims that the name became extremely popular toward the end of the nineteenth century (143), which would make it a rather ordinary name for someone born in 1901. Grant also cites Dugdale, who claims that "Stencil the conspiracy theorist" from Freud's "The Psychotic Dr. Shreber" may be the origin of the name (25).

Stencil, Sidney (V)

See Stencil, Herbert. The name is also appropriate for the father, in that he, too, seeks patterns, albeit politico-historical ones.

Stephen (MMV)

This nickname given to Siegel by his roommate Grossmann in the context of "guilt" and a "Jesuit voice" (197) is clearly a reference to Stephen Dedalus in Joyce's *Portrait of the Artist as a Young Man* and *Ulysses*, where Stephen's roommate often chastises him for his "Jesuit" tendencies. In fact, Siegel's roommate Grossman (Big man) may be modelled on Joyce's, stately, plump Buck Mulligan, although Grossmann is a very minor character in this story.

Stephens (M&D)

Stephens is a common surname. As the *Seahorse* and Captain Smith are real, one imagines Stephens may be, but Pynchon's source is uncertain.

Steve (GR)

Common name.

"Steve"/"Ramón" (ATD)

Both assumed names for this fugitive are common, one in the U.S., the other in Mexico where he resides in this passage.

Stick, Joaquin (GR)

One of several simple-pun names, it is spoken "walkin' stick." As with many characters in the novel, he does not exist beyond a name and is not developed at all: a simple joke.

Stig (M&D)

The word *stig* is Swedish for "path" or "track." As a robust Swedish axman whose job it is to clear the "visto," Stig is appropriately named.

Still, Dr. A[ndrew] T[aylor] (ATD)

"American physician who founded osteopathy" (AH4).

Stinnes, Hugo (GR)

Weisenburger identifies the historical industrialist (151).

Stockton, Bob (ATD)

Robert D. "Bob" Stockton and C.W. Hunsicker operated a gambling house in Denver called the Richlieu Hotel, later taken over by Ed Chase and renamed the Navarre (Parkhill 68–9).

Stone, the Reverend Edmund of Chipping Norton (M&D)

Although his dates are not commonly known, this historical figure did make the discovery about willow bark mentioned in the narrative. He found this forerunner of aspirin in 1763.

Stonybloke, Will (GR)

As the "character" is introduced with several of Slothrop's Harvard classmates who have real names of prominent families, we expect Stonybloke to be the same. The name may be a real one, but from a family not nearly as prominent as Pitt, Kennedy, or even Biddle or Villard. The name may be charactonymic and meant to apply broadly to the wealthy and powerful. The adjective *stony* means "hardhearted or unemotional" and *bloke* is British slang for "a man." Thus, "heartless man."

Stresemann (GR)
Ware identifies the German statesman and 1926 Nobel peace prize winner, Gustav Stresemann (*"Gravity's Rainbow"*).

Stuggles, Constable (GR)
This police officer has a comic sounding surname with no obvious meaning. It may derive from *stug*, an obsolete word meaning "pig trough" or the adjective *stuggy*, "stocky" (OED). The former possibility seems consistent with Pynchon's portrayal of the police.

Sturgeon, John (M&D)
See Abraham.

Suárez, Pino (ATD)
José María Pino Suárez ran for Vice President with Madero and was assassinated with him by Huerta's officers (Cookcroft 85, 212).

Suckling, Darby (ATD)
A Darby is a plasterer's tool, slang for handcuffs, a short term for Derby ale and a variant pronunciation of the town of Derby, but it is also a common name. The name may also allude to the 1959 Disney film, *Darby O'Gill and the Little People*, offering an oblique reference to this character's youth. A suckling is "a young mammal that has not been weaned" (AH4), appropriate for this character described as "the 'baby' of the crew" (3). There may also be an allusion to Sir John Suckling, seventeenth-century British poet.

Sukhomlinoff, General (ATD)
The reference is to Genberal Vladimir Sukhomlinov, Russian Minister of War.

Sullivan, Mr. [Laurence] (M&D)
He is said to be "lock'd in a struggle" with Clive "for the Soul of the [East India] Company" (162). Although the spelling varies slightly, the reference is clear: "Clive returned to England in 1760 with a large fortune, in the defence of which he was drawn into bitter rivalry with Laurence Sulivan who had been the dominant figure in the Court of Directors for some years" (Marshall 28).

Surd the drunken yeoman, Howie (V)
Harder cites the definition of *surd* as "an irrational number." The OED also lists "irrational" (in human terms), "senseless," and "stupid." There is no textual evidence of overwhelming stupidity, so perhaps the name refers to his drunkenness, a senseless state. The whole name approximates the phrase "how absurd."

Susans (GR)
See Girls, Slothrop's.

Svegli, Professor(e) (ATD)
The surname is a comic invention rooted in the Italian verb *svegliàre* (to wake up): he is Professor Wake Up. Or the name could derive from the related word *sveglio* (quick witted or clever), appropriate to this expert on the Sfinciuno Itinerary. The English title Professor is used on 248, the Italian on 569.

Swallowfield, Gus (ATD)
Lew Basnight's alias combines the common name Gus with the name of a village in Berkshire England. Given his role as an insurance agent, we might read *Swallowfield* as a pun on "flood."

Swanlake, Jessica (GR)
The surname, taken from the famous Tchaikovsky ballet, is probably meant to describe the character's beauty and (balletic) grace. It may be intended ironically, however, as the plot of the story on which the ballet is based describes a doomed love that ultimately triumphs over evil, unlike the idyllic wartime relationship between Roger Mexico and Jessica Swanlake that fails with the arrival of peace. The tale has various endings, most of which are not happy, but even the common ending in which Odette and Siegfried are drowned together by Rothbart still represents a kind of triumph absent from the complete

failure of Roger and Jessica's relationship. There is a slight possibility that Pynchon is also playing with a probable etymology of Jessica, from the Hebrew *Yiskah*, meaning "he beholds" (Withycombe 167). In this case, the full name could be glossed "he beholds beauty," referring to Mexico's feelings for Jessica.

Sweet, Mr. [Benjamin] (M&D)
Headlee identifies the historical axman (6).

Swift, Brother Tom (ATD)
Like the Chums of Chance, Tom Swift is the protagonist in a series of boys' adventure books. Notice that the balloon boys, the anarchists, and the capitalists all refer to colleagues at some point as "Brother."

Swivett, Mr. (M&D)
The character is purple-faced with agitation as he rails against the forces of calendar reform. The surname derives from *swivet*, "a state of agitation; a fluster or panic" (OED).

Swome, Lionel (ATD)
The first name is common. *Swome* is a dialect variation of the past tense of *swim* (OED). The character seems a parody of British officiousness, so perhaps the name is meant to capture this in part by sound: merely pronouncing the name puts one's mouth in an unpleasant piscine purse.

Swope, Mr. (GR)
Weisenburger identifies the historical newspaperman and FDR "buddy" (243).

Sybil (MMV)
A common name, but like several other names applied to minor characters in the story, one that has an application to the story itself rather than to the character. The name recalls the epigraph to T.S. Eliot's *The Waste Land*: "For once I saw with my own eyes the Cumean Sibyl hanging in a jar, and when the boys asked her, 'Sibyl, what do you want?' she answered, 'I want to die'" (Eliot 3 note 1). By implication, the name conjures up a sense of doom at the party, and as the Sibyl was a prophet, strong foreshadowing as well. The Cumean Sibyl in a jar is also echoed by the pig foetus tacked above the entrance to the apartment (198). Pynchon suggests another borrowing from T.S. Eliot in the introduction to SL (15), but MMV has two obvious Eliot allusions besides the reference to the Sibyl/Sybil. Lupescu first quotes Eliot's lines from Baudelaire at the end of *The Waste Land*'s first part ("The Burial of the Dead" — another significant reference given our story's end): "*Mon semblable ... mon frère*" (198). Then, after leaving, he pokes his head back in to say "Mistah Kurtz — he dead" (199), Eliots epigraph to *The Hollow Men*.

Sylvia (V)
Common name.

Symons, Arthur [William] (ATD)
The reference is to the prolific author and literary critic. The statement about "how sensitive Arthur is" (945) may refer to the mental breakdown he suffered in 1908 (Beckson).

Szabó, Zsu Zsa (M&D)
Although *szabó* means "tailor" in Hungarian, it is a common surname. It seems to be used for its alliteration. Zsu Zsa seems to be a nickname or familiar form of the common Hungarian name Zsuzsanna.

Sztup, Mme. (GR)
Weisenburger identifies the Yiddish origin of the surname as the word *sztup* or *shtup*, ultimately meaning "to fornicate with" (214), an appropriate name within the context of the Anubis orgy.

Tabor, Baby Doe (ATD)
Elizabeth McCourt ("Baby") Doe was a "young and beautiful divorcée" whom H.A.W. Tabor married after divorcing his first wife (Federal Writers' Project — CO 170).

Tabor, Haw (ATD)
H.A.W. Tabor was an immensely wealthy Leadville mine owner, who acted as mayor and postmaster when the town was incorporated, served for 30 days as U.S. Senator, and lost everything in the silver collapse of 1893 (Federal Writers' Project — CO 170-1).

Takeshi (GR)
This kamikaze pilot has what seems to be a fairly common Japanese name, but the word *takeshi* is a variant of *takeki*, a Japanese word meaning "valiant, brave, or fearless" (Yoshitaro 1893-94), appropriate for a kamikaze. Spelled Takashi it is also a common name (at least four Takashis, who were fallen WWII era Japanese soldiers have had their final letters published) (Nihon Senbotsu Gakusei Kinen-Kai 107, 138, 172, 205). The collection includes letters from kamikaze pilots, although the four Takashis in the collection were not kamikazes.

Talbot, Larry (Vine)
Not a character, the name refers to the "Wolfman in those old Hollywood monster movies" (Diebold and Goodwin); that is the name of the character played by Lon Chaney in the 1941 film, *The Wolfman*.

Tallihoe of Virginia (M&D)
The character places Mason and Dixon on "a Coach of peculiar Design" that whisks them — without stopping — to meet George Washington (273-4); the surname derives from *tally-ho*, "fast coach," but the term did not come into use until 1823 (OED).

Tamara (GR)
An ordinary name, but seemingly employed for Slothrop's pun: "At this rate, Tamara's gonna get here before tonight."

Tancredi, Andrea (ATD)
Thomas Pynchon Wiki sees a pop-culture allusion in the surname: "Tancredi is a time-travelling character in *City of Death*, a four-part serial in the British science fiction television series *Dr. Who* which involves time travel and bilocation." The *Wiki* goes on to point out interesting parallels between the serial and themes and details from ATD. *Tancredi* is also a Rossini opera in which the main character is an exiled soldier named Tancredi. Both the given- and the surname, however, are quite common.

Tassis, Omedio (Lot 49)
Omodeo Tasso (or Tassis) did organize the Thurn and Taxis couriers around 1290 (Harlow 59). Pynchon may have found his spelling in another source.

Tchitcherine, Vaslav (GR)
Weisenburger cites Von Kármán on a Frank Tchitcherine associated with Kerenesky and Seed on Georgi Tchitcherine involved in negotiating the Rapallo treaty (although the narrator says Vaslav is not related to him) (153). In an earlier article, Weisenburger claimed that the character Tchitcherine derived from Gogol's character Chichikov, "a travelling-agent for death" ("Origins" 39), but as he does not repeat the claim in his 1988 companion to the novel, he may have decided against this reading.

Teflon, Morris (V)
Depending on one's interpretation of the first name, this character can be read in different ways. The OED offers several definitions of *morris*: "an elongated, flat eel-like fish now regarded as the aborted young of the conger eel; to dance; to move away rapidly; to move at a rapid pace." Harder reads the name as "animate plus inanimate" (75). It can also be taken as a name of doubling: teflon reduces friction, thus enabling rapid motion. Both speed and slipperiness are appropriate for a character whose main activity is photographing friends and strangers having sex in his apartment and then selling the prints to sailors. But if we read *morris* as "aborted eel" and *teflon* as an inanimate

substance, we have a name of inanimate doubling. While we use the word *teflon* to describe any non-stick surface (even figuratively to describe people unaffected by attacks), Teflon is actually the proprietary name for a non-stick coating (polyetrafluoroethylene) patented by Dupont in 1945 (OED).

Telangiecstasis, Spyro ("Spider") (GR)

A good example of a fairly hidden joke. The surname sounds as if it could be Greek, but, as Fowler points out, means a disease of the capillaries (278). (The common spelling is *telangiectasis*.) The condition is commonly referred to as *spider veins*.

Teledu (V)

According to the OED, *teledu* is a skunk-like carnivorous animal of Java and Sumatra, also called stinking badger or stinkard. The name demonstrates Pynchon's love of obscure words as well as names used seemingly for humorous effect alone. On the other hand, some negative names applied to very minor characters who cannot be shown to deserve derision may be used to identify many of the little people who make up the massive preterite class. That is, they are viewed as pariahs or vulgarians by the elect.

Ten Eyck, Al (V)

Common name.

Tenebrae (M&D)

Dewey compares the name Tenebrae to the other light-related names in the novel (Wicks and LeSpark) and glosses it as "a gloomy, heavy darkness" (120). The word *Tenebræ* is a religious term designating certain Holy-Week lauds and matins "at which the candles lighted at the beginning of the service are extinguished one by one after each psalm" (OED). This may refer to her role of keeping Wicks in check as he tells his stories.

Ter Meer, [Fritz] (GR)

Weisenburger identifies the historical I.G. Farben bigwig (272).

Teresa (V)

See also Augustine, Bartholomew, Ignatius, Paul, and Veronica. Fairing probably names this rat for Teresa of Avila, sixteenth-century Spanish mystic, writer, and reformer.

Teresa (ATD)

It is said of this youthful infatuation of Webb's that he would never forget her name (87). Yet it is a common name. There is not enough context to suggest a link with the saint or any other well-known bearer of this name.

Tesla, Nikola (ATD)

This Serbian-born inventor, physicist, and engineer appears throughout the novel both as character and background to strange experiments and a powerful weapon.

Thanatz, Miklos (GR)

The name sounds plausibly Greek, and of course the last name points both to the Greek word for death and the Freudian death instinct (*thanatos*). The character first appears as elect, along with other passengers on the *Anubis*, which Weisenburger points out is also the name of "the jackal-headed god of Egyptian mythology who conducted the dead to judgment" (213). Thus the elect connection to death forces is heightened, just as the mindless pleasures of the preterite are associated with life. Interestingly, Thanatz seems to shift to the preterite (see especially 667).

Thapsia (Vine)

Thapsia is a Mediterranean herb known for its purgative and emetic qualities (OED). The character is only mentioned twice, so there is no way of knowing whether the name is descriptive. It may refer to the rebirth of interest in herbalism during the 1960s and again among new-age enthusiasts of the 1980s.

Theign, Derrick (ATD)

Derrick is a common name, deriving from the Old German Theodoric (Withycombe 78), meaning ruler of people (Withycombe 264). It is appropriate for one who controls others, even their lives and deaths, as this character does. The spelling is no longer common (Withycombe 78), suggesting the noun *derrick*, "a machine for hoisting or moving heavy objects" (AH4), also appropriate for one who controls, but the machine element suggests his role in working for the existing power structure. This association is echoed in the surname. *Theign* is an obsolete verb, meaning "to be a servant or minister, to perform the duties of an office" (OED). This clearly describes his position.

Theophile (GR)

Larsson points out that the name derives from the Greek for "lover of God" (V247.14). He is seen trying to get a tank to smuggle to Palestine; perhaps his love of God translates into the type of Zionism first seen in V's character Da Conho, who dreams of gunning down Arabs.

Thickley, Sheriff (M&D)

The context suggests that he could be real, but there is no clear source. The surname may suggest thickness, in the sense of stupidity, and might be directed at law enforcement agents in general.

Thiel, Dr. (GR)

Weisenburger identifies the historical researcher (200).

Thomas (M&D)

See Abraham.

Thomas, Lowell (GR)

Weisenburger identifies the historical writer/adventurer (139).

Thorn, Ryder (ATD)

Thorn is a common name, but may also refer to the sharp spike on a plant, such as a rose bush. It is descriptive of the unpleasant information he imparts to Miles (554). The name also connects him to another who has access to the future, El Espinero (The Thorn Man). Ryder may refer to the Rider-Waite tarot deck (also used to read the future), mentioned throughout the text, or Rider Haggard, author of adventure novels with more than a little in common with the Chums of Chance novels as depicted in the text.

Thornton, Eleanor (ATD)

She was the model for the Rolls Royce hood ornament, known as the Spirit of Ecstasy, as described in the novel. Her lover Lord Montagu had her immortalized in this fashion after she died when the SS *Persia* was sunk in 1915. He survived (Mansfield).

Thorvald (ATD)

This persistent tornado is given the name Thorvald, presumably because its first syllable is sounded the same as the first syllable in *tornado*.

Thoth, Mr. (Lot 49)

Hollander identifies Thoth as the "Egyptian god of communication and writing" ("Pynchon, JFK and the CIA" 73). Seed offers a more extensive gloss on the meaning and significance of Thoth:

> The naming of Mr. Thoth who Oedipa sees in an old people's home offers yet another mockery of the sacred. Thoth was the lord of ritual and magic; according to Harold Innis, "he represented creation by utterance and production by thought and utterance," but the rambling old man Oedipa speaks to offers anything but enlightenment [*Fictional Labyrinths* 131].

Colvile links the root of Thoth to the German *Tod* or "death" (370), referring, perhaps, to the character's advanced age. Grant cites Neuman on Thoth as the god of scribes, indicating by his age the decay of the written word and Madsen on Thoth's role in introducing plurality in language;

he also cites a connection with the theme of hieroglyphics (72). While all of these shades of meaning can enrich our understanding of the text, the primary reading clearly links the character to the god of communication and communication as one of the central themes of the novel.

Throsp, Corydon (GR)

Weisenburger identifies the character as fictional, "as his name, from the pastoral tradition, suggests" (17). Corydon is a "generic proper name in pastoral poetry for a rustic" (OED). This seems to suggest preterition, as do the bohemian qualities of the neighborhood and house, detailed briefly by Weisenburger (17). *Throsp* does not seem to be a common name or an English word. It is a near anagram of Slothrop, however, missing only an *l* and a second *o*. This could be read as another indication of preterition.

Throwster, Aaron (GR)

Larsson mentions the biblical Aaron (Moses's brother) and points out that a throwster is "one who makes threads out of silk," but states that the name is a common one in Britain (V82.11). *Throwster* is also an obsolete word for a thrower, particularly of dice. The silk thread reference could refer to Throwster's occupation as surgeon (mentioned on 113), while the connotation of a *thrower* could refer to his "throwing a fit" (227–28).

Throyle, Hastings (ATD)

Hastings is common as a surname, but not a given one. It inevitably recalls the battle of Hastings in 1066. Throyle sounds like "the royal," perhaps an arrogant opinion of his ideas in the context of his argument with Blope.

Thyssen (GR)

Weisenburger identifies the historical financier (151).

'Ti Bruce, Chef (Vine)

The name means "little Bruce." According to Diebold and Goodwin, "Ti is Cajun slang for petite and the character may refer to a well-known Bay area chef named 'Big Bruce' Aidells."

Tiffany (M&D)

McHale glosses this as a "fashionable nineties name" (48). According to the Social Security Administration, Tiffany was among the top 20 female baby names from 1980 to 1989 (excepting 1985 when it ranked 23rd) ("Popular Baby Names").

Tifkira (V)

The character is described as "an unscrupulous merchant." *Tifkira* is a Maltese word for "souvenir" (Falzon). The name may refer to the fact that Tifkira and his hoard of wine act as impetus for remembering (the point of a souvenir) a meeting between Fausto and Dnubietna. This is supported by Cassola's gloss of the word: "remembrance" (330). The name could also be descriptive in that souvenir shops are often thought to be dens for unscrupulous merchants forcing the naive to buy overpriced trinkets.

Tiny (ATD)

One of many ironic names, the massive bouncer named Tiny is 7 feet 6 inches and stout (399).

Tisonnier, Professor (M&D)

Tissonier is French for "poker." The name is appropriate for a fencing instructor.

Tito (V)

Although a fairly common Hispanic name, Tito, who makes a living selling pornographic pictures to servicemen, could refer to the Spanish *títere*, meaning "puppet" or "nincompoop."

Toadflax, Captain Q. Zane (ATD)

Zane is a common name, but may be a reference to Western author Zane Grey. Toadflax refers to a genus of narrow-leaved flowering plants (AH4).

Togo, Admiral (GR)
Weisenburger identifies the historical Japanese naval commander (175).

Toko, a Negritoe or Asian Pygmy (M&D)
The name could be an anachronistic reference to the Toko Corporation, manufacturers of electronic components. *Toko* is also a variant spelling of *toco*, "corporal punishment" (OED).

Toledo, Don Garcia de (V)
Grant identifies the historical military commander (195).

Tom (M&D)
See Jefferson, Thomas.

Tondeghho (M&D)
See Abraham.

Tongue, Leroy (V)
Hollander has pointed out that one source of Pynchon character names, from his earliest short fiction, involves parts of the body ("Pynchon, JFK and the CIA" 67). This is one example of such a name, where there is probably no additional meaning beyond the comic-grotesque. Following Bakhtin on Rabelais, however, we should notice that such body-part names often have to do with consumption of food and drink, or sexuality (or both in the case of Mr. Tongue). Such names invariably stand for some subversion or transgression in regard to the established order or elect.

Tonio (ATD)
Common Italian name.

"Topor" (ATD)
As he is Siberian, one looks to Russian for the name, where it means "coarse." But our brief glimpse shows an intelligent, thoughtful, well-spoken, highly skilled artisan, making this reading unmotivated. The name may be an allusion to French artist/writer/filmmaker, Roland Topor. If we keep the sound but change the spelling, we have the English verb *toper* (to cause to fall or topple), appropriate for one who is a "short-ax genius" (788) who fells trees, or (to drink immoderately), a comic name, not directed at the character himself (OED).

Torpidini, "Two-Ton" Carmine (Vine)
Torpidini sounds plausibly Italian, but is no common surname. It is formed from the English *torpid* ("slow or sluggish") and would aptly describe someone whose girth has earned him the name *Two-Ton*. Of course the diminutive *-ini* undercuts the nickname and the root *torpid*, unless the surname is read "a little slow."

Tourneur the ship's barber (V)
The name appears to have no significance since we know nothing of the character other than that he is a barber, but one wonders if Pynchon did not confuse horror-film director Jacques Tourner with George King, who gave us *Sweeny Todd the Demon Barber of Fleet Street*, whose haircutting "hero" cuts the throats of his patrons and has them baked into pies. The name could also allude to Elizabethan dramatist Cyril Tourneur whose play *The Revenger's Tragedy* (although sometimes attributed to Thomas Middleton) is in part a model for *The Courier's Tragedy* in Lot 49.

Tox, Timothy (M&D)
This fictional author of the *Pennsylvaniad* is obviously, as Charles Clerc points out, modeled on John Barth's fictionalized Ebenezer Cooke who works on his epic *Marylandiad* in *The Sot-Weed Factor* (*Mason* 91). The alliterative name hints at some of the poetic excess we find in his doggerel couplets, emphasized by the surname sound tox(ic).

Toy, Yup (ATD)
Not a common Chinese name, it sounds more like a stereotypical "Chinese name" invented by Americans. In fact, there was

a character named Yup Toy played by H.T. Tsiang who appeared in the 1960 television program *Sugarfoot*. *Thomas Pynchon Wiki* suggests that the name is a joke, "yuppie toy": "expensive yuppie gadget."

Tracy, Alfonso (GR)
Common name.

Tracy, Mabel (GR)
Common name.

Tran, Thi Ahn (Vine)
The name is composed of common Vietnamese names and seems only to identify the character as Vietnamese.

Traverse, Cooley (ATD)
The given name of Webb's father is a variant of *cooly* or *coolie*, used primarily as a term for cheap laborers, especially from China or India; it can also be used to describe a member of the lower class (OED). These associations are relevant to the Traverse clan, especially in how they are viewed by owners and managers. *See* Traverse, Webb for the surname.

Traverse, Frank (ATD)
Although called Francisco once (200), Francis (also used to refer to him [217]) is the likely name from which the more common Frank is derived. The adjective *frank* can mean open, sincere, straightforward (AH4), all appropriate to his character. Francis recalls Saint Francis of Assisi, whose dedication to the poor is well known. This seems linked to Frank's interest in revolution and anarchy and his being on the side of the oppressed, against the interests of the wealthy and powerful, epitomized by Scarsdale Vibe.

Traverse, Jess (Vine)
Slade reads the surname as a suggestion of "angles at variance to officialdom" ("Communication" 74). The quality of resisting official control is passed from father Jess to daughter Sasha. One could read the entire name Jess Traverse as "just contrary," or someone who refuses to conform or give in.

Traverse, Jesse (ATD)
Given the character Jesse's birth in ATD and the character Jess Traverse's advanced age in Vine, they appear to be one and the same. *See* Traverse, Jess. The reading "just contrary" seems to summarize aptly the entire Traverse family's resistance to authority, social convention, and the mechanisms of capitalism the former are used to uphold.

Traverse, Kit (ATD)
Kit is short for Christopher, which he is also called (334, 673). It is a common name. *See* Traverse, Webb for the surname.

Traverse, Lake (ATD)
Lake is not a common name, but combined with the surname, it forms a geographical reference to Lake Traverse, located on the borders of Minnesota, South Dakota, and North Dakota. This multistate location, embodied in the name, prefigures the scene where Lake Traverse is placed with elbows and knees in four different states while Sloat and Deuce have their way with her (269). *See* Traverse, Webb for the surname.

Traverse, Reef (ATD)
Unlike his brothers, Reef has a name that is not a shortened form of some common name. Nor is it commonly used as a name itself. It does allow for his brothers to refer to him familiarly as "Reefer" (199 et al.), a pun on the slang term for a marijuana cigarette. The word *reef* has many associations appropriate, not so much to the character as to the novel and the author. In nautical terms (terms familiar to the sailor Pynchon), a reef is a horizontally folded section of sail, used to reduce the surface area of the sail, exposing less of it to the wind (OED). Most are familiar with *reef* as a chain of rocks, coral, etc. under water, but the same word in gold

mining terms (appropriate to ATD) means a vein of quartz containing gold (OED). Finally, as a slang verb, *reef* can mean to feel someone's genitals (OED). This last offers an apt, metonymic description of the largely sexual nature of the relationship between Reef and Yashmeen. See Traverse, Webb for the surname.

Traverse, Webb (ATD)

While Traverse is a fairly common surname, Pynchon must be playing with the wide range of meanings of this semantically dense word. As a verb, *traverse* can mean to pass across or through, to cross and recross, and to move diagonally (AH4), all of which relate to this character's, indeed this family's, growth and development. But it also means "to go counter to; thwart" and as a legal term "to deny formally" (AH4), meanings that reflect charactonymically every member of the Traverse family, but especially Webb's consistent defiance of the seemingly irresistible force of capitalism. These qualities are also reflected in some of the meanings of *traverse* as a noun: "defensive barrier" or "something that obstructs or thwarts" (AH4). Webb is typically a surname, but may double the preceding associations by way of an allusion to outlaw John Joshua Webb, who did not let his occasional involvement in law enforcement prevent him from moonlighting as a criminal (O'Neal 334–5), much as Webb Traverse does not let his mine work prevent him from using dynamite in furthering the interests of organizing miners against the mine owners. Webb is also "a pet form of Webster" (Kolatch 238).

Treacle (ATD)

Dick Counterfly's third wife has a name meaning "molasses" or "cloying speech or sentiment" (AH4). She bestows her sweet attentions on Chick Counterfly, and presumably many other young men.

Treacle, Edwin (GR)

Larsson suggests *treacle* as the British term for "molasses," as an old term for "antidote to a poison," and as a description of something "excessively sweet and sticky" (V85.25). None of these possibilities suggests a promising connection to our character, a famous Freudian. *Treacle* is also anything cloying, especially speech or sentiment. AH4 defines *cloying* as causing "distaste or disgust by supplying with too much of something originally pleasant." Perhaps the name suggests that orthodox Freudianism has outgrown its usefulness.

Treemorn, Rica (ATD)

The context suggests that this is Lake Traverse's companion in her initial foray into prostitution. The name is not listed in MacKell's study of Colorado prostitution in the era. Rica is a fairly common name, but also Spanish for "rich," suggesting one impetus for entering prostitution. Treemorn, not a common name, suggests both nature (*tree*) and new beginning (*morn*), but also the sadness of a loss by sound association: "mourn," capturing both the loss of nature through mining and the loss of innocence.

Trefoil, Gavin (GR)

As Weisenburger suggests, a trefoil is a trifoliate plant. He cites the comparison of Trefoil to Krishna and offers a very good analysis of how *trefoil* refers to Hindu mythology and, by extension, captures the driving contraries of GR: "love and hate, white and black, salvation and destruction" (86).

Tremaine, Winthrop (Winner) (Lot 49)

The swastika salesman takes both of his names from two prominent surnames of whiteness and the elect. Winthrop, of course, suggests John Winthrop, early founding figure in New England, and Tremaine is an old British name (Reaney and Wilson 453). The nickname Winner further suggests alignment with the Puritan elect, but through theories of racial supremacy rather than piety. Grant suggests that Tremaine might refer to the television program Johnny Tremaine, acting as a "diminution of the American past" (122).

Trench (V)
There are three possibilities for this name. The OED defines the noun *trench* as "a cut, scar, furrow, or deep wrinkle in the face." As a verb, *trench* means to cut, carve or gash. Either of these meanings could be appropriate for a cosmetic surgeon's assistant. We might also read *trench* as a synonym for gutter, a place frequently occupied by this character's mind.

Trent (Vine)
Common name.

Trent (M&D)
A common given name. If the character was the actual coachman for Elizabeth, Lady Barnard (about whom biographical evidence is somewhat scarce), no obvious source mentions him.

Trespassers, the (ATD)
This shadowy group is ambiguous. The name and initial description suggest something sinister (424), then they appear to be intent on warning humanity of its inexorable doom (554). The name captures both the physical and temporal aspects of these visitors from the future.

Triggerman, Ernie (Vine)
Triggerman is variously defined as "gunman" (AH4) or more generally, "hired thug" (OED). Triggerman represents Hollywood, so the reference seems to be to the mercenary nature of producers in general.

Trillium (Vine)
Trillium is a North American herb, also called wake-robin (OED). The name seems metonymically appropriate for a young hippie, and part of a group of names in the novel taken from the 1960s' preoccupation with nature, freedom, and radical politics.

Tripping, Geli (GR)
Fowler (158) and Weisenburger (155) both point out the obvious pun: gaily tripping, that is the enjoyment of LSD-induced mind alteration. Like other names derived from drugs, sexuality, etc., Geli Tripping identifies Pynchon's young witch as a transgressive figure. Fowler also suggests that Pynchon may have come across the name Geli in some source on Hitler: Geli Raubel was the name of the niece with whom Hitler had been in love (15).

Tristero y Calavera, Hernando Joaquín de (Lot 49)
As Grant points out, *calavera* means "skull" in Spanish, suggesting, he says, "the threatening nature of the Tristero" (127). He also cites Mendelson on the name Tristero (tryst, *tristesse*), Palmeri who sees a sinister quality in *tryst* and *tristia* as melancholy, Tanner who adds "terror" to *triste* to identify sadness and terror in America, and suggests *triste* and *eros* as a final possibility (44). Together what do the names suggest? A love of sadness and death? Romantic melancholy? Sadness at the need to kill to defend the disinherited? The terror of sadness and death? Or perhaps the need to love (or at least recognize) mortality as well as persistent sadness. This is another name with multiple interpretive possibilities.

Tromblay, Skip (Vine)
Tromblay is a not uncommon surname, but it may be meant as a pun for trompe l'oeil (usually used for art pieces that give the illusion of reality). As Tromblay is a news anchor, this could be a reference to the media and its trickery and superficiality.

Trudi, the blond (GR)
Common name.

Tsangarakis, Tony (ATD)
Both given- and surname are common in Greek, appropriate for a character referred to as "the Greek" (1042).

Tsurigane, Miss Umeki (ATD)
Umeki is a common Japanese name. There may be a reference to Japanese actress Miyoshi Umeki. But the definition of the Japanese word *umeki* is "inserting a piece of wood into a crack or hole" (*Brinkley's J-ED* 1563). Given the physical nature of the character's relationship and her physical attractiveness, some play on the sexual connotations of the word seem likely. Tsurigane is not a common name. The word means "a large hanging bell" (*Brinkley's J-ED*). As she is a mathematician, this could be a reference to a bell curve. Or, keeping with a sexual reading, the hollow bell may be read as a vaginal image.

Tubby (ATD)
While not a character as such, this trained pig does interact with Edwarda Vibe, who later describes their relationship as "closest friends" (161). Tubby recalls the pig theme that was so prevalent in GR. The name is obviously charactonymic for a pig.

Tubsmith, Root (ATD)
Root is fairly common as a surname, but not a given name. It may be another math reference referring to: "a number that when multiplied by itself an indicated number of times forms a product equal to a specified number" (AH4). The last name sounds Dickensian. Based on such words as locksmith or wordsmith, where one works with or on something, he works with a tub. The suggestion is of a large belly, worked on by what appears to be a largely liquid diet.

Tulsa, Aunt (Vine)
D.L.'s aunt is only mentioned once as a religious person who tended to read things as messages from beyond. Perhaps the name Tulsa is meant to refer to the Bible Belt by way of one of its better-known cities.

Tumbling (M&D)
This neighbor of the historical Harland may be real, but he is not mentioned in Mason's journal (although a Tumblestone does appear [191]).

Tunadoras (M&D)
See Abraham.

Turner, Freddie (ATD)
This colleague of Vanderjuice's from Harvard is historian Frederick Jackson Turner, who did give the talk on the frontier in American history as described in the text (52). He was not at Harvard, however, until 1910 ("Turner, Frederick Jackson").

Turnstone, Willis (ATD)
Willis is a common name. A turnstone is a wading bird named for its manner of finding food (AH4). If charactonymic meaning is intended, "turn stone" suggests the kind of forceful manipulation often employed by chiropractors, and illustrated by Turnstone's ad hoc treatment of Jimmy Drop (310). The name also recalls the common saying "leave no stone unturned."

Twiford, Mr. (M&D)
Host to Mason and Dixon mentioned in Mason's Journal (63).

Uchida, Mr. Ryohei (ATD)
As *Thomas Pynchon Wiki* says, Uchida was a Japanese nationalist and member of the Black Dragon Society mentioned by Pynchon.

Uckenfay, Des (ATD)
The surname is a joke, translating from pig Latin to "Fucken." The gender of this obese one year old is not given, but Des could be short for Desmond, Desiree, Desdemona or similar common names. Read together with the pig Latin translated, the names approximate "They's Fuckin'."

Ulrich, Johann (M&D)

Although the name is fairly common, the context suggests a reference to the Pied Piper of Hamelin (who is not named in any version of the tale). Ulrich is said in the novel to have been a famed fifer from Hanover (just north of the German city of Hamelin) who taught his skills to Slowcombe.

Umberto I (V)

Grant identifies the historical Italian king (103).

Unchleigh, Lieutenant (M&D)

One expects a derisive name for a character who embodies both timidity and incompetence (36), yet the name is enigmatic. It does not seem to be used as a surname. It could be loosely charactonymic if we read the name as *unch* obsolete form of inch (OED)and *-ly*, or one who does things by inches (timidly). Or we could read the surname as pig Latin for *lunch*, thus he would be the comically named Lieutenant Lunch.

Urania (M&D)

The name is often used as a "title of a book or poem dealing with celestial or astrological themes" (OED). It is an amusing name for Dixon's dance partner, although it would have been more appropriate had she danced with the astronomer, Mason.

Ursula (GR)

The name of Ludwig's pet lemming is common enough as a given name that it need not have any specific signification. Ware suggests that the name is appropriate for a lemming by citing the history of St. Ursula, who was massacred with 11,000 virgins in Cologne during the fifth century ("*Gravity's Rainbow*").

Utgarthaloki, Frau (GR)

See Utgarthaloki, Stefan. Interestingly, the narrator says "nobody is certain what her first name is."

Utgarthaloki, Stefan (GR)

"He is named for the Teutonic god Utgarthaloki (Loki of Outgard), a giant and personification of evil" (Weisenburger 296). An appropriate name for this member of the elect whose home is the place where powerful figures representing "the System" machinate against Roger Mexico. The name ideally represents the immense strength and seeming invincibility of the forces of economic and political power.

Valentiner, Max (ATD)

While the name Valentiner would be an ironic creation for a U-Boat captain who sinks a passenger ship, Max Valentiner is the actual name of the German submarine commander who sank the passenger liner SS *Persia* without firing a warning shot or allowing the passengers time to escape (Manfield).

Vámos, Mihály (ATD)

Mihály is the Hungarian form of the common name Michael. Given that he is a motorcycle racer and hill-climbing champion (951) the surname may derive from the Spanish *vamos* (let's go), implying hurried departure. Vámos does seem to be a fairly common Hungarian surname, though.

Vamplet, Miss Oomie (ATD)

A vamp is "a woman who uses her sex appeal to entrap and exploit men" (AH4). So, Vamplet is "little vamp." If the given name is pronounced "OOH MY!," it would aptly describe a typical male response to such a creature.

Van der Groov, Frans (GR)

Weisenburger glosses the name as "Frank the Groove" (60). Of course the Dutch for *groove* is *groef*. If we retain the English reading of the last part of the name, it would be "Frans of the groove." Perhaps *groove* refers to the rifling (spiral groove in the barrel) of his ubiquitous gun with which he hunts the dodoes.

Van der Groov, Hendrik (GR)
Hendrik is a common name in Germany, Belgium, and the Netherlands. *See* Van der Groov, Frans for the surname.

Van Meter (Vine)
Common name.

van Niekerk, Sargeant (V)
Another plausible Dutch name, van Niekerk could have been taken from Pynchon's voluminous background material, but the source is uncertain.

van Wijk, Willem (V)
Grant cites Pittas-Giroux, who claims the name is a joke referring to a historical figure of the same name who sided with the whites against his tribesmen (116).

Vanderjuice, Professor Heino (ATD)
He is referred to as Heino Vanderjuice of New Haven (6) and of Yale University (29), emphasizing his affiliation with an academic institution, hence he is in thrall to larger powers, especially the capitalists who help endow the university. This is emphasized, too, in the comic name Vanderjuice that echoes the famous Vanderbilt family of immense wealth, yet undercuts the sense of power by making the name sound ridiculous. It could also be read as a multilingual pun: *van der juice*, translating to " of the Jews," though he is not depicted as being Jewish. *Thomas Pynchon Wiki* suggests "wonder juice" or "wander juice" or "fond o' juice." The last seems most likely and would be one of several names suggesting a strong fondness for alcohol. Heino is a common name, popular in Denmark, the Netherlands, and Germany.

Vane, Sir Henry (the younger) (M&D)
The DNB identifies the politician and author (Mayers).

Vanya (GR)
Vanya is the "token Slav" in the Pökler collective (155). The name appears to be an ethnic marker.

Varkumian the pimp (UR, V)
Harder suggests that the name is "a play on the German word for 'dissolute,' or 'squalid'" (68). Presumably he means *verkommen*, an adjective usually rendered in English as "seedy" or "depraved." It could also derive from the German verb *verkümmern*, meaning "to become stunted." Grant argues that the name is modelled on the character Youkoumian in Evelyn Waugh's *Black Mischief* (41). In UR he is introduced as "a pimp named Varkumian" (126) instead of the name followed by the occupational epithet as in V.

Vaseline (ATD)
The name of this maid to Edwarda Vibe comes from the popular brand of petroleum jelly; R.A. Cheesbrough introduced the proprietary term Vaseline in 1872 (OED), just prior to the time of the novel. The use of the name of this early lubricant may have comic sexual connotations, but nothing that has any direct application to this very minor character. There may be some slight charactonym intended, as Vaseline helps Edwarda slip away from her husband.

Vásquez, Emilio (ATD)
Emilio Vásquez-Gómez was one of Madero's early cabinet members (Gonzales 81–2).

Vásquez, Sargeant Amparo (ATD)
Amparo means "shelter" in Spanish, ironic for a prison guard, but appropriate in a way. It is also a common Hispanic name, as is the surname Vásquez.

Vásquez Brothers Marimba Quartet (M&D)
One of Pynchon's musical inventions, the name has no clear reference. Vásquez is a common Chicano surname. There is a possible reference to DJ Junior Vasquez. By the 1980s, he was one of the most well-known DJs in New York City.

Vaucanson, Jacques de (M&D)
The French inventor is identified by the *Encyclopaedia Britannica* ("Vaucanson, Jacques de").

Vaucanson's Duck (M&D)
Any standard reference listing Vaucanson will mention the famous duck. While this is one of many instances of fact being stranger than fiction in Pynchon, the duck in M&D is, needless to say, fictionalized. The *Encyclopaedia Britannica* mentions the duck's ability to eat, drink, and "digest." Love is Pynchon's addition.

Veery, Cosmo and Damian (M&D)
The Veery brothers are named for the famous saintly brothers Cosmas (also spelled Cosmos or Cosmo) and Damian. A veery is a type of bird, a thrush (OED). The meaning of this surname is unclear in reference to these two effigy makers. Veery is also an anagram of every, perhaps suggesting "Everyman" as revolutionary.

Veevle (M&D)
This name has no apparent meaning or external reference. It is not a common surname. There may be an allusion to "weevil" or "evil" by sound association.

Venusbergs, the (V)
The name seems to be a convoluted joke. Wagner had originally intended to call *Tannhäuser, Der Venusberg* (The Mount or Hill of Venus), but decided against it when he heard about reactions from some of the public (purportedly medical students and faculty), focusing on vulgar jokes (Newman 5). The jokes must revolve around a pun: the mount of Venus, or mons veneris, is the female pubic mound. The reference may be to the fat Venusberg daughter who tried to "lure young Profane into the bathroom" (379).

Verbena (ATD)
She is only mentioned as a friend of Katie McDivott. The name is not common, but one of several in the novel derived form the names of flowering plants.

Veronica (V)
See also Augustine, Bartholomew, Ignatius, Paul, and Teresa. The mysterious V-rat is named by Fairing after the disputed Saint Veronica. Unlike the other rats, who are named for accepted saints, Veronica's name and identity have been questioned for years: the name comes from *vera icon* (true image) and was most likely invented for the fabled woman said to have wiped Christ's face when he fell on the way to Calvary (Farmer 477).

Vesna (ATD)
Common Slavic name.

Vibe, Colfax (ATD)
Colfax is a common city name in the United States, but not common as a personal name. It doesn't couple with Vibe (vibration), like many of the other family names, to produce any sort of meaning. It may have been chosen solely to produce the anachronistic/technological nickname "Fax."

Vibe, Cragmont (ATD)
Unlike other Vibes, such as Scarsdale, Fleetwood, and Wilshire, whose location-based names give off the vibration of wealth and power, Cragmont has a name drawn from a neighborhood in Berkeley, California. It is appropriate for a boy who ran off with the circus, married a "trapeze girl," and started "an enormous family" (150). The name suggests Berkeley's liberal reputation.

Vibe, Dittany (ATD)
One would expect this enthusiastic recipient of spankings to have a delightfully suggestive, if not pornographic name. Dittany is "an aromatic woolly plant" (AH4). She is one of several female characters in the novel named for plants or flowers.

Vibe, Edwarda Beef (ATD)
Edwarda is a feminine form of the name Edward, but much less common. She is also called "Eddie" (160–1), suggesting

perhaps masculinity, but the little description we have seems to undercut this, although her attractiveness is described with the more typically masculine word *handsome* (161). The name was probably chosen along with the maiden name as a joke/pop culture reference: Edwarda Beef ("where's the beef?"), referring to the popular television ads for Wendy's Restaurant from the 1980s featuring this phrase.

Vibe, Fleetwood (ATD)
Like Scarsdale and Wilshire, Fleetwood gives off the vibration of wealth, being the name of a wealthy New York Suburb as well as the Cadillac Fleetwood automobile. There may also be a pop culture reference to the rock band Fleetwood Mac.

Vibe, R. Wilshire (ATD)
Like Fleetwood and Scarsdale, Wilshire has a name suggesting the vibration of wealth associated with Los Angeles's Wilshire Boulevard, which runs through Beverly Hills. But it also travels through Hollywood, appropriate to this decadent producer of "horrible 'musical dramas'" (161).

Vibe, Scarsdale (ATD)
Vibe is slang for vibration, describing the force or message felt to emanate from a person or thing. It is often used in the phrase "bad vibes" referring to a person, place, or thing to which one has an immediately negative reaction. Presumably, the Scarsdale Vibe would be a sense of wealth and power associated with the very affluent New York suburb, Scarsdale.

Vicki (Vine)
Common name.

Villa, Gastón and his Bughouse Bandoleros (ATD)
This Pynchon band name echoes in its style Enrico Eddie and His Hong Kong Hotshots from Vine. *Bughouse* is slang for an insane asylum (AH4) and *bandolero* is Spanish for "brigand." Although both Gastón and Villa are common names, the surname alludes to Pancho Villa, the Mexican revolutionary.

Villa, Pancho (ATD)
Mexican revolutionary and organizer of the El Dorado cavalry (Gonzales 79).

Villard, Dumpster (GR)
AH4 lists the Villards as a prominent monied family involved in railroads and publishing. The character is another classmate of Slothrop's at Harvard. The name Dumpster seems to be a swipe at the ruling class.

Villiers, M. de (UR, V)
Grant identifies the source for this name as the 1899 Baedeker guide to Egypt (45). Villiers was the Russian vice-consul at Alexandria (Baedeker 5). One wonders if Pynchon does not intend the reader to recall another Villiers here. Villiers de l'Isle-Adam was the author of *L'Eve Futur*, in which Thomas Edison creates a female automaton named Hadaly based on a woman compared to the Venus Victrix (note the double V). The automaton shares some superficial qualities with V.

Vince, Sister (Vine)
Purely a joke, Sister Vince is the Harleyite Order's theologian. The name reinforces the comedy of a group of bikers who would reconstitute their gang as a group of nuns "for tax purposes" (358).

Vincent (LL)
Common name.

Vincent (MMV)
Common name. He is one of Brennan's friends. Since Brennan is Krinkles Porcino's roommate and a Vincent and a Krinkles both appear in E (81), this is likely the same Vincent.

Vincent (E)
Common name.

Vincenzo (ATD)

This common name is Italian for Vincent.

Viola, Mme. (V)

The name seems chosen for its first letter: Stencil leaves Malta in search of another clue related to V., said to be in the possession of "one Mme. Viola" (451). The name is a fairly common one.

Violetta (LL)

A common Italian name, the word for violet. There may be an ironic reference to the beautiful courtesan Violetta in Verdi's *La Traviata*; our Violetta is only mentioned as a fortune teller from the past: "The old woman with the eye patch" (76).

Virbling, Booth (ATD)

Booth is a common name. *Thomas Pynchon Wiki* suggests that, as a crime writer, Virbling would favor the use of verbs over other parts of speech. We might also read the name as "verbaling," based on *verbalist*, "one skilled in the use of words" (AH4). Hence Virbling (verbaling) would be "skillfully using words," also appropriate for a writer.

Virginia (GR)

Common name.

Viridian (ATD)

The name has no obvious application to the character: the word means "a durable bluish-green pigment" (AH4), termed "Veronese green" by the OED. Like many of Pynchon's odd character names, this one may reflect primarily his love for obscure words.

Vishinsky (GR)

Weisenburger identifies the historical Soviet state prosecutor (258).

Vittorio (Lot 49)

Another character from *The Courier's Tragedy*, Vittorio has the Italian form of Victor for his name. Since he is a toady to Angelo, his name may suggest being part of the elect, rather than the ur-preterite founders of the Trystero. *See also* Niccoló.

Vlasta (GR)

This Herero's name seems to come from the Russian *vlast-*, meaning "rule" or "dominate." Like Enzian, whose father was Russian, Vlasta probably represents a union between Africa and Europe. The European side always represents domination.

Voam, Professor (M&D)

The "camp naturalist" (321) has a name derived from the common abbreviation for the volt-ohm-amp meter (VOAM), a device used to measure voltage, impedance, and current.

Vogelsang, Hedwig (V)

Vogelsang is a common German surname derived from the words for "bird" and "singing." Grant cites Stark and Haarhof on a possible reference to Heinrich Vogelsang, an agent for "the first and most aggressive German appropriator of land in Southwest Africa" (121). Perhaps Pynchon means for Hedwig to be his descendant. The name Hedwig comes from an old German "female personal name composed of the elements *hadu* contention and *wīg* war" (Hanks and Hodges 151). The name is appropriate for an aggressive, sadistic, and sexually precocious member of the siege party, whose violent surroundings only fuel the excitement of the revelers.

Vogt (V)

In English, the word means "steward or bailiff." Harder defines it as "overseer" or "boss" (76). Vogt does run a musical instrument factory, so the name may be descriptive of character function. There is also a possible comic reading. The character is Austrian, so the pronunciation of the name would approximate "fucked." Vogt is, however, a common surname.

Volcanoe, Captain (M&D)
This is another appropriate name for a rebel who is waiting for revolution to erupt.

Volodya (ATD)
Common Russian name, familiar for Vladimir.

von Braun, Wernher (GR)
Weisenburger identifies the historical scientist (128).

von Göll, Gerhardt (GR)
Goll, without the umlaut, seems a fairly common German surname. *Von Göll* has no clear meaning. The German pronunciation approximates "fun girl," perhaps a reference to the pornographic films the character had directed in the past.

von Hartmann, Hr. (UR)
German consul at Alexandria, Egypt at the time period covered in the story (Baedeker 5).

von Maltzan (GR)
Weisenburger identifies the historical German baron (96).

von Stradonitz, Friedrich August Kekulé (GR)
Weisenburger identifies the historical chemist (197).

von Trotha, General Lothar (V)
Grant identifies the historical proto-Nazi monster who was responsible for the slaughter of 80% of Southwest Africa's Hereros (118).

Vond, Brock (Vine)
Cowart points out that *brock* is Anglo Saxon for "badger" (178), recalling both the vicious animal known to fiercely defend itself when threatened and the act of persistently harassing someone. But *badger* also means "one who wears a special kind of badge" (OED). All of these definitions apply to this federal agent. Cowart also suggests that Vond does not fit into *Vineland*'s image of family by suggesting a Dutch etymology of the surname: *Vondeling*, "foundling" (188).

Vongolli (M&D)
The name refers to little clams popular in Brazilian cuisine. It is certainly an odd name for "a Sidekick, a French-Shawanese half-breed Renegado" (707).

Vormance, Dr. Alden (ATD)
Alden is a common name. Vormance is not. It can be reassembled as V-romance, recalling Vhiessu in V, described by Evan Godolphin at one point as a bedtime story (193). Hugh Godolphin stumbled on this eerie place during an expedition much like the Vormance expedition.

Vouziers, Comte Raoul Antoine de, Marquis de Tour et Tassis (Lot 49)
In the absence of historical evidence to the contrary, Grant suggests that this name is made up (132). Vouziers is a city in France, but the name does not seem to mean anything. It does suggest the global force of Thurn and Taxis and, given the context of "aristocrats" controlling world affairs, the long history of "the establishment."

Vowtay, the Brothers (M&D)
Vowtay has no clear meaning. The brothers set out to Bengal to derive great riches, unsuccessfully. The name may derive from *vow* "promise" and *tay* a variant of *tael*, "fluctuating money of account" (OED), reflecting the vagaries of "Nabobickal" success.

Vroom, Cornelius (M&D)
Although Vroom is a common Dutch surname, there seems to be some deliberate play on its meaning. *Vroom* is Dutch for "pious or devout." There is a clear intention of demonstrating the hypocrisy of Christian slave holders on the Cape and in other locations throughout the novel. There is also deep irony in this family name in that all the members of the

family are described in terms of violence and perversion (Cornelius), greed and sexual hunger (Johanna), or sexual precocity (Jet, Greet, and Els). The novel's depiction of Cape attitudes toward religion is instructive: "the only reason for anyone to endure church all day Sunday is to be reminded of the Boundaries there to be o'erstepp'd. The more aware of their Sins as they commit them, the more pleas'd be the Cape folk" (80).

Vroom, Els (M&D)
Els is the Dutch equivalent of Alice. *See* Vroom, Cornelius for the surname.

Vroom, Greet (M&D)
Greet seems a variation of Griet, the Dutch equivalent of Peg or Meg. *See* Vroom, Cornelius for the surname.

Vroom, Jet (M&D)
Jet is the Dutch equivalent of Harriet. *See* Vroom, Cornelius for the surname.

Vroom, Johanna (M&D)
Johanna is the Dutch equivalent of Jane or Joan. *See* Vroom, Cornelius for the surname.

Vumb, B.F. (ATD)
Thomas Pynchon Wiki suggests "bum fuck" and sees a rhyming reference to "dumb" in the surname. Given the shared vowel sound, this is plausible. B.F. given as initials with no names divulged is strongly suggestive of B.F. Skinner, the American psychologist. Vumb, an engineer, recalls professor Voam, a naturalist, in M&D.

Waddington, Robert (M&D)
Cope identifies Waddington as Maskelyne's assistant at St. Helena where he observed the transit of Venus ("Some Contacts" 233).

Wade (Vine)
Common name.

Wafna, Count (GR)
The name comes from one gambling song within *Carmina Burana*, "*Ego sum abbas*" ("The Abbot of Cockaigne"). The abbot sings that anyone who visits him in the tavern in the morning will be fleeced of his clothing by evening and cry out against fate. The exclamation in the original is *Wafna! Wafna!* Parlett translates this as "Save me!" (178). He notes that *Wafna* "is cognate with 'weapons' (cf. modern German *Waffen*) and so equivalent to *aux armes!* as a cry for help" (241). The word is translated variously by different interpreters of the verse, but Pynchon almost certainly refers to the "*Ego sum abbas*" through this character, who is last seen wearing only a bow tie and lurching across the deck of the Anubis, "hands full of red, white, and blue chips that spill and clatter on deck, and he'll never cash them in" (491).

Wagner, Professor (GR)
Weisenburger identifies the historical scientist (119).

Wagwheel, Tansy (ATD)
The Dickensian sounding Wagwheel has no clear meaning and is not a common name. It could be short for "wagon wheel": her job for Lew Basnight is said to "drive [her] screaming down Fifteenth Street" (178), a fate slightly embodied in the name. Tansy is a flowering plant. It is fairly common as a surname.

Wahmke, Dr. (GR)
Weisenburger identifies the historical scientist (195).

Waite, Arthur Edward (ATD)
Historical occultist who created the Rider-Waite tarot deck illustrated by Pamela Colman Smith (Kaplan 23).

Waite, Mr. A.E. (GR)
Weisenburger identifies the historical tarot expert (305).

Waldetar the conductor (V)
Waldetar is not a common Portuguese given name; one might expect the more common Waldemar or Valdemar. It is

possible that the name refers to the Brazilian actor Waldetar de Souza, who played Chico in Marcel Camus's 1959 *Black Orpheus*. In the film, the main character (played by Breno Mello) is a streetcar conductor. The occupational epithet Pynchon attaches to the character's name may allude obliquely to the film.

Walker, Foley (ATD)
Both names are common as surnames. *Foley* also refers to an individual who creates sound effects for movies, after Jack Foley, who edited sound effects for Universal Studios in the 1930s (AH4). Several websites suggest that such sound effect creators were often referred to as foley walkers, after the popular sound effect of footsteps.

Wallace (Vine)
Common name.

Wallace (M&D)
This Philadelphia land speculator is not listed in Mason's journal or other key sources. The surname is relatively common. If the character is real, Pynchon's source is uncertain.

Warford, Mr. Joseph (M&D)
Browne identifies the historical Maryland justice (131).

Warford, Mrs. (M&D)
Browne identifies the wife of Justice Warford (133).

Warp, Delver (M&D)
We can read the name as one who delves into that which is twisted or perverted. He is said to have returned from Bengal as "non–Nabobickal as when [he] went out" (100), reflecting the perverted desires of those who would profit from colonialism.

Warpe (Lot 49)
See Warpe, Wistfull, Kubitschek and McMingus.

Warpe, Wistfull, Kubitschek and McMingus (Lot 49)
Since none of these "characters" exists beyond the name of the law firm, it is best to examine them together. Hollander offers a comic reading and dismisses it as a joke: "an emotionally twisted, yearning, Czech bebopper (Charlie Mingus)" ("Pynchon, JFK and the CIA" 70). He does identify the name of Kubitschek as an allusion to "Brazilian social reformer" Juscelino Kubitschek, who served as president from 1956 to 1961 (70). This ties in to Hollander's fascinating reading of the novel as an allegory of the JFK assassination. Colvile ties the name of Warpe into the weaving motif in the novel (most prominent in Oedipa's recounting of the Remedios Varo Painting *Bordando el Manto Terrestre*) by glossing the name as *warp(e)*: "One of the two directions of the thread or wool in weaving" (12). Grant suggests it is a "warm-up" for later inventions of firm names (11). We could read Warpe as "warped," but there does not seem to be a clear unifying notion bringing the names together.

Warren, "Rabbit" (Lot 49)
The name is another simple pun — this one quite obvious: a place where rabbits breed, but also a term for a brothel (OED).

Washington, George (M&D)
A clear reference to revolutionary war hero and first American president.

Washington, Martha (M&D)
Another clear historical reference: the first, first lady.

Wasp and Winsome, Attorneys at Law (LL)
The first of Pynchon's ridiculously named law firms, this one, too, is meant largely to poke fun at the legal profession. Behind the charm of Winsome is the stinger of the Wasp. Or the acronym for White Anglo-Saxon Protestant suggests

Water Giant, the (GR)
See Moss Creature, the.

Wawazume, Professor (Vine)
The closest sounding Japanese word may be Watatsumi, referring to a deity of the sea. This is loosely appropriate in the context of this character's mentioning Chipco's change of an "inland marine policy" to protect against "all forms of animal life" just prior to an attack on a lab by an apparent sea monster (142).

Waxwing, Blodgett (GR)
Blodgett is commonly used as a surname, not a given name and derives from two Dutch words: *bloed* ("blood") and *goet* ("good"); it is probably a modernization of the old Dutch surname Bloedgoet. Obviously, the name was meant to suggest nobility or pure blood line, but here we also see a contrast to *bad blood*. Here *good blood* is also used to overthrow conventional notions of human value as it is applied to a petty criminal (a preterite soul). Larsson (V246.35) and Caesar (7) are undoubtedly correct in the suggestion that Waxwing is a quiet homage to Nabokov's *Pale Fire*, whose central poem begins "I was the shadow of the waxwing slain." The fact that a waxwing is a bird might also refer to Waxwing's freedom, "well-known escapee from ... the worst stockade in the ETO.... He has been AWOL off and on since the Battle of the Bulge" (246).

Wayne, Corporal (GR)
Although Wayne is a common surname, the character, batman or servant to Prentice, is introduced as his driver. The OED lists *wayn(e)* as a variant of *wain*, meaning "wagon" as a noun, or "to carry in a wagon" as a verb. The name is appropriate for a character who is only seen driving during his brief appearance in the novel. Winston points out that the name is also an allusive pun referring to Bruce Wayne, the alter-ego of the comic hero Batman (73).

Wayvone, Ralph, Jr. (Vine)
Diebold and Goodwin suggest a play on the popular rock refrain, "rave on." Wayvone itself does not seem to mean anything. It is not a common surname, but seems to be used occasionally as a given name. The sound of the surname is the same as the Chicano slang term *juevon* (lazy, or someone who does no work) (Vasquez and Vasquez 49).

Wayvone, Ralph, Sr. (Vine)
Ralph is a common name. See Wayvone, Ralph, Jr. for the surname.

Wayvone, Vincent (Vine)
Vincent is a common name. See Wayvone, Ralph, Jr. for the surname.

Webern, Anton (GR)
Weisenburger identifies the historical composer (206).

Wedge, Duke (V)
As a minor character, Duke Wedge has a name that functions purely as a charactonym. The character defines himself by his sexual conquests. *Duke* functions as an obvious masculine signifier. We may read *wedge* as a noun suggesting something (a penis) used to pry something (a vagina) apart or as a verb describing this action.

Weedon (ATD)
The reference is to Weedon Grossmith, brother of and collaborator with comic actor and writer George Grossmith, mentioned in this same passage (494).

Weichensteller (GR)
As Weisenburger points out, *Weichensteller* is the German term for a "pointsman or switchman" (211) — appropriate for a member of the rocket's re-entry team. The name also echoes that of the character Pointsman.

Weissmann, Lieutenant (V, GR)

Literally "white man" in German, the name is appropriate for a Nazi. First introduced in V, the character plays a larger role in GR. In his guide to V, Grant quotes Richter on the character: "A professional Aryan even in name" (120). Weisenburger discusses how the color white is connected to death throughout GR, so it is no coincidence that the "white man" (*see also* Blicero) is the figure most connected to death in the novel. Harder glosses the name as "wise man," (78) presumably because he "breaks" the supposed code in the sferics recorded by Mondaugen in V, but this reading seems doubtful.

Wells, Buck (ATD)

Buckley Wells (the source of Pynchon's spelling "Bulkley" [279] is uncertain) was the manager of the Smuggler mine (Backus 11), as depicted by Pynchon.

Wenk (GR)

Achtfaden's Nordhausen code name, like the names Spörri and Hawasch, is drawn from Fritz Lang's film *Dr. Mabuse, der Spieler* (Fowler 198).

Wensleydale (ATD)

A close business associate of Lew Basnight, Wensleydale is named for a region of Yorkshire, England, known especially for its eponymous cheese. It is uncertain how this could apply to such a minor character, but perhaps its proper, aristocratic sound suggests his priggishness: he denounces Basnight for some unspecified transgression (37–8).

Werfner, Professor Doktor Joachim at Göttingen (ATD)

Both Renfrew and Werfner are fairly common names, but Werfner is chosen as it reverses the spelling of Renfrew, his double or part of his bilocated self. Even the given names are similar: Joachim is a variant of Yehoyachim, meaning "God will establish" (Kolatch 250), echoing Jothim ("God is upright"). Each is also presented with a tag describing his physical location as part of the theme of bilocation in the novel. Werfner may derive from the German noun *Werfen* (distortion), suggesting that Werfner is merely a distortion of Renfrew, as in a warped mirror image, showing something backward, even the letters in a name.

Wernher the bartender (V)

Common German name.

Wesley, [John] (M&D)

The DNB identifies Wesley as the founder of Methodism (Rack).

Wetherburn, Mr. [Henry] (M&D)

Henry Wetherburn owned Wetherburn's tavern in colonial Williamsburg, Virginia. The building still exists and has been fully restored.

Whappo (GR)

The name is connected to whipping (Hohmann 22), presumably onomatopoeically. He is described as "baiting his master in hopes of getting a leather-keen stripe or two across [his] dusky Afro-Scandanavian buttocks" (69).

Wharfinger, Richard (Lot 49)

Grant cites Sondergard's clever suggestion that the name is a conflation of "Webster, Heywood, Marston, and Massinger," creating a composite tragedian of the era (58). He also cites Colvile and Cowart on the word's meaning, "manager of a commercial wharf" (59). Obviously, this provides links, not only to Driblette's suicide, but to numerous water images in the novel. The OED defines *wharfinger* as "the owner or keeper of a wharf." This points to an intriguing possibility: given the prominent image of tapestry and weaving, *wharf* may be a conflation of *warp* and *woof*, in other words, the entire pattern. As keeper of the "wharf," Wharfinger (and his play) is thought by Oedipa to contain the key to meaning.

Wheat, Catherine (M&D)
Browne identifies the unwed mother described in the text (131).

Wheat, Conrad (M&D)
Browne identifies the historical father of Catherine Wheat (131, 155).

Wheeler, Prairie (Vine)
Berger reads *prairie* as "a site of openness" (par 21). Cowart suggests that the name is charactonymic and offers the French *prairie* ("meadow"), the month *Prairial* from the French Revolutionary Calendar of 1793, and a possible reference to Miss Prairie Dawn from *Sesame Street* ("Continuity" 178). The charactonymic quality of these readings is unclear. Slade reads the entire name *Prairie Wheeler* as a union of "the twin symbols of Earth and Fortuna (Fortune's wheel, or chance)" ("Communication" 74). We should also consider it as a 1960s nature-based name.

Wheeler, Zoyd Herbert (Vine)
"Zoyd is a father with the qualities of a mother, a father without the phallus, whose penis is only a penis. He is not quite a void — some figure for feminine absence entirely outside the symbolic order; he is ... a Zoyd: passive but capable" (Berger par 21). Diebold and Goodwin point out that Zoyd rhymes with *void* also, and that it shares a *Z* with Zuñiga, although they offer no explanation of the significance of this. According to Slade, the surname Wheeler leaves Zoyd "associated with the unpredictability of Fortune's turning wheel" ("Communication" 75). Zoyd is uncertain as a reference to *void* or a variation of it. The probable reference is to the avant garde rock/classical/jazz group of the 1970s and 1980s, Art Zoyd. The French group has used strings, horns, and keyboard (Zoyd's instrument in Vine), without percussion (Robbins 22).

Whike, Mr. (M&D)
It is unclear if the name may refer to a real person, but Whike seems to be a relatively common Scots surname.

Whimbrel, Mr. (M&D)
The OED identifies *whimbrel* as a term applied to some species of curlew (a type of shore bird). We know nothing of the minor character bearing this name except that he is a publisher. Perhaps the name comically alludes to some actual publisher with an avian name (Pelican or Penguin).

White, Mr. (M&D)
Common name.

Whitefield, [George] (M&D)
The DNB identifies this Methodist leader (Schlenther).

Whitestreet (GR)
This "Fallen Officer" listed in the *Times* is fictional (Weisenburger 134). The name's reference to the color white links this character to death, prefiguring his death, in that the color white is associated with death throughout the novel. While Whitestreet does not appear to be a common surname, there is an English village named Whitestreet Green.

Whitpot, Mr. (M&D)
According to the OED, *whitpot* is an obsolete variant of *white-pot*, "a kind of pudding or custard made by boiling milk with other ingredients." Since the character is described as an "itinerant Stove-Salesman," we may read it as a specialized description based in metonymy. The connection to boiling or heating implied by the name may also apply to this minor character's temper, revealed when he draws vigorously on his pipe and responds to a fop who has called for a New York style non-smoking area, that "what's needed is a No-Idiots Area" (365).

Whittaker, Edmund (ATD)
British mathematician at Cambridge in the late nineteenth century ("Edmund Taylor Whittaker").

Wiener, Tex (Vine)
Tex is a very masculine name and *Wiener* ("sausage or frankfurter") is clearly

phallic. The name is doubly a masculine identifier.

Wieselsberger (GR)
Weisenburger identifies the historical researcher (210).

Wigglesworth, Brenda (V)
Grant cites Safer who points out the ironic parallel with "devout Puritan poet Michael Wigglesworth" (190), but there is more here. The character is described as an American WASP. "Wigglesworth" is listed among the names of Mayflower descendants (McAuslin 817), so the name itself defines her as a WASP. It is also clear that her travelling, soul-searching, and experience-seeking is all part of a perfunctory college-girl game and that she will enter the realm of Puritan elect "come marriage and the Good Life, someday soon now" (452).

Wild, Mr. (M&D)
This is a mystery. Mason clearly states that Wild was "Mr. Bodley's Librarian" (558) and the context identifies the year as 1752. In 1752, Mr. Bodley's Librarian was Humphrey Owen (Philips 92). Philips lists no librarian named Wild from the founding of the library until 1800.

William (I) of Orange (Lot 49)
Sixteenth-century Dutch prince and instigator of the eighty years war, which freed the Dutch from Spain.

Williams, Ralph Vaughn (ATD)
The reference is to the twentieth-century British composer, whose first name is pronounced "Rafe," whose beautiful *Fantasia on a Theme of Thomas Tallis* is still widely played.

Willow (ATD)
The name comes from a type of tree, but is fairly common as a female name.

Wim (GR)
The name is common in Germany, Belgium, and the Netherlands.

Wim (M&D)
The name is common in Germany, Belgium, and the Netherlands.

Wimpe, V-Mann / the I.G. man (GR)
V-mann stands for *Verbindungsmann*, or "agent" (Weisenburger 89). Weisenburger states that *wimpe* means nothing in German, but "suggests the American slang 'wimp'—a weakling" (96). Larsson identifies the pop cultural reference: "Popeye's hamburger-mooching pal J. Wellington Wimpy" (V152.19).

Winsome, Gouverneur "Roony" (V)
See also Charisma and Fu. Unlike the first Whole-Sick-Crew trio we meet in the novel (Raoul, Slab, and Melvin), each of these names is odd, producing an effect opposite to grounding the odd within the ordinary. The strangeness of these names taken together makes them all seem ordinary, much like the crew itself. We have little evidence that Winsome is what his name implies — charming. Of course, the word *winsome* suggests charm that is childlike or naive (AH4). This may suggest the basic immaturity of the crew. Grant cites Pittas-Giroux, who suggests that Roony derives from *The Education of Henry Adams*, where Adams's friend Roony Lee, son of Robert E. Lee, appears (71). The "southern" connection is clear. The spelling of "Gouverneur" suggests a French association, but there is no textual support for this. More likely, the name refers to Gouverneur Morris (1752–1816), a signer of The Articles of Confederation, who, like Winsome, lived in New York.

Winsome, Mafia (V)
Grant suggests that the character is a caricature of Ayn Rand (71), but the name itself seems unconnected to this reading. On the one hand, it is a simple contradiction, a name combining violence and charm. On the other hand, each part of the name describes her: Mafia describes the mercenary nature of her "theory"

(125), Winsome, her popularity as a writer of vulgar romance novels.

Winthrop, Governor [John] (GR)
Weisenburger identifies the historical Massachusetts Bay Colony governor (112).

Winthrop, Matilda (V)
Grant cites Safer on a reference to John Winthrop meant to contrast the contemporary world with the ideals of the original American colonies (142). Of course, GR paints a very negative picture of John Winthrop and the ideas spawned by his Puritan orthodoxy (554–6). The reference to Winthrop, however, in the name of an aging, African-American brothel manager, may be taken ironically. But many African-American surnames derive from the names of their slave-ancestor's owners (the elect owned *and* named the preterite). The first name suggests the character's success in the world through her role in an alternate economy, opposed to the legal structures established by the elect: Matilda derives from the Old German *Mahthildis*, meaning might or strength in battle (Withycombe 202).

Wistfull (Lot 49)
See Warpe, Wistfull, Kubitschek and McMingus.

Wivern, General (GR)
Fowler identifies the wivern as a "two-legged dragon with wings" (276). If there is any significance to the name, it may be that the dragon image is connected to Wivern's high rank and position in "the system"—a fearful creature of the modern day.

Woevre, Piet (ATD)
Piet is a very common Dutch name. The Woevre is a region in northeast France, the sight of bitter fighting during WWI. This may be linked to this character's brutality and involvement in the business of weaponry.

Woffington, Mrs. [Margaret (Peg)] (M&D)
The DNB identifies this actress (Cave).

Wofte, Protasia (M&D)
This character from *The Ghastly Fop* sequence of the novel has a relatively common surname. Although Protasia is not terribly common, Withycombe cites its use in England in the seventeenth century (236). As Withycombe says, the etymology is uncertain.

Wolfe, [James] (M&D)
The DNB identifies this British army officer (Reid).

Womack, Flash (GR)
See Brennan, Peewee. Womack is a common surname, and Flash seems to be a common nickname.

Wren, Mildred (UR, V)
The name of Victoria's younger sister probably has no special significance, although Withycombe points out that the name had fallen from favor before it became very popular again in the nineteenth century (208), making it appropriate in the context of the historical chapter (taking place at the end of the nineteenth century) where it appears.

Wren, Sir Alastair (UR, V)
Tanner speculates that the name Wren echoes that of architect Christopher Wren (44). The name Alastair is spelled several different ways by different families, and we may see a connection with the mystic Aleister Crowley, suggesting a sinister ancestor for Victoria Wren.

Wren, Victoria (UR, V)
As numerous critics have pointed out, this first manifestation of V. begins with the queen's name, specifically the queen most associated with empire and colonialism, some of whose sinister political qualities are associated with V. Grant also identifies a pun on *Wren* (*reine*) (45). This reading establishes a doubling in the name (Victoria

"Queen"). Grant also cites Chambers on the importance of the wren in several myth systems, as identified by Frazer and held to be sacred (45). Grant also mentions Tanner's speculation on a connection to the seventeenth-century architect Christopher Wren. This allusion seems particularly appropriate for the extremely religious Victoria Wren: Christopher Wren designed 53 churches in London ("Wren, Sir Christopher"). The OED identifies *wren* as a slang term for a young woman, also appropriate for this first appearance of the youthful V. Note that some of these glosses are more relevant to the character in the context of the novel V than in the story UR.

Wuxtry-Wuxtry, Mickey (GR)

Another preposterous sounding hyphenated name, Wuxtry-Wuxtry derives from "the archetypal newsboy's cry: 'Wuxtry! Wuxtry!' [Extra! Extra!] Read all about it!' The spelling was commonly used in the 1940s" (Larsson V738.19) [square bracketed translation in the original]. The reference to the newsboy's cry encapsulated in the name presumably refers to the character's startling "revelation" that Slothrop was "in love, in sexual love, with his and his race's death" (738). It seems to also indicate the character's inflated opinion of his interpretation, and perhaps that of analysts in general.

Wyman, Pap (ATD)

Charles E. "Pap" Wyman did own a notorious saloon in Leadville, Colorado in the late nineteenth century (Noel 175).

X, Elliot (Vine)

Hill reads the name as a "telling combination of first- and last-namesakes" that simultaneously recalls Malcolm X and T.S. Eliot through a character who "refuses to plod institutional racism's path into an ecumenically white waste land" (206). The reference to T.S. Eliot is by no means certain, but the reference to Malcolm X for this member of Black Panther parody BAAD is unmistakable.

Xemxi, Elena (V)

Grant cites Inglott on Elena as the "inevitable name for the wife of a Faust" (referring to Helen) and Cassola on the Maltese meaning of Xemxi ("sunny") (149). The name also helps explain part of the meaning of Fausto's phrase "a terrible misalliance" when referring to the Maijstral-Xemxi combination that led to Paola's birth (314). The strong wind of *maijstral* suggests a storm in contrast to the pleasant meteorological association of *xemxi* ("sunny").

Yoder Boys, the (M&D)

The surname is fairly common, but these very minor characters do not appear to be historical, judging by their brief appearance among characters who are all fictional, save Mason and Dixon themselves.

Yogi, the (ATD)

The reference is to former New York Yankee Yogi Berra, known for his double talking and garbled language.

Yolande (GR)

Common name.

Yomama, Michiko (Vine)

The first name is a relatively common Japanese one and the surname sounds plausibly Japanese (close to Yamana or even Yamamoto), but as Diebold and Goodwin point out, puns on "the black insult, 'Yo' Mama!'"

Youngblood, Tiger (V)

While the term *young blood* once suggested the rake or "fast man," it now suggests "the vigor that a youth brings to his setting" (OED). Tiger also suggests vigor, thus yielding a doubling.

Yrjö (GR)

Weisenburger points out that this fictional king appeared in Pynchon's short story "The Secret Integration" (76). Yrjö is a common Finnish name.

Yrjö, King (SI)
He is fictional. Yrjö is a common Finnish name.

Yusef the factotum (V)
Yusef, or Yusuf, is the Muslim name for Joseph: the name captures the ideal of physical beauty associated with the biblical Joseph and also means "prophet" (Ahmed 223–24). Our character is introduced whilst vainly combing his mustaches, and is shown to prophesy chaos and anarchy.

Yutts, Clovis (ATD)
Clovis is not a common name. Stewart does not list it in his *American Given Names*. It recalls Clovis I, fifth-to-sixth-century king of the Franks, but he is known as a unifier, having brought together Gaul as a single kingdom (AH4), surely ironic for this klansman and drooling sadist. *Clovis* also refers to "a prehistoric human culture widespread throughout North America from about 12,000 to 9,000 B.C." (AH4), perhaps suggesting this character's extremely primitive nature. The surname is quite appropriate to this klansman: Yutts is a variation of *yutz*, Yiddish for "jerk."

Yvonne (GR)
Common name.

Yzhitza (ATD)
An enigmatic name for a prostitute, Yzhitza is not a common name and has no clear meaning or sound association.

Zack (M&D)
The context suggests that he is a grandson of Thomas Cresap. Bailey mentions grandchildren, but does not name them. The Cresap genealogy lists a Zachary, but he was not born until 1983 (Cresap and Cresap 633).

Zack (ATD)
Common name.

Zaharoff, [Sir] Basil (ATD)
This financier and arms dealer or "merchant of death" was real ("Zaharoff, Sir Basil").

Zaim (ATD)
Common Slavic name.

"Zanni" (ATD)
Theign's name for an invented agent derives from the commedia dell'arte. *See* Zanni. This is supposed to be a local operative in Venice, referred to as "this city of masks" (708). The commedia dell'arte stock characters, including Zanni, were also referred to as masks ("Commedia dell'Arte"). As a code name, "Zanni" itself is a mask.

Zanni (ATD)
The name of this young pilot from the Italian counterparts of the Chums of Chance is drawn from the commedia dell'arte theatre. The Zanni was one of the stock characters, a "madcap servant," often an acrobat who relied on physical comedy ("Commedia dell'Arte"). The character Zanni is described as a "comically anxious but good-hearted Italian" with "drops of perspiration flying off his face at all angles" (243). His name and behavior also recall the English adjective *zany*.

Zapata, Emiliano (ATD)
Mexican revolutionary and leader of peasant uprisings (Gonzales 39).

Zapf (Lot 49)
Zapf is a German surname, possibly derived from the verb *zapfen*, meaning to tap or draw (beer, for example). As the character is the owner of a bookstore, the name probably refers to Hermann Zapf (b. 1918), world famous book and type designer.

Zarpazo, Father, the Wolf of Jesus (M&D)
Zarpazo is Spanish for "thud, bang, or bump," and probably refers to the

character's brutality, which is echoed in the epithet "Wolf of Jesus" (viciousness in the service of the Lord). Ware suggests an allusion to a notorious Colombian bandit from the mid-twentieth century also named Zarpazo ("*Mason & Dixon*").

Zeeman (M&D)

Although Zeeman is a common Dutch name, Pynchon may be alluding to physics terminology again, by way of the Zeeman effect: "The splitting of single spectral lines of an emission spectrum into three or more polarized components when the radiation source is in a magnetic field" (AH4).

Zeit the doctor (MMV)

Zeit is German for "time." Joined with the occupational epithet, it sends a grim message: If time is the doctor and time's ultimate progression is to death, the prognosis is poor indeed. Miriam's husband curses him after she dies and the wording is suggestive: "cursing Zeit" (196), or cursing time, mortality, etc. These same associations are echoed later in the paragraph, in a different context, by the phrase "racing against time" (196).

Zeitsuss, Mr. (V)

Although Harder glosses the name as "sweet spirit" (76), the literal translation from German would yield "sweet time" (*süss* ["sweet"] and *Zeit* ["time"]). Since Zeitsuss aspires to be a union organizer, the name may refer to a proletarian age of milk and honey that could come through unionizing. On the other hand, the name could refer to the phrase "taking one's sweet time," possibly referring to negative interpretations of unions. There is not sufficient evidence to support any single reading here, and the name could be purely comical.

Zenobia (LL)

Kolatch claims the name derives from the Greek for sign or symbol (450). Pynchon may have lifted the name from the Baedeker guide to Egypt, which he admits to having used as background for UR (SL 17). Zenobia was an Egyptian queen of the third century A.D. (Baedeker cviii). It seems an odd name for one described as "an Armenian refugee" (71).

Zenobia the Copt (V)

This name overheard in a conversation refers to a contemporary (at the time of the chapter) character, but the allusion is to the historical Queen Zenobia of Palmyra who conquered Alexandria in 259 CE ("Alexandria" 55). In this context, Copt refers to a pre–Islamic Egyptian (AH4).

Zermelo, [Ernst] (ATD)

Late nineteenth-century German mathematician ("Ernst Zermelo").

Zhang, Dr./Captain (M&D)

One meaning of the Chinese *zhang* is "open" or "spread" (Jingrong 876). This might reflect his antipathy to the boundary line or any unnatural means of confinement or division used against both nature and people. Zhang is a fairly common Chinese surname, though.

Zhao, Dr. (ATD)

Common Chinese name.

Zhdaev, Major (GR)

This is a plausibly Russian sounding name, but the closest common Russian surname seems to be Zhdanov.

Zhivka (ATD)

A common Bulgarian name, Zhivka derives from the stem *Zhiv-*, meaning "living" in Bulgarian, Russian, and Serbo-Croation. Even in the trying circumstances of warfare, she has many children and a beautiful rose garden, suggesting the triumph of life over death embodied in the name.

Zhlubb, Richard M. (GR)

Numerous critics have identified this reference to Richard M. Nixon. "Richard

M. Zhlubb (i.e. 'schlub' or 'jerk') is a parody of Nixon's paranoia" (Seed, *Fictional Labyrinths* 203).

Zilberfeld, Yitzhak (ATD)
Yitzhak is a variant of Yitzchak (Hebrew for "he will laugh"), commonly Anglicized to Isaac (Kolatch 255). Zilberfeld seems to come from the German *silber* (pronounced "zilber") (silver) and *feld* (field), though our character is more interested in gold (167). The mining association is appropriate to the novel, but most likely both given- and surname were chosen to suggest the Jewish ethnicity of this "Zionist agent" (165).

Zip (ATD)
Presumably a nickname, Zip seems appropriate for this minor boy balloonist, perhaps meant to suggest his youthful attraction to fast flying.

Zippo, Antoine (V)
Here is another minor character whose name is probably pure paronomasia. We can sound all but the last letter as "and to unzip" (obvious bodily function/sexual connotations). Harder claims that this "pseudo-Italian" name "connote[s] liveliness" (74). The surname itself recalls the popular windproof lighter developed in 1932.

Zipyagin, Grigori Nikolaevitch (ATD)
The given name and patronymic are common. The surname is not. There is a probable reference to a Russian minister of the interior named Dmitry Sergeyevich Sipyagin. The spelling of his surname varies according to source—Sipyagin, Sipiagin, Sipiaguine, Zipyagin. He was a reactionary assassinated by a socialist revolutionary in 1902 ("Sipyagin, Dmitry Sergeyevich").

Zogheb, Comte de (UR)
Danish consul-general at Alexandria, Egypt during the time period covered by the story (Baedeker 6).

Zoltan (ATD)
This common Hungarian given name sets the stage for the vampire jokes, as the slavic region (one thinks of Transylvania, long part of Hungary, when one thinks of vampires) was the origin of vampire legends. There is also a pop culture reference to a 1978 B-movie, *Zoltan, Hound of Dracula*.

Zombini, Bria (ATD)
Bria may be short for Brianna, a feminized version of Brian, and unlike the names of her siblings, not specifically Italian. *See* Zombini, Luca for the surname.

Zombini, Cici (ATD)
Cici is probably a familiar form of Cecilia, a common name among Italians and others. *See* Zombini, Luca for the surname.

Zombini, Concetta (ATD)
Concetta is a common Italian name. *See* Zombini, Luca for the surname.

Zombini, Dominic (ATD)
Dominic is a common Italian name. *See* Zombini, Luca for the surname.

Zombini, Elijah (ATD)
This Zombini ancestor is one of the only family members whose given name is not Italian. Elijah means "God" (Hamilton 41) or "the Lord is my God" (Kolatch 79). He is described as making the "first lasagna south of the Mason-Dixon" (570). That he has a distinctly religious name may allude to the religious fervor common to the southern region of the United States. It is, however, a common name. *See* Zombini, Luca for the surname.

Zombini, Luca (ATD)
On the Web, one can find a series of Living Dead Dolls featuring a Great Zombini, although it is unlikely that Pynchon is referring to this figure. The Italian ending *-ini* completes a name beginning Zombi, a variant spelling of *zombie* (a reanimated corpse), frequently featured

in Pynchon's beloved horror films. It is an appropriately sinister name for this "mysterious" illusionist. There may also be comic play on the Italian *zombese* (to tramp or trounce) or even Zamboni, the name of those street-sweeper-looking vehicles that resurface ice-skating/hockey rinks. Luca is a common Italian name.

Zombini, Lucia (ATD)
Lucia is a common Italian name. *See* Zombini, Luca for the surname.

Zombini, Niccolò dei (ATD)
Niccolò is a common Italian name, but was perhaps more common in centuries past. There may be a reference to Renaissance philosopher Niccolò Machiavelli. This allusion may be an oblique reference to the early business practices of the Zombini family: "Corporations today are gentle and caring compared to those early factory owners, whose secrecy and obsession just got meaner and meaner as the years and generations passed" (569). Niccolò escapes this Machiavellian world. *See* Zombini, Luca for the surname.

Zombini, Nunzi (ATD)
One would ordinarily read Nunzi as a familiar form of the common Italian name Annunziata, but this character is a boy. Nunzi is a common Italian surname. It also recalls the character name Nunzi Passarella in SI. *See* Zombini, Luca for the surname.

Zoot, Dr. (ATD)
This comic name derives from the zoot suit: "characterized by full-legged, tight-cuffed trousers and a long coat with wide lapels and heavily padded, wide shoulders" (AH4).

Zsuzsa (ATD)
This common name is a shortened form of the Hungarian Zsuzsanna, spelled Susanna in English.

Zuñiga, Debbi (Vine)
See Zuñiga, Hector.

Zuñiga, Hector (Vine)
The fist name is obvious, from *hector* (v. "to intimidate," n. "a bully"). There does not seem to be any connection to the mythological Hector of the *Iliad*, but Slade sees a reference to Hecate, as he reads Zuñiga as an alter ego of Frenesi, whom he associates with Proserpine ("Communication" 74). This would link Brock Vond to Pluto as abductor of Proserpine and ruler of Hades. Zuñiga is a common Hispanic surname, but given Hector's addiction to television and the novel's film references, the name could be a reference to television and film actor Daphne Zuniga, who rose to prominence in the early 1980s.

Zvi (Lot 49)
Zvi is a relatively common Jewish name. It is a variant of the Hebrew name Zevi or Tz'vee, which means "a deer" (Kolatch 152–3). Hilarius tells of Nazi experiments he took part in trying to render Jews insane or catatonic: "A catatonic Jew was as good as a dead one" (137). His most successful attempt was on Zvi, rendered insane permanently by Hilarius's face. If there is any intended meaning, besides identifying Zvi as a Jew, the name suggests, in context, "a deer caught in the headlamps," rendered nearly catatonic.

Zwitter (GR)
As Weisenburger points out, *Zwitter* means "hermaphrodite" in German (160). Since we are given no information about his sexuality, we may read the name as one of many non-specific derisive names. But the term is not wholly derisive. Volkswagen Beetles with split rear windows (produced in the 1950s) were called zwitters.

Bibliography

Adonis, Andrew. "Fitzmaurice, Henry Charles Keith Petty—fifth marquess of Landsdowne (1845–1927)." *Oxford Dictionary of National Biography*. Ed. H. C. G. Matthew and Brian Harrison. 2004. Oxford: Oxford University Press, May 2006. 4 June 2007. <http://www.oxforddnb.com/view/article/35500>.
Ahmed, Salahuddin. *A Dictionary of Muslim Names*. New York: New York University Press, 1998.
"Aleksandrov, Pavel Sergeevich." *Encyclopaedia Britannica*. 2007. Encyclopaedia Britannica Online. 22 June 2007. <http://search.eb.com/eb/article-9000496>.
"Alexandria." *The Oxford Encyclopedia of Ancient Egypt*. Vol. 1. Ed. Donald B. Redford. Oxford: Oxford University Press, 2001. 54–57.
Alvord, Clarence Walworth. *The Mississippi Valley in British Politics: A Study of the Trade, Land Speculation, and Experiments in Imperialism Culminating in the American Revolution*. Cleveland: The Arthur H. Clark Company, 1917.
Anderson, John. *The International Politics of Central Asia*. Manchester: Manchester University Press, 1997.
"Arnold, Benedict." *Encyclopaedia Britannica*. 2007. Encyclopaedia Britannica Online. 24 July 2007. <http://search.eb.com/eb/article-9009576>.
Backus, Harriet Fish. *Tomboy Bride*. Boulder, CO: The Pruett Press, 1969.
Baedeker, Karl, ed. *Egypt: Handbook for Travellers*. Leipsic: Karl Baedeker, Publisher, 1898.
Bailey, Kenneth P. *Thomas Cresap: Maryland Frontiersman*. Boston: The Christopher Publishing House, 1944.
Bakhtin, Mikhail. *Rabelais and His World*. Bloomington: Indiana University Press, 1984.
Baldwin, Olive, and Thelma Wilson. "Davies, Mary Ann (1743/4–1818)." *Oxford Dictionary of National Biography*. Ed. H. C. G. Matthew and Brian Harrison. 2004. Oxford: Oxford University Press, 2004. 6 Sept. 2005. <http://www.oxforddnb.com/view/article/7252>.
Barbour, Elizabeth, and the Telluride Historical Museum. *Images of America: Telluride*. Mount Pleasant, SC: Arcadia Publishing, 2006.
The Baseball Encyclopedia: The Complete and Official Record of Major League Baseball. New York: Macmillan, 1969.
Beckett, J. V., and Peter D. G. Thomas. "Grenville, George (1712–1770)." *Oxford Dictionary of National Biography*. Ed. H. C. G. Matthew and Brian Harrison. 2004. Oxford: Oxford University Press, Aug. 2005. 18 Aug. 2005. <http://www.oxforddnb.com/view/article/11489>.

Beckson, Carl. "Symons, Arthur William (1865–1945)." *Oxford Dictionary of National Biography*. Ed. H. C. G. Matthew and Brian Harrison. 2004. Oxford: Oxford University Press, 2004. 8 May 2007. <http://www.oxforddnb.com/view/article/36400>.
Bedini, Silvio A. "History Corner: William Mayo (1684–1744) Surveyor of the Virginia Piedmont, Part II." *Professional Surveyor*. 15 Oct. 2002. <http://www.profsurv.com/ps_scripts/article.idc?id=571>.
Bell, E. T. *Men of Mathematics*. New York: Simon and Schuster, 1937.
Bellesîles, Michael A. "Allen, Ethan (1738–1789)." *Oxford Dictionary of National Biography*. Ed. H. C. G. Matthew and Brian Harrison. 2004. Oxford: Oxford University Press, 2004. 6 Sept. 2005. <http://www.oxforddnb.com/view/article/70404>.
Berger, James. "Cultural Trauma and the 'Timeless Burst': Pynchon's Revision of Nostalgia in *Vineland*." *Postmodern Culture* 5.3 (1995). 13 Sept. 2001. <http://muse.jhu.edu/journals/postmodern_culture/v005/5.3berger.html>.
Berressem, Hanjo. "Godolphin, Goodolphin, Goodol'phin, Goodol'Pyn, Good ol'Pym: A Question of Integration." *Pynchon Notes* 10 (1982): 3–17.
Bilger, Burkard. "The Riddler: Meet the Marquis de Sade of the Puzzle World." *The New Yorker*. 4 March 2002. 64–71.
"Blinky Morgan Case." *The Encyclopedia of Cleveland History*. 11 Apr. 2007. <http://ech.case.edu/ech-cgi/article.pl?id=BMC>.
Blumberg, David. "Umlauts and Oz: Signifiers within the Textual Zone of Pynchon's *Gravity's Rainbow*." *American Journal of Semiotics* 9.4 (1992): 69–76.
Boersema, David B. "Wittgenstein on Names." *Essays in Philosophy: A Biannual Journal*. Vol. 1.2. 2000. 07 June 2005. <http://www.humboldt.edu/~essays/paper2.html>.
"Boscovich, Ruggero Giuseppe." *Encyclopaedia Britannica*. 2005. Encyclopaedia Britannica Online. 7 Sept. 2005. <http://search.eb.com/eb/article-9080803>.
"Bouguer, Pierre." *Encyclopaedia Britannica*. 2005. Encyclopaedia Britannica Online. 7 Sept. 2005. <http://search.eb.com/eb/article-9015907>.
Bowen, H. V. "Clive, Robert, first Baron Clive of Plassey (1725–1774)." *Oxford Dictionary of National Biography*. Ed. H. C. G. Matthew and Brian Harrison. 2004. Oxford: Oxford University Press, 2004. 6 Sept. 2005. <http://www.oxforddnb.com/view/article/5697>.
Bradley, Ian, ed. *The Complete Annotated Gilbert and Sullivan*. Oxford: Oxford University Press, 1996.
Brazeau, Robert. "A Note on 'Pierce Inverarity.'" *Pynchon Notes* 30–31 (1992): 185–187.
Brewer, E. Cobham. "Cock Lane Ghost." *Dictionary of Phrase and Fable*. Philadelphia: Henry Altemus, 1898. Bartleby.com, 2000. 19 Sept. 2002. <http://www.bartleby.com/81/3784.html>.
Brinkley's Japanese-English Dictionary. Vol. II M–Z. Ann Arbor: University of Michigan Press, 1963.
Brown, Raymond E., Joseph A. Fitzmeyer, Roland E. Murphy, eds. *The New Jerome Biblical Commentary*. Upper Saddle River, NJ: Prentice Hall, 1990.
Caesar, Terry, and Takashi Aso. "Japan, Creative Masochism, and Transnationality in *Vineland*." *Critique: Studies in Contemporary Fiction* 44.4 (2003): 371–387.
Caesar, Terry P. "A Note on Pynchon's Naming." *Pynchon Notes* 5 (1981): 5–10.
Camp, Roderic A. *Mexican Political Biographies, 1884–1935*. Austin: University of Texas Press, 1991.
Cannon, John. "Stanhope, Philip Dormer, fourth earl of Chesterfield (1694–1773)." *Oxford Dictionary of National Biography*. Ed. H. C. G. Matthew and Brian Harrison. 2004. Oxford: Oxford University Press, 2004. 6 Sept. 2005. <http://www.oxforddnb.com/view/article/26255>.
"Cargill Gliston Knott." *Penicuik Community Development Trust*. 21 June 2007. <http://www.penicuikcdt.org.uk/Cargill_Knott.html>.

Carter, Philip. "Penn, John (1729–1795)." *Oxford Dictionary of National Biography*. Ed. H. C. G. Matthew and Brian Harrison. 2004. Oxford: Oxford University Press, 2004. 23 Aug. 2005. <http://www.oxforddnb.com/view/article/21849>.
Cassola, Arnold. "Pynchon, V., and the Malta Connection." *Journal of Modern Literature* 12.2 (1985): 311–331.
Castillo, Debra A. "Borges and Pynchon: The Tenuous Symmetries of Art." *New Essays on* The Crying of Lot 49. Ed. Patrick O'Donnell. Cambridge: Cambridge University Press, 1991. 21–46.
Cave, Richard Allen. "Woffington, Margaret [Peg] (1720?–1760)." *Oxford Dictionary of National Biography*. Ed. H. C. G. Matthew and Brian Harrison. 2004. Oxford: Oxford University Press, 2004. 23 Aug. 2005. <http://www.oxforddnb.com/view/article/29820>.
Clarke, Tristram. "Short, James (1710–1768)." *Oxford Dictionary of National Biography*. Ed. H. C. G. Matthew and Brian Harrison. 2004. Oxford: Oxford University Press, 2004. 23 Aug. 2005. <http://www.oxforddnb.com/view/article/25459>.
Clasper, David. *Harry Clasper: Hero of the North*. Exeter: Gateshead, 1990.
Clennell, W. H. "Bodley, Sir Thomas (1545–1613)." *Oxford Dictionary of National Biography*. Ed. H. C. G. Matthew and Brian Harrison. 2004. Oxford: Oxford University Press, 2004. 6 Sept. 2005. <http://www.oxforddnb.com/view/article/2759>.
Clerke, A. M. "Bevis, John (1695–1771)." The Rev. Anita McConnell. *Oxford Dictionary of National Biography*. Ed. H. C. G. Matthew and Brian Harrison. 2004. Oxford: Oxford University Press, 2004. 6 Sept. 2005. <http://www.oxforddnb.com/view/article/2330>.
Clifton, Gloria. "Dollond family (per. 1750–1871)." *Oxford Dictionary of National Biography*. Ed. H. C. G. Matthew and Brian Harrison. 2004. Oxford: Oxford University Press, 2004. 6 Sept. 2005. <http://www.oxforddnb.com/view/article/49855>.
Colvile, Georgiana M. M. *Beyond and Beneath the Mantle: On Thomas Pynchon's* The Crying of Lot 49. Amsterdam: Editions Rodopi B.V., 1988.
"Commedia dell'Arte." *Encyclopaedia Britannica*. 2007. Encyclopaedia Britannica Online. 11 June 2007. <http://search.eb.com/eb/article-9024948>.
Cook, Alan. "Halley, Edmond (1656–1742)." *Oxford Dictionary of National Biography*. Ed. H. C. G. Matthew and Brian Harrison. 2004. Oxford: Oxford University Press, 2004. 18 Aug. 2005. <http://www.oxforddnb.com/view/article/12011>.
Cookcroft, James D. *Intellectual Precursors of the Mexican Revolution, 1900–1913*. Austin: Von Boeckmann-Jones Company, 1968.
Cooper, Thompson. "Maire, Christopher (1697–1767)." The Rev. G. Bradley. *Oxford Dictionary of National Biography*. Ed. H. C. G. Matthew and Brian Harrison. 2004. Oxford: Oxford University Press, 2004. 18 Aug. 2005. <http://www.oxforddnb.com/view/article/17815>.
Cowart, David. *Thomas Pynchon: The Art of Allusion*. Carbondale: Southern Illinois University Press, 1980.
Cresap, Joseph Ord, and Bernarr Cresap. *The History of the Cresaps*. Revised ed. Gallatin, Tennessee: Cresap Society, 1987.
"Darlington and the Tees Vale." *North East England History Pages*. 19 Jan. 2005. <http://www.thenortheast.fsnet.co.uk/Darlington%20and%20the%20Tees%20Vale.htm>.
Davenport-Hines, Richard. "Gordon, Charles George (1833–1885)." *Oxford Dictionary of National Biography*. Ed. H. C. G. Matthew and Brian Harrison. 2004. Oxford: Oxford University Press, 2004. 30 Aug. 2005. <http://www.oxforddnb.com/view/article/11029>.
———. "Shirley, Laurence, forth Earl Ferrers (1720–1760)." *Oxford Dictionary of National Biography*. Ed. H. C. G. Matthew and Brian Harrison. 2004. Oxford: Oxford University Press, 2004. 27 Sept. 2005. <http://www.oxforddnb.com/view/article/25432>.

"Delisle, Joseph-Nicolas." *Encyclopaedia Britannica*. 2005. Encyclopaedia Britannica Online. 7 Sept. 2005. <http://search.eb.com/eb/article-9029834>.
Dewey, Joseph. "The Sound of One Man Mapping: Wicks Cherrycoke and the Eastern (Re)solution." *Pynchon and* Mason & Dixon. Ed. Brooke Horvath and Irving Malin. Newark, New Jersey: University of Delaware Press, 2000. 112–131.
Diebold, John, and Michael Goodwin. *Babies of Wackiness: A Reader's Guide to Thomas Pynchon's* Vineland. 1998. 29 July 2002. <http://www.mindspring.com/~shadow88/>.
Earle, James W. "Freedom and Knowledge within the Zone." *Approaches to* Gravity's Rainbow. Ed. Charles Clerc. Columbus: Ohio State University Press, 1983. 229–250.
"Edmund Taylor Whittaker." *The Mathematics Genealogy Project*. 21 June 2007. <http://genealogy.math.ndsu.nodak.edu/html/id.phtml?id=18571>.
"Edward Hawke, 1st Baron Hawke." *Encyclopaedia Britannica*. 2004. Encyclopaedia Britannica Online. 12 Aug. 2004. <http://search.eb.com/eb/article?eu=40434>.
Eliot, T. S. *The Waste Land*. Norton Critical Edition. Ed. Michael North. New York: W. W. Norton and Company, 2001.
"Ernst Zermelo." *The Mathematics Genealogy Project*. 24 June 2007. <http://genealogy.math.ndsu.nodak.edu/html/id.phtml?id=46828>.
Falzon, Grazio. *Basic English-Maltese Dictionary*. 1997. 21 Jan. 2002. <http://www.aboutmalta.com/language/engmal.htm>.
Farmer, David Hugh. *The Oxford Dictionary of Saints*. 3rd ed. Oxford: Oxford University Press, 1992.
Featherling, Dale. *Mother Jones: The Miner's Angel*. Carbondale: Southern Illinois University Press, 1974.
Federal Writers' Program of the Work Projects [sic] Administration of the State of Colorado. *Colorado: A Guide to the Highest State*. 1941 New Revised Edition. Ed. Harry Hansen. New York: Hastings House, 1970.
Federal Writers' Program of the Works Progress Administration of Massachusetts. *The Berkshire Hills*. New York: Funk and Wagnalls, 1939.
Friedman, Alan J., and Manfred Puetz. "Science as Metaphor: Thomas Pynchon and *Gravity's Rainbow*." *Critical Essays on Thomas Pynchon*. Ed. Richard Pierce. Boston: G.K. Hall & Co., 1981. 69–81.
Gaddis, William. *The Recognitions*. 1955. New York: Penguin, 1993.
Gascoigne, John. "Banks, Sir Joseph, baronet (1743–1820)." *Oxford Dictionary of National Biography*. Ed. H. C. G. Matthew and Brian Harrison. 2004. Oxford: Oxford University Press, Sept. 2005. 6 Sept. 2005. <http://www.oxforddnb.com/view/article/1300>.
Gates, Henry Lewis. "Who Calculated the Speed of the Moon?" *Little Known Black History Facts*. McDonalds Corporation, 2000. 5 June 2007. <http://www.infoage.org/mcdonalds2000.html>.
"Georg Ferdinand Frobenius." *The Mathematics Genealogy Project*. 14 June 2007. <http://genealogy.math.ndsu.nodak.edu/html/id.phtml?id=4642>.
Gerasimov, Vadim. *Tetris Story*. 26 Apr. 2007. <http://vadim.oversigma.com/Tetris.htm>.
Gestwicki, Ronald. *An English-Herero, Herero-English Dictionary*. Windhoek, South West Africa: Anglican Church, 1966.
"Gibbs, J. Willard." *Encyclopaedia Britannica*. 2007. Encyclopaedia Britannica Online. 25 Jan. 2007. <http://search.eb.com/eb/article-9036747>.
"Gobineau, Joseph Arthur, comte de." *Encyclopaedia Britannica*. 2007. Encyclopaedia Britannica Online. 2007. 10 July 2007. <http://search.eb.com/eb/article-9037141>.
Gonzales, Michael J. *The Mexican Revolution*. Albuquerque: University of New Mexico Press, 2002.
Gosse, Philip. *St. Helena 1502–1938*. London: Cassel, 1938.
Grant, J. Kerry. *A Companion to* The Crying of Lot 49. Athens: University of Georgia Press, 1994.

___. *A Companion to* V. Athens, Georgia: The University of Georgia Press, 2001.
Guicciardini, Niccolò. "Hutton, Charles (1737–1823)." *Oxford Dictionary of National Biography*. Ed. H. C. G. Matthew and Brian Harrison. 2004. Oxford: Oxford University Press, 2004. 18 Aug. 2005. <http://www.oxforddnb.com/view/article/14300>.
Guzman, Martín Luis, ed. *Memoirs of Pancho Villa*. Austin: University of Texas Press, 1965.
Hamilton, E.N. *Bible Names*. Chicago: Linden Printing Company, 1939.
Hanham, A. A. "Dodington, George Bubb, Baron Melcombe (1690/91–1762)." *Oxford Dictionary of National Biography*. Ed. H. C. G. Matthew and Brian Harrison. 2004. Oxford: Oxford University Press, 2004. 6 Sept. 2005. <http://www.oxforddnb.com/view/article/7752>.
Hanks, Patrick, and Flavin Hodges. *A Dictionary of First Names*. Oxford: Oxford University Press, 1990.
Hannam, June. "Parkhurst, (Estelle) Sylvia (1882–1960)." *Oxford Dictionary of National Biography*. Ed. H. C. G. Matthew and Brian Harrison. 2006. Oxford: Oxford University Press, May 2006. 15 May 2007. <http://www.oxforddnb.com/view/article/37833>.
Harder, Kelsie B. "Names in Thomas Pynchon's *V.*" *Literary Onomastics Studies* 5 (1972): 64–80.
Harlow, Alvin F. *Old Post Bags: The Story of the Sending of a Letter in Ancient and Modern Times*. New York: D. Appleton and Company, 1928.
Harris, Eileen. "Halfpenny, William (d. 1755)." *Oxford Dictionary of National Biography*. Ed. H. C. G. Matthew and Brian Harrison. 2004. Oxford: Oxford University Press, 2004. 27 Sept. 2005. <http://www.oxforddnb.com/view/article/11922>.
Harvey, Sir Paul, ed. *The Oxford Companion to Classical Literature*. Oxford: Oxford University Press, 1974.
___. "Shovell, Sir Cloudesley (bap. 1650, d. 1707)." *Oxford Dictionary of National Biography*. Ed. H. C. G. Matthew and Brian Harrison. 2004. Oxford: Oxford University Press, 2004. 14 July 2005. <http://www.oxforddnb.com/view/article/25470>.
Hayes, Peter L. "Pynchon's Cunning Lingual Novel: Communication in *Lot 49*." *The University of Mississippi Studies in English* 5 (1984–1987): 23–28.
Hayles, N. Katherine. "'A Metaphor of God Knew How Many Parts': The Engine that Drives *The Crying of Lot 49*." *New Essays on* The Crying of Lot 49. Ed. Patrick O'Donnell. Cambridge: Cambridge University Press, 1991. 97–125.
Headlee, A. J. W. *The Accopmt of the Hands Settling the Lines between Maryland and Pennsylvania*. Morgantown, West Virginia: Published by permission of the Historical Society of Pennsylvania, 1976.
Henderson, William. *Notes on the Folk Lore of the Northern Counties of England and the Borders*. 1866. East Ardsley, England: E.P. Publishing Ltd., 1973.
"Henry Parker Manning." *The Mathematics Genealogy Project*. 14 June 2007. <http://genealogy.math.ndsu.nodak.edu/html/id.phtml?id=38191>.
"Hergesheimer, Joseph." *Encyclopaedia Britannica*. 2007. Encyclopaedia Britannica Online. 23 Jan. 2007. <http://search.eb.com/eb/article-9040140>.
"Hermann Amandus Schwartz." *The Mathematics Genealogy Project*. 14 June 2007. <http://genealogy.math.ndsu.nodak.edu/html/id.phtml?id=7487>.
Herzogenrath, Bernd. "A Possible Source for the Name Oedipa Maas." *Pynchon Notes* 40–41 (1997): 107–109.
"Hilarius of Sexten." *The Catholic Encyclopedia* Vol. VII. Ed. Charles G. Herkermann et al. New York: Robert Appleton Company, 1910. 348.
"Hilbert, David." *Encyclopaedia Britannica*. 2007. Encyclopaedia Britannica Online. 24 July 2007. <http://search.eb.com/eb/article-9040439>.
Hill, Robert R. "Decoding Community in Pynchon's *Vineland*: Problematic Definitions for Readers and Characters." *Pynchon Notes* 40–41 (1997): 197–217.

Hite, Molly. "Feminist Theory and the Politics of *Vineland.*" *The* Vineland *Papers: Critical Takes on Pynchon's Novel.* Ed. Geoffrey Green, Donald J. Greiner, and Larry McCaffery. Normal, Illinois: Dalkey Archive Press, 1994. 135–153.
___. *Ideas of Order in the Novels of Thomas Pynchon.* Columbus: Ohio State University Press, 1983.
Hohmann, Charles. *Thomas Pynchon's* Gravity's Rainbow: *A Study of its Conceptual Structure and of Rilke's Influence.* New York: Peter Lang, 1986.
Hollander, Charles. "Does McClintic Sphere in Pynchon's *V.* Stand for Thelonious Monk?" *Notes on Contemporary Literature* 30 (2000): 4–7.
___. "Pynchon, JFK and the CIA: Magic Eye Views of *The Crying of Lot 49.*" *Pynchon Notes* 40–41 (1997): 61–106.
___. "Pynchon's Politics: The Presence of an Absence." *Pynchon Notes* 26–27 (1990): 5–59.
The Honours Register of the University of Oxford: A Record of University Honours and Distinctions, Completed to the End of Trinity Term, 1883. Oxford: The Clarendon Press, 1883.
Howat, Gerald M.D. "Grace, William Gilbert [W.G.] (1848–1915)." *Oxford Dictionary of National Biography.* Ed. H. C. G. Matthew and Brian Harrison. Oxford: Oxford University Press, 2004. 25 June 2007. <http://www.oxforddnb.com/view/article/33500>.
Howse, Derek. "Maskelyne, Nevil (1732–1811)." *Oxford Dictionary of National Biography.* Ed. H. C. G. Matthew and Brian Harrison. 2004. Oxford: Oxford University Press, 2004. 18 Aug. 2005. <http://www.oxforddnb.com/view/article/18266>.
___. "Mason, Charles (1728–1786)." *Oxford Dictionary of National Biography.* Ed. H. C. G. Matthew and Brian Harrison. Oxford: Oxford University Press, 2004. 14 Jan. 2005. <http://www.oxforddnb.com/view/article/18268>.
"Internal Macedonian Revolutionary Organization." *Encyclopaedia Britannica.* 2007. Encyclopaedia Britannica Online. 21 June 2007. <http://search.eb.com/eb/article-9042560>.
"iron mask, the man in the." *Encyclopaedia Britannica.* 2007. Encyclopaedia Britannica Online. 24 July 2007. <http://search.eb.com/eb/article-9042804>.
An Irving Berlin Songography. 15 Apr. 2002. <http://www.thepeaches.com/music/composers/berlin/songography.html>.
Jasper, Allison T. "Thomas Pynchon's Absurd Truths: Puns and Metaphor in *The Crying of Lot 49.*" *The Arkansas Review: A Journal of Criticism* 5.1–5.2 (1996): 39–67.
Jingrong, Wu, ed. *The Pinyin Chinese-English Dictionary.* Beijing: The Commercial Press, 1979.
"John Edensor Littlewood." *The Mathematics Genealogy Project.* 20 June 2007. <http://genealogy.math.ndsu.nodak.edu/html/id.phtml?id=10463>.
Johnston, John. "Toward the Schizo-Text: Paranoia as Semiotic Regime in *The Crying of Lot 49.*" *New Essays on* The Crying of Lot 49. Ed. Patrick O'Donnell. Cambridge: Cambridge University Press, 1991. 47–78.
Josephson, Matthew. *The Robber Barons: The Great American Capitalists 1861–1901.* New York: Harcourt Brace and Company, 1934.
Kaplan, Stuart R. *The Encyclopedia of Tarot.* New York: U.S. Game Systems, Inc., 1978.
"Kentigern, Saint." *Encyclopaedia Britannica.* 2007. Encyclopaedia Britannica Online. 24 July 2007. <http://search.eb.com/eb/article-9045116>.
Kharpertian, Theodore D. *A Hand to Turn the Time: The Menippean Satires of Thomas Pynchon.* London: Associated University Presses, 1990.
Kolatch, Alfred J. *Complete Dictionary of English and Hebrew First Names.* Middle Village, New York: Jonathan David Publishers, 1984.
Kolbe, F.W. *An English-Herero Dictionary with an Introduction to the Study of Herero and Bantu in General.* London: Trübner and Company, n.d.
Kulisheck, P. J. "Pelham, Henry (1694–1754)." *Oxford Dictionary of National Biography.*

Ed. H. C. G. Matthew and Brian Harrison. 2004. Oxford: Oxford University Press, 2004. 23 Aug. 2005. <http://www.oxforddnb.com/view/article/21789>.
"Lacaille, Nicolas Louis de." *Encyclopaedia Britannica.* 2005. Encyclopaedia Britannica Online. 7 Sept. 2005. <http://search.eb.com/eb/article-9046736>.
"La Condamine, Charles-Marie de." *Encyclopaedia Britannica.* 2005. Encyclopaedia Britannica Online. 7 Sept. 2005. <http://search.eb.com/eb/article-9046607>.
"Lalande, Jérôme." *Encyclopaedia Britannica.* 2005. Encyclopaedia Britannica Online. 7 Sept. 2005. <http://search.eb.com/eb/article-9046905>.
Larsson, Donald F. *A Companion's Companion: Illustrated Additions and Corrections to Steven Weisenburger's* A Gravity's Rainbow Companion. 5 May 2002. 7 Sept. 2005. <http://www.english.mankato.msus.edu/larsson/grnotes.html>.
Laughton, J. K. "Jenkins, Robert (d. 1743)." The Rev. Richard Harding. *Oxford Dictionary of National Biography.* Ed. H. C. G. Matthew and Brian Harrison. 2004. Oxford: Oxford University Press, 2004. 18 Aug. 2005. <http://www.oxforddnb.com/view/article/14734>.
Leithauser, Brad. "Any Place You Want." Rev. of *Vineland* by Thomas Pynchon. *New York Review of Books* 37.4 (1990): 7–10.
Lemay, J. A. Leo. "Franklin, Benjamin (1706–1790)." *Oxford Dictionary of National Biography.* Ed. H. C. G. Matthew and Brian Harrison. 2004. Oxford: Oxford University Press, 2004. 6 Sept. 2005. <http://www.oxforddnb.com/view/article/52466>.
Le Vot, André. "The Rocket and the Pig: Thomas Pynchon and Science Fiction." *Caliban* 12 (1975): 111–118.
Levy, Avigdor, ed. *The Jews of the Ottoman Empire.* Princeton: The Darwin Press, Inc., 1994.
Liberman, Mark. "Rinehart." *Language Log.* 9 Dec. 2006. 12 June 2007. <http://itre.cis.upenn.edu/~myl/languagelog/archives/003880.html>.
"Liman von Sanders, Otto." *Encyclopaedia Britannica.* 2007. Encyclopaedia Britannica Online. 5 June 2007. <http://search.eb.com/eb/article-9048279>.
"Lombroso, Cesare." *Encyclopaedia Britannica.* 2007. Encyclopaedia Britannica Online. 31 May 2007. <http://search.eb.com/eb/article-9002414>.
Lossing, Benson J. *Pictorial Field Book of the Revolution.* Vol. 2. 1850. 19 Jan. 2005. <http://freepages.history.rootsweb.com/~wcarr1/Lossing1/chap54.html#e025>.
Loughlin, James F. "Colonna." *Catholic Encyclopedia.* 30 Aug. 2005. <http://www.newadvent.org/cathen/04125c.htm>.
___. "St. Ambrose." *The Catholic Encyclopedia.* 20 Jan. 2005. <http://www.newadvent.org/cathen/01383c.htm>.
Lowry, Donal. "Jameson, Sir Leander Starr, baronet (1853–1917)." *Oxford Dictionary of National Biography.* Ed. H. C. G. Matthew and Brian Harrison. 2004. Oxford: Oxford University Press, 2006. 8 May 2007. <http://www.oxforddnb.com/view/article/34155>.
"Lugosi, Bela." *Encyclopaedia Britannica.* 2007. Encyclopaedia Britannica Online. 24 July 2007. <http://search.eb.com/eb/article-9049304>.
MacKell, Jan. *Brothels, Bordellos, and Bad Girls: Prostitution in Colorado, 1860–1930.* Albuquerque: University of New Mexico Press, 2004.
Malone, Kemp. "Meaningful Fictive Names in English Literature." *Names and Their Varieties: A Collection of Essays in Onomastics.* Ed. Kelsie B. Harder. New York: University Press of America, 1980. 53–65.
Mansfield, Susan. "Salvaging a Sense of History." *The Scotsman.* 19 Jan. 2004. 24 July 2007. <http://living.scotsman.com/index.cfm?id=64032004>.
Marshall, P. J. *Problems of Empire: Britain and India, 1757–1813.* London: George Allen and Unwin Ltd., 1968.
Mayers, Ruth E. "Vane, Sir Henry, the younger (1613–1662)." *Oxford Dictionary of National*

Biography. Ed. H. C. G. Matthew and Brian Harrison. 2004. Oxford: Oxford University Press, 2004. 7 Sept. 2005. <http://www.oxforddnb.com/view/article/28086>.

McAuslin, William Alexander. *Mayflower Index*. Clinton, Massachusetts: The General Society of Mayflower Descendants, 1932.

McConnell, Anita. "Bird, John (1709–1776)." *Oxford Dictionary of National Biography*. Ed. H. C. G. Matthew and Brian Harrison. 2004. Oxford: Oxford University Press, 2004. 6 Sept. 2005. <http://www.oxforddnb.com/view/article/2448>.

McHale, Brian. "Mason and Dixon in the Zone, or, a Brief Poetics of Pynchon-Space." *Pynchon and* Mason & Dixon. Ed. Brook Horvath and Irving Malin. Newark, New Jersey: University of Delaware Press, 2000. 43–62.

Mendelson, Edward. "The Sacred, the Profane and *The Crying of Lot 49*." *Pynchon: A Collection of Critical Essays*. Ed. Edward Mendelson. Englewood Cliffs, N.J.: Prentice-Hall, 1978. 97–111.

Metcalf, Pauline C. "de Wolfe, Elsie." *American National Biography Online*. February 2000. 12 Apr. 2007. <http://www.anb.org/articles/17/17-00215.html>.

"Michelson-Morley experiment." *Encyclopaedia Britannica*. 2007. Encyclopaedia Britannica Online. 25 Jan. 2007. <http://search.eb.com/eb/article-9052479>.

"Mikimoto Kokichi." *Encyclopaedia Britannica*. 2007. Encyclopaedia Britannica Online. 21 May 2007. <http://search.eb.com/eb/article-9052631>.

Millard, Bill. "Ducking the Snovian Distinction: The 'Both/And' Logic of *Mason & Dixon*." *International Pynchon Week*. 12 June 1998. 1 Mar. 2002. <http://www.columbia.edu/~ubm1/snovian.html>.

Miller, David Philip. "Birch, Thomas (1705–1766)." *Oxford Dictionary of National Biography*. Ed. H. C. G. Matthew and Brian Harrison. 2004. Oxford: Oxford University Press, 2004. 6 Sept. 2005. <http://www.oxforddnb.com/view/article/2436>.

Moore, Steven. *A Reader's Guide to William Gaddis's* The Recognitions. 21 Apr. 2002. <http://www.williamgaddis.org/recognitions/trguide.html>.

Moore, Thomas. *The Style of Connectedness:* Gravity's Rainbow *and Thomas Pynchon*. Columbia: University of Missouri Press, 1987.

Newman, Ernest. *Stories of the Great Operas and Their Composers*. 1928. Philadelphia: The Blakiston Company, 1945.

New, Melvyn. "Profane and Stencilized Texts: In Search of Pynchon's *V.*" *The Georgia Review* 33 (1979): 395–412.

Nihon Senbotsu Gakusei Kinen-Kai (Japanese Memorial Society for the Students Killed in the War), ed. *Listen to the Voices from the Sea*. Scranton: The University of Scranton Press, 2000.

Noel, Thomas J. *Colorado: A Liquid History and Tavern Guide to the Highest State*. Golden, CO: Fulcrum Publishing, 1999.

O'Donnell, Patrick. "Introduction." *New Essays on* The Crying of Lot 49. Ed. Patrick O'Donnell. Cambridge: Cambridge University Press, 1991. 1–20.

O'Neal, Bill. *Encyclopedia of Western Gunfighters*. Norman: University of Oklahoma Press, 1979.

Oglethorpe, James. *Letters to the Duke of Newcastle, January 22, 1740*. 19 Jan. 2005. <http://msit.gsu.edu/dhr/gacolony/letters/JO_Newcastle_1740_January.htm>.

Olster, Stacey. "When You're a (Nin)jette, You're a (Nin)jette All the Way — or Are You?: Female Filmmaking in *Vineland*." *The* Vineland *Papers: Critical Takes on Pynchon's Novel*. Ed. Geoffrey Green, Donald J. Greiner, and Larry McCaffery. Normal, Illinois: Dalkey Archive Press, 1994. 119–134.

Oppenheim, Janet. *The Other World: Spiritualism and Psychical Research in England, 1850–1914*. Cambridge: Cambridge University Press, 1985.

Orr, N. Lee. "Alfredo Barilli: Atlanta Musician, 1880–1935." *American Music* 2.1 (1984): 43–60.

Orwell, George. "London Letter to *Partisan Review*." *My Country Right or Left 1940–1943. Volume Two of the Collected Essays, Journalism, and Letters*. Boston: Godine Publishers, 2000. 112–123.
Osur, Alan M. "The Role of the Colorado National Guard in Civil Disturbances." *Military Affairs* 46.1 (1982): 19–24.
"Pamela Colman Smith Collection, 1896–1900." *Bryn Mawr College Library Special Collections*. 2003. 25 Jan. 2007. <http://www.brynmawr.edu/Library/speccoll/guides/smith.shtml>.
Parkhill, Forbes. *The Wildest of the West*. New York: Henry Holt, 1951.
Parlett, David, trans. *Selections from the Carmina Burana*. New York: Penguin, 1986.
Passage, Charles E. *Character Names in Dostoevsky's Fiction*. Ann Arbor: Ardis, 1982.
Petillon, Pierre-Yves. "A Re-Cognition of Her Errand into the Wilderness." *New Essays on* The Crying of Lot 49. Ed. Patrick O'Donnell. Cambridge: Cambridge University Press, 1991. 127–170.
"philately." *Encyclopaedia Britannica*. 2007. Encyclopaedia Britannica Online. 17 July 2007. <http://search.eb.com/eb/article-9059643>.
Philip, Ian. *The Bodleian Library in the Seventeenth and Eighteenth Centuries*. Oxford: Oxford University Press, 1983.
Pierce, Richard A. *Russian Central Asia 1867–1917*. Berkeley: University of California Press, 1960.
Plato. *Great Dialogues of Plato*. Trans. W. H. D. Rouse. New York: Mentor Books, 1956.
"Popular Baby Names." *Social Security Online*. 01 July 2006. <http://www.ssa.gov/OACT/babynames>.
Porch, Douglas. *The Conquest of Morocco*. New York: Alfred A. Knopf, 1983.
Porter, Roy, ed. *The Biographical Dictionary of Scientists*. 2nd ed. New York: Oxford University Press, 1994.
Pynchon, Thomas. *Against the Day*. New York: Penguin, 2006.
———. *The Crying of Lot 49*. 1965. New York: Perennial Library/Harper and Row, 1990.
———. *Gravity's Rainbow*. 1973. New York: Penguin, 1987.
———. Letter. *New York Times Book Review*. 17 July 1966. 22, 24.
———. *Mason & Dixon*. New York: Henry Holt and Company, 1997.
———. *Slow Learner*. 1984. Boston: Little, Brown and Company, 1998.
———. *V.* 1963. New York: Perennial Library/Harper and Row, 1990.
———. *Vineland*. Boston: Little, Brown and Company, 1990.
Pynchon — Film & TV: Buckaroo Banzai. 14 Feb. 2003. <http://www.themodernworld.com/pynchon/pynchon_film_bb.html>.
Quinn, David B. "Cabot, John (c.1451–1498)." *Oxford Dictionary of National Biography*. Ed. H. C. G. Matthew and Brian Harrison. 2004. Oxford: Oxford University Press, 2004. 6 Sept. 2005. <http://www.oxforddnb.com/view/article/66135>.
Rack, Henry D. "Wesley, John (1703–1791)." *Oxford Dictionary of National Biography*. Ed. H. C. G. Matthew and Brian Harrison. 2004. Oxford: Oxford University Press, 2004. 7 Sept. 2005. <http://www.oxforddnb.com/view/article/29069>.
Raudaskoski, Heikki. "'The Feathery Rilke Mustaches and Porky Pig Tattoo on Stomach': High and Low Pressures in *Gravity's Rainbow*." *Postmodern Culture* 7.2 (1997). 03 Apr. 2002. <http://muse.jhu.edu/journals/posmodern_culture/v007/7.2raudaskoski.html>.
Reaney, P.H. *The Origin of English Surnames*. London: Routledge & Kegan Paul, 1968.
Reaney, P.H., and R.M. Wilson. *A Dictionary of English Surnames*. 3rd ed. Oxford: Oxford University Press, 1997.
Reich, Angela. "Re-Reading *The Crying of Lot 49*: A Note on the *Oz* Connection." *Pynchon Notes* 30–31 (1992): 179–84.
Reid, Stuart. "Wolfe, James (1727–1759)." *Oxford Dictionary of National Biography*. Ed.

H. C. G. Matthew and Brian Harrison. 2004. Oxford: Oxford University Press, 2004. 23 Aug. 2005. <http://www.oxforddnb.com/view/article/29833>.

Reynolds, Philip K. "The Banana in Chinese Literature." *Harvard Journal of Asiatic Studies* 5.2 (1940): 165–81.

Richwell, Adrian Emily. "*The Crying of Lot 49*: A Source Study." *Pynchon Notes* 17 (1985): 78–80.

Robbins, Ira A., ed. *The New Trouser Press Record Guide*. 3rd ed. New York: Collier Books, 1985.

Robinson, H.W. "A Note on Charles Mason's Ancestry and His Family." *Proceedings of the American Philosophical Society* 93.2 (1949): 134–36.

___. "Jeremiah Dixon (1733–1799) A Biographical Note." *Proceedings of the American Philosophical Society* 94.3 (1950): 272–4.

Rogers, Pat. "Johnson, Samuel (1709–1784)." *Oxford Dictionary of National Biography*. Ed. H. C. G. Matthew and Brian Harrison. 2004. Oxford: Oxford University Press, 2004. 18 Aug. 2005. <http://www.oxforddnb.com/view/article/14918>.

"Róheim, Geza." *Encyclopaedia Britannica*. 2003. Encyclopaedia Britannica Online. 01 Dec. 2002. <http://search.eb.com/eb/article?eu=85940>.

Rolfe, Frederick. *Hadrian the Seventh*. 1904. New York: New York Review of Books, 2001.

Rolleston, T.W. *Celtic Myths and Legends*. 1917. New York: Dover, 1990.

Rushdie, Salman. "Still Crazy after all These Years." Rev. of *Vineland* by Thomas Pynchon. *The New York Times Book Review*. 12 Jan. 1990. 1, 36–37.

Sante, Luc. *Low Life: Lures and Snares of Old New York*. New York: Farrar, Straus, and Giroux, 1991.

Schaffer, Simon. "Cavendish, Henry (1731–1810)." *Oxford Dictionary of National Biography*. Ed. H. C. G. Matthew and Brian Harrison. 2004. Oxford: Oxford University Press, 2004. 6 Sept. 2005. <http://www.oxforddnb.com/view/article/4937>.

Schermerhorn, Elizabeth W. *Malta of the Knights*. n.p.: Wm. Heinemann Ltd., 1929.

Schlenther, Boyd Stanley. "Whitefield, George (1714–1770)." *Oxford Dictionary of National Biography*. Ed. H. C. G. Matthew and Brian Harrison. 2004. Oxford: Oxford University Press, 2004. 23 Aug. 2005. <http://www.oxforddnb.com/view/article/29281>.

"Schmitt, Jacob W." *The Encyclopedia of Cleveland History*. 11 Apr. 2007. <http://ech.case.edu/ech-cgi/article.pl?id=SJW>.

Schweizer, Karl Wolfgang. "Stuart, John, third earl of Bute (1713–1792)." *Oxford Dictionary of National Biography*. Ed. H. C. G. Matthew and Brian Harrison. 2004. Oxford: Oxford University Press, 2004. 6 Sept. 2005. <http://www.oxforddnb.com/view/article/26716>.

The Shotton Dobby. 10 Jan. 2005. <http://www.seaham.i12.com/sos/shotton.html>.

"Shunkichi Kimura." *The Mathematics Genealogy Project*. 5 June 2007. <http://genealogy.ams.org/html/id.phtml?id=38055>.

Siegel, Jules. "Who Is Thomas Pynchon ... and Why Did He Take off with My Wife?" *Playboy* 24.3 (March 1977): 97, 122, 168–170, 172, 174.

Simmon, Scott. "Beyond the Theatre of War: *Gravity's Rainbow* as Film." *Critical Essays on Thomas Pynchon*. Ed. Richard Pierce. Boston: G.K. Hall & Co., 1981. 124–139.

"Sipyagin, Dmitry Sergeyevich." *Encyclopaedia Britannica*. 2007. Encyclopaedia Britannica Online. 25 July 2007. <http://search.eb.com/eb/article-9067974>.

"Sir Pierre Louis Napoleon Cavagnari." *Encyclopaedia Britannica*. 11th ed. 1911. 21 June 2007. <http://www.1911encyclopedia.org/Sir_Pierre_Louis_Napoleon_Cavagnari>.

"Siraj-ud-Dawlah." *Encyclopaedia Britannica*. 2004. Encyclopaedia Britannica Online. 10 June 2004. <http://search.eb.com/eb/article?eu=69740>.

Slade, Joseph W. "Communication, Group Theory, and Perception in *Vineland*." *The Vineland Papers: Critical Takes on Pynchon's Novel*. Ed. Geoffrey Green, Donald J. Greiner, and Larry McCaffery. Normal, Illinois: Dalkey Archive Press, 1994. 68–88.

———. "Religion, Psychology, Sex, and Love in *Gravity's Rainbow.*" *Approaches to* Gravity's Rainbow. Ed. Charles Clerc. Columbus: Ohio State University Press, 1983. 153–198.
"Slezak, Leo." *Encyclopaedia Britannica*. 2007. Encyclopaedia Britannica Online. 22 May 2007. <http://search.eb.com/eb/article-9068910>.
Speck, W. A. "James II and VII (1633–1701)." *Oxford Dictionary of National Biography.* Ed. H. C. G. Matthew and Brian Harrison. 2004. Oxford: Oxford University Press, 2004. 18 Aug. 2005. <http://www.oxforddnb.com/view/article/14593>.
Spence, Lewis. *British Goblins and Demons.* 20 Sept. 2005. <http://www.belinus.co.uk/folklore/Spencebritishgoblins.htm>.
Spence, Richard. *Trust No One: The Secret World of Sidney Reilly.* Los Angeles: Feral House, 2002.
"Srinivas Ramanujan." *The Mathematics Genealogy Project.* 14 June 2007. <http://genealogy.math.ndsu.nodak.edu/html/id.phtml?id=91561>.
Sterling, Christopher H. "de Forest, Lee." *American National Biography Online.* February 2000. 19 Mar. 2007. <http://www.anb.org/articles/13/13-00416.html>.
Stevick, Phillip. "Prologomena for the Study of Fictional *Dreck.*" *Comic Relief: Humor in Contemporary American Literature.* Ed. Sarah Blacker Cohen. Urbana: University of Illinois Press, 1978. 263–280.
Stewart, George R. *American Given Names: Their Origin and History in the Context of the English Language.* New York: Oxford University Press, 1979.
Symons, A.J.A. *The Quest for Corvo: An Experiment in Biography.* 1934. New York: New York Review of Books, 2001.
Tabbi, Joseph. "Pynchon's Groundward Art." *The* Vineland *Papers: Critical Takes on Pynchon's Novel.* Ed. Geoffrey Green, Donald J. Greiner, and Larry McCaffery. Normal, Illinois: Dalkey Archive Press, 1994. 89–100.
Tanner, Tony. *Thomas Pynchon.* London: Methuen, 1982.
Ted and Company Theater Works. 2006. 16 July 2007. <http://www.tedandlee.com/ABOUTTL/History/tabid/66/Default.aspx>.
Thomas Pynchon Wiki: Against the Day. Feb.–July 2007. <http://against-the-day.pynchonwiki.com/wiki/index.php?title=Main_Page>.
Thompson, David. "Ellicott, John (1702/3–1772)." *Oxford Dictionary of National Biography.* Ed. H. C. G. Matthew and Brian Harrison. 2004. Oxford: Oxford University Press, 2004. 6 Sept. 2005. <http://www.oxforddnb.com/view/article/8654>.
Thomson, Peter. "Garrick, David (1717–1779)." *Oxford Dictionary of National Biography.* Ed. H. C. G. Matthew and Brian Harrison. 2004. Oxford: Oxford University Press, 2004. 18 Aug. 2005. <http://www.oxforddnb.com/view/article/10408>.
Thurn und Taxis: Telecom Pioneers by Phonebook of the World. 12 Aug. 2005. <http://www.thurnundtaxis.com>.
Tololyan, Kachig. "War as Background in *Gravity's Rainbow.*" *Approaches to* Gravity's Rainbow. Ed. Charles Clerc. Columbus: Ohio State University Press, 1983. 31–67.
"Turkey." *Encyclopaedia Britannica.* 11th ed. 1911. 25 June 2007. <http://www.1911encyclopedia.org/Turkey>.
Turnbull, Gordon. "Boswell, James (1740–1795)." *Oxford Dictionary of National Biography.* Ed. H. C. G. Matthew and Brian Harrison. 2004. Oxford: Oxford University Press, 2004. 6 Sept. 2005. <http://www.oxforddnb.com/view/article/2950>.
"Turner, Frederick Jackson." *Encyclopaedia Britannica.* 2007. Encyclopaedia Britannica Online. 24 July 2007. <http://search.eb.com/eb/article-9073867>.
"Twins Killed in Horror Car Smash." *Independent.* 7 May 2000. 16 July 2007. <http://www.independent.ie/national-news/twins-killed-in-horror-car-smash-514197.html>.
"Uskoks." *Encyclopaedia Britannica.* 11th ed. 1911. 19 June 2007. <http://www.1911encyclopedia.org/Uskoks>.

Vasquez, Dr. Librado Keno, and Maria Enriqueta Vasquez. *Regional Dictionary of Chicano Slang*. Austin: Jenkins Publishing Company, 1975.
"Vaucanson, Jacques de." *Encyclopaedia Britannica*. 2005. Encyclopaedia Britannica Online. 23 Aug. 2005. <http://search.eb.com/eb/article-9074908>.
Veech, James. *Mason and Dixon's Line: A History*. Pittsburgh: W.S. Haven, 1857.
Vian, Alsager. "Emerson, William (1701–1782)." Rev. by Niccolò Guicciardini. *Oxford Dictionary of National Biography*. Ed. H. C. G. Matthew and Brian Harrison. 2004. Oxford: Oxford University Press, 2004. 6 Sept. 2005. <http://www.oxforddnb.com/view/article/8784>.
Waddell, Helen. *The Wandering Scholars*. Boston: Houghton Mifflin Company, 1927.
Ware, Tim. "Etymologies." *ThomasPynchon.com*. 27 Sept. 2001. <http://www.hyperarts.com/pynchon/mason-dixon/extra/ety.html>.
___. "Further Information 2." *ThomasPynchon.com*. 12 Aug. 2004. <http://www.hyperarts.com/pynchon/mason-dixon/extra/info2.html>.
___. "*Gravity's Rainbow*: An Ever Expanding Web-Guide." *ThomasPynchon.com*. 12 July 2002. <http://www.hyperarts.com/pynchon/gravity/index.html>.
___. "*Mason & Dixon*." *ThomasPynchon.com*. 27 Sept. 2001. <http://www.hyperarts.com/pynchon/mason-dixon/index.html>.
Warrington, John. *Everyman's Classical Dictionary*. London: J.M. Dent and Sons, 1961.
Weisenburger, Steven. *A Gravity's Rainbow Companion: Sources and Contexts for Pynchon's Novel*. Athens: The University of Georgia Press, 1988.
___. "The Origin of Pynchon's Tchitcherine." *Pynchon Notes* 8 (1982): 39–42.
"Welsh Cartoonist Retires to 'Aberflyarff.'" *BBC News*. 11 June 1999. 16 July 2007. <http://news.bbc.co.uk/2/hi/uk_news/366957.stm>.
Wentworth, Harold, and Stuart Berg Flexner, eds. *Dictionary of American Slang*. n.p.: Thomas Y. Crowell Company, 1960.
West, Rebecca. *Black Lamb and Grey Falcon: A Journey through Yugoslavia*. 1941. New York: Penguin, 1955.
White, Allon. "Pigs and Pierrots: The Politics of Transgression in Modern Fiction." *Raritan* 2 (1982): 51–70.
"Will Divide." "Location, Location, Biolocation." [weblog posting] 23 April 2007. *The Chumps of Choice*. 28 July 2007. <http://chumpsofchoice.blogspot.com/search?q=moss+gatlin>.
Williams, Mari E. W. "Bradley, James (bap. 1692, d. 1762)." *Oxford Dictionary of National Biography*. Ed. H. C. G. Matthew and Brian Harrison. 2004. Oxford: Oxford University Press, 2004. 22 Aug. 2005. <http://www.oxforddnb.com/view/article/3187>.
Williamson, Karina. "Smart, Christopher (1722–1771)." *Oxford Dictionary of National Biography*. Ed. H. C. G. Matthew and Brian Harrison. 2004. Oxford: Oxford University Press, 2004. 23 Aug. 2005. <http://www.oxforddnb.com/view/article/25739>.
Willmoth, Frances. "Flamsteed, John (1646–1719)." *Oxford Dictionary of National Biography*. Ed. H. C. G. Matthew and Brian Harrison. 2004. Oxford: Oxford University Press, 2004. 17 Aug. 2005. <http://www.oxforddnb.com/view/article/9669>.
Winner, Thomas G. "Problems of Alphabetic Reform Among the Turkic Peoples of Soviet Central Asia, 1920–1941." *The Slavonic and East European Review* 31 (1952): 133–47.
Winston, Mathew. "A Comic Source of *Gravity's Rainbow*." *Pynchon Notes* 15 (1984): 73–76.
Withycombe, E.G. *The Oxford Dictionary of English Christian Names*. 2nd ed. London: Oxford University Press, 1963.
Wright, Joseph, ed. *The English Dialect Dictionary*. Vol. 3. New York: G. P. Putnam's Sons, 1902.
Yoshitaro, Takenobu, ed. *Kenkyusha's New Japanese-English Dictionary*. American ed. Cambridge, Massachusetts: Harvard University Press, 1942.

"Zaharoff, Sir Basil." *Encyclopaedia Britannica.* 2007. Encyclopaedia Britannica Online. 21 May 2007. <http://search.eb.com/eb/article-9078200>.

Zaleski, Carol, and Philip Zaleski, eds. *The Book of Heaven: An Anthology of Writings from Ancient to Modern Times.* Oxford: Oxford University Press, 2000.

www.ingramcontent.com/pod-product-compliance
Lightning Source LLC
Chambersburg PA
CBHW032100300426
44116CB00007B/828